YESTERDAY'S
TOMORROWS

"He went to the railings of the balcony and leant forward... The place into which he looked was an aisle of Titanic buildings, curving away in a spacious sweep in either direction."

YESTERDAY'S
TOMORROWS

THE STORY OF CLASSIC BRITISH
SCIENCE FICTION IN 100 BOOKS

MIKE ASHLEY

BRITISH LIBRARY

FRONTISPIECE: *When the Sleeper Wakes*, H.G. Wells, illustrated by Henri Lanos from *The Graphic*, 21 January 1899. Lanos (1859–1929) was a French artist who had also studied architecture and illustrated several French science-fiction stories as well as a later translation of Wells's *The War of the Worlds* when serialized in *Je sais tout* in 1905.

First published in 2020 by
The British Library
96 Euston Road
London NW1 2DB

Cataloguing in Publication Data
A catalogue record for this publication is available from the British Library

ISBN 978 0 7123 5371 7

Front cover design by Jason Anscomb

Text design and typesetting by Tetragon, London
Printed and bound in Malta by Gutenberg Press

CONTENTS

List of Illustrations   10

Introduction: *The Start of It All*   11

I   WELLS, WELLS AND WELLS AGAIN   21

    1   *The Time Machine*   H.G. Wells (1895)   23

    2   *The War of the Worlds*   H.G. Wells (1898)   26

    3   *When the Sleeper Wakes*   H.G. Wells (1899)   28

    4   *The Country of the Blind and Other Stories*   H.G. Wells (1911)   31

II   WARS TO END ALL WARS   33

    5   *The Outlaws of the Air*   George Griffith (1895)   36

    6   *The Invasion of 1910*   William Le Queux (1906)   38

    7   *When William Came*   Saki (1913)   40

    8   *The Struggle for Empire*   Robert W. Cole (1900)   42

III   DOOM AND DISASTER   45

    9   *The Crack of Doom*   Robert Cromie (1895)   46

    10   *The Violet Flame*   Fred T. Jane (1899)   48

    11   *The Purple Cloud*   M.P. Shiel (1901)   50

    12   *The Machine Stops*   E.M. Forster (1909)   53

IV FUTURES NEAR AND FAR   55

  13 *The Napoleon of Notting Hill* G.K. Chesterton (1904)   57
  14 *With the Night Mail* Rudyard Kipling (1909)   59
  15 *The Night Land* William Hope Hodgson (1912)   62
  16 *The Elixir of Life or 2905 A D* Herbert Gubbins (1914)   65

V THE OLD AND THE NEW   69

  17 *The Hampdenshire Wonder* J.D. Beresford (1911)   71
  18 *The Lost World* Arthur Conan Doyle (1912)   74

VI ESCAPE OR REALITY?   77

  19 *A Drop in Infinity* Gerald Grogan (1915)   79
  20 *The Terror* Arthur Machen (1916)   82
  21 *The New Moon* Oliver Onions (1918)   84
  22 *Meccania, the Super State* Owen Gregory (1918)   86
  23 *When the World Shook* H. Rider Haggard (1919)   89
  24 *A Voyage to Arcturus* David Lindsay (1920)   92

VII BRAVE NEW WORLDS   97

  25 *The People of the Ruins* Edward Shanks (1920)   99
  26 *The Secret Power* Marie Corelli (1921)   101
  27 *Theodore Savage* Cicely Hamilton (1922)   104
  28 *Number 87* Harrington Hext (1922)   106
  29 *Nordenholt's Million* J.J. Connington (1923)   108
  30 *Ultimatum* Victor MacClure (1924)   110
  31 *Menace from the Moon* Bohun Lynch (1925)   112
  32 *Man's World* Charlotte Haldane (1926)   115
  33 *To-morrow* Alfred Ollivant (1927)   117
  34 *Concrete* Aelfrida Tillyard (1930)   120

VIII SUPER, SUB OR NON-HUMAN?   125

    35 *The Blue Germ* Martin Swayne (1918)   128
    36 *Back to Methuselah* George Bernard Shaw (1921)   130
    37 *The Cheetah Girl* Christopher Blayre (1923)   134
    38 *The Clockwork Man* E.V. Odle (1923)   136
    39 *The Collapse of Homo Sapiens* P. Anderson Graham (1923) 139
    40 *The Last of My Race* J. Lionel Tayler (1924)   142
    41 *The Amphibians* S. Fowler Wright (1925)   143
    42 *The Emperor of the If* Guy Dent (1926)   147
    43 *The Man with Six Senses* Muriel Jaeger (1927)   150
    44 *Kontrol* Edmund Snell (1928)   153
    45 *The Ant Heap* Edward Knoblock (1929)   155
    46 *Brain* Lionel Britton (1930)   157
    47 *The Seventh Bowl* Miles (1930)   160
    48 *Brave New World* Aldous Huxley (1932)   163

IX PHILOSOPHICAL SPECULATIONS   169

    49 *The World, the Flesh and the Devil* J.D. Bernal (1929)   171
    50 *If It Had Happened Otherwise* J.C. Squire (1931)   173

X INTO THE COSMIC   177

    51 *To-morrow's Yesterday* John Gloag (1932)   181
    52 *Gay Hunter* J. Leslie Mitchell (1934)   182
    53 *Adrift in the Stratosphere* A.M. Low (serial 1934; book, 1937) 184
    54 *Planet Plane* John Beynon (1936)   187
    55 *Crisis! —1992* Benson Herbert (1936)   191
    56 *Star Maker* Olaf Stapledon (1937)   193
    57 *Out of the Silent Planet* C.S. Lewis (1938)   195
    58 *Sinister Barrier* Eric Frank Russell (1939)   197

XI PREPARING FOR WAR   201

59   *Lost Horizon*   James Hilton (1933)   203
60   *The Peacemaker*   C.S. Forester (1934)   206
61   *The Strange Invaders*   Alun Llewellyn (1934)   208
62   *Land Under England*   James O'Neill (1935)   210
63   *Woman Alive*   Susan Ertz (1935)   212
64   *Swastika Night*   Murray Constantine (1937)   215
65   *The Hopkins Manuscript*   R.C. Sherriff (1939)   217

XII OUR DARKEST HOURS   221

66   *The Twenty-Fifth Hour*   Herbert Best (1940)   224
67   *Loss of Eden*   Douglas Brown & Christopher Serpell (1940)   225
68   *Secret Weapon*   Bernard Newman (1942)   228
69   *The Golden Amazon*   John Russell Fearn (1944)   230
70   *Four-Sided Triangle*   William F. Temple (1949)   232

XIII POST-ATOMIC DOOM   235

71   *Death of a World*   J. Jefferson Farjeon (1948)   238
72   *Nineteen Eighty-Four*   George Orwell (1949)   239
73   *Time Marches Sideways*   Ralph L. Finn (1950)   242
74   *The Day of the Triffids*   John Wyndham (1951)   244
75   *The Last Revolution*   Lord Dunsany (1951)   246
76   *The Sound of His Horn*   Sarban (1952)   248
77   *The Magicians*   J.B. Priestley (1954)   250

XIV SCIENCE FICTION BOOM   253

78   *The Quatermass Experiment*   Nigel Kneale (TV, 1953; book, 1959)   256
79   *Journey Into Space*   Charles Chilton (radio, 1953; book, 1954)   258

80 *Childhood's End* Arthur C. Clarke (1953)   260
81 *The Echoing Worlds* Jonathan Burke (1954)   264
82 *One in Three Hundred* J.T. McIntosh (1954)   266
83 *Alien Dust* E.C. Tubb (1955)   268
84 *City Under the Sea* Kenneth Bulmer (1957)   271
85 *Non-Stop* Brian W. Aldiss (1958)   273
86 *Deadly Image* (aka *The Uncertain Midnight*) Edmund Cooper (1958) 276
87 *Hospital Station* James White (1962)   278
88 *Calculated Risk* Charles Eric Maine (1960)   280
89 *A for Andromeda* Fred Hoyle & John Elliot (TV, 1961; book, 1962)   282

XV OLD WORLDS FOR NEW   287

90 *Facial Justice* L.P. Hartley (1960)   289
91 *The Drowned World* J.G. Ballard (1962)   291
92 *The World in Winter* John Christopher (1962)   294
93 *Memoirs of a Spacewoman* Naomi Mitchison (1962)   296
94 *Telepath* Arthur Sellings (1962)   298
95 *To Conquer Chaos* John Brunner (1964)   300
96 *The Dark Mind* Colin Kapp (1964)   303
97 *Doctor Who* David Whitaker (1964)   305
98 *FROOMB!* John Lymington (1964)   308
99 *The Sundered Worlds* Michael Moorcock (1965)   310
100 *The Garbage World* Charles Platt (1966)   313

Select Bibliography   317
Acknowledgements   319
Index   321

LIST OF ILLUSTRATIONS

Frontispiece. "He went to the railings of the balcony and leant forward…" from *When the Sleeper Wakes*, H.G. Wells, illustrated by Henri Lanos from *The Graphic*, 21 January 1899.

Plate 1. "Coming through the bushes by the white sphinx were the heads and shoulders of men running." from *The Time Machine*, H.G. Wells (New York: Henry Holt, 1895), illustrated by W.B. Russell.

Plate 2. "Wiped out" from *The War of the Worlds* by H.G. Wells, illustrated by Warwick Goble from *Pearson's Magazine*, June 1897.

Plate 3. "The Invasion of 1910" by William Le Queux, as serialized in the *Daily Mail* from 10 March 1906. *The Crack of Doom* by Robert Cromie (London: Digby, Long, 1895). *The Violet Flame* by Fred T. Jane (London: Ward, Lock, 1899).

Plate 4. "With the Night Mail" by Rudyard Kipling (New York: Doubleday, Page, 1909) illustrated by Frank X. Leyendecker.

Plate 5. "Suddenly, out of the darkness…" from *The Lost World*, Arthur Conan Doyle, illustrated by Harry Rountree, from *The Strand Magazine*, June 1912.

Plate 6. *Menace from the Moon* by Bohun Lynch (London: Jarrolds, 1925); *The Clockwork Man* by E.V. Odle (London: Heinemann, 1923) illustrated by C. Paine.

Plate 7. *Brave New World* by Aldous Huxley (London: Chatto & Windus, 1932), dustjacket by Leslie Holland.

Plate 8. *Star Maker* by Olaf Stapledon (London: Methuen, 1937), dustjacket by Bip Pares.

Plate 9. *Sinister Barrier* by Eric Frank Russell (Reading, PA: Fantasy Press, 1948), dustjacket by Andrew J. Donnell.

Plate 10. *Four Sided Triangle* by William F. Temple (London: John Long, 1949), dustjacket by Roger Hall.

Plate 11. *Death of a World* by J. Jefferson Farjeon (London: Collins, 1948), dustjacket by Norman Manwaring; *The Day of the Triffids* by John Wyndham (London: Michael Joseph, 1951), dustjacket by Patrick Gierth; *The Last Revolution* by Lord Dunsany (London: Jarrolds, 1951), dustjacket by Ley Kenyon.

Plate 12. *The Sound of His Horn* by Sarban (New York: Ballantine Books, 1960), cover by Richard M. Powers.

Plate 13. *The Magicians* by J.B. Priestley (London: Heinemann, 1954), dustjacket by Val Biro.

Plate 14. *Childhood's End* by Arthur C. Clarke (London: Sidgwick & Jackson, 1954), dustjacket by Deborah Jones.

Plate 15. *One in Three Hundred* by J.T. McIntosh (New York: Doubleday, 1954), dustjacket by Mel Hunter.

Plate 16. *The Dark Mind* by Colin Kapp (London: Corgi Books, 1965), cover by Josh Kirby.

INTRODUCTION

The Start of It All

THIS BOOK PROVIDES A GUIDE TO SOME OF THE INNOVATIVE
and creative science fiction by British writers published in the United
Kingdom from the mid-1890s to mid-1960s, a period I shall define as
"classic". We will need to explore definitions, and not just what I mean
by "classic" but what I mean by "science fiction" (or "sf" as my preferred
abbreviation), especially as the term did not come into the popular idiom
until 1929, and then only in the United States.[*]

In 1952 the American writer and critic Damon Knight found it impossible to define science fiction and satisfy everybody and so simply said that
science fiction "is what we point to when we say it." It's rather like "beauty
is in the eye of the beholder" in that we recognize a work of science fiction
without having to define it, and that's rather what it's been like through
much of the history of science fiction in Britain.

Few would argue with the suggestion that H.G. Wells was the father
of science fiction, at least in Britain. But he would not have recognized
the term. He referred to his work as "fantastic and imaginative romances"

---

[*]   It is true that the poet William Wilson used the term "science fiction" in 1851 to describe a work
from the viewpoint of an artist in how various creatures would perceive an object. The chemist H.B.
Mason also used the term when describing the occult adventure *Etidorhpa* by John Uri Lloyd in 1897,
in this case inappropriately as the book is anti-science, but these were one-off references which did
not catch on.

but came to accept the term "scientific romances" which had been used by many reviewers and had previously been applied to translations of the works of Jules Verne. During the 1890s, the word "romance" did not mean a love story as we think of it now, but still related to its original medieval usage which meant a fanciful or heroic adventure. To all intents, a scientific romance was an adventure story where science is a key element and that definition could apply loosely to most science fiction. These days we also have techno-thrillers where science plays a key part, but in the scientific romance, as in science fiction, there is a speculative element. The scientific part of the story, whether physical, technical or sociological, revolves around some feature which does not exist at the time of writing but could well exist in the future or elsewhere in the universe. Crucially the science must seem feasible and possible, even if it stretches credulity. If it is impossible, then it is not science fiction but fantasy.

I should, perhaps, qualify that by saying it had to seem possible at the time of writing. There is much that once seemed possible but which we now believe impossible, such as travelling beyond the speed of light, but that does not stop us using that possibility alongside some scientific gobbledegook to rationalize it. As Arthur C. Clarke once said, "Any sufficiently advanced technology is indistinguishable from magic." Science fiction requires a significant suspension of disbelief amongst its readers in order that they can delight in the sense of wonder.

Arthur C. Clarke was one of the giants of science fiction, and one of his works is discussed in this book. Many might regard him as a modern writer rather than classic, but his writing career goes back to the mid-1940s, and he published a few stories and essays even earlier, mostly in amateur magazines. Most of his work fits into the classic mode. So, what is significant about the dates I have set to define "classic" science fiction?

One might argue that science fiction in Britain dates back at least to Thomas More's *Utopia*, first published in 1516 in Antwerp and elsewhere in Europe, all editions in Latin. The first English translation, published in England, was in 1551. It is really a philosophical discussion of an ideal society. It features little scientific speculation but much that is sociological. A stronger case can be made for *New Atlantis* by Sir Francis Bacon, published just after his death in 1626. This ideal society, called Bensalem, encourages the pursuit of science though little is described. Bacon was knocking at the door of science fiction but not quite opening it.

Bishop Francis Godwin's *The Man in the Moone*, published in 1638, qualifies as science fiction inasmuch as it describes a voyage to the moon, but since the voyage is made in a vehicle pulled by geese, it offers little by way of scientific speculation. The lunar society is rather more interesting, however, especially as the inhabitants can fly by using propelling fans. At the time he was writing this was an innovative idea.

Also of interest around this time is *The Description of a New World, called the Blazing-World* by Margaret Cavendish, the Duchess of Newcastle, published in 1666. Not only was she the first British woman to write a work of science fiction, she was an amateur scientist and infuriated members of the fledgling Royal Society in 1667 by insisting upon attending their discussions even though women were not usually allowed. Her book may best be described as eccentric and is full of weird and wonderful ideas and theories about ideal societies.

I will not catalogue all the early works of what we can call proto-science fiction but simply note that they include *The Consolidator* (1705) by Daniel Defoe, *Gulliver's Travels* (1726) by Jonathan Swift, *The Life and Adventures of Peter Wilkins* (1751) by Robert Paltock and similar fantastic voyages before we come, at length, to *St. Leon* (1799) by William Godwin, where immortality is achieved by chemical means. More importantly, Godwin's daughter, Mary, better known as Mary Shelley, was the author of *Frankenstein; or, The Modern Prometheus* (1818), which Brian W. Aldiss honoured as the first true work of science fiction in his study *A Billion Year Spree* in 1973, and with good reason. This remarkable novel, where electricity is used to infuse the life spark in a being assembled from parts of dead humans, uses the scientific knowledge of the day to rationalize how life may be created. What's more, Mary Shelley was no one-hit wonder. She wrote other works classifiable as science fiction: *The Last Man* (1826), "The Mortal Immortal" (1834) and other fragments, so we may also hail her as the first science-fiction writer.

The ball now gathers pace as writers came to terms with new scientific achievements and how they might influence society and the future of humanity. Much of the advance in science fiction was not in Britain but in France, most notably with Jules Verne, but also through the visions of Albert Robida, the philosophical mysticism of Camille Flammarion and the complex concepts of J.-H. Rosny the elder. Verne's work was translated into English but dumbed down and marketed as juvenile fiction, often serialized in boys' magazines. Here was sown the seed of what would become an increasing problem for science fiction in Britain as it came to be seen as fiction for adolescents rather than adults.

A growing number of British writers were producing the occasional science fiction story. Edward Bulwer Lytton, better known for his supernatural and occult stories, wrote *The Coming Race* in 1871 where an advanced race of humans had established a utopian society beneath Britain. That same year Sir George Chesney, writing anonymously, caused a stir with "The Battle of Dorking" where an unprepared Britain is overrun by Germany. It gave rise to the future-war theme which we will find repeatedly in the works covered by this book.

Perhaps the best known work of British science fiction pre-H.G. Wells was *The Strange Case of Dr. Jekyll and Mr. Hyde* (1886) by Robert Louis Stevenson, which explored how science might release the beast within us.

Few British writers made science fiction a regular part of their output. One exception was the Canadian-born Grant Allen who had lived in England since his teenage years. The majority of his scientific imaginings appeared as short stories such as "Pausodyne" (1881) which dealt with suspended animation and "A Child of the Phalanstery" (1884) which looked at the purity of the human race through eugenics.

The latter half of the nineteenth century had seen a dramatic rise in the number of magazines devoted to fiction, and in the 1890s the old-style titles such as *Blackwood's Magazine*, *The Cornhill* and *Chambers's Journal*, were rivalled by the new heavily illustrated monthlies including *The Strand*, *Pearson's* and *The Idler*. They encouraged a more sensational form of fiction and became a cauldron for both science fiction short stories and serialized novels. It was in this world that science fiction exploded in Britain, chiefly in the hands of one writer, H.G. Wells. There were contemporaries who produced a considerable amount of science fiction, both short and long, including George Griffith, M.P. Shiel and Arthur Conan Doyle, all of whom have representative books covered here, but none produced such a remarkable body of work as Wells in so short a space of time. Wells' output not only shaped the nature of science fiction and more or less defined the field, but also established it as a distinct genre. One can regard the emergence of Wells as a base camp in science fiction, so that the years before him saw the fledgling field steadily developing and coming to terms with itself, but after him it was established and maturing.

Wells, therefore, is our starting point.

It is far less easy to define an end to the classic period of science fiction, because the traditional form of the field which continued to mature during the start of the twentieth century continues to be written by some today. But there were further moments in the field's evolution where it took quantum leaps. The two most obvious were the two world wars. Writers had long predicted a global war with the result that the First World War gave science fiction, or at least the future-war element of it, some credibility. The war also gave science fiction a new momentum as the public realized the horror of mechanized warfare, the power of science, and the effects upon the world economy that could cause strife and catastrophe. Unlike the development of science fiction in America which looked to science to improve the world and benefit mankind, in Britain science fiction reflected the fears for the future.

The Second World War, and in particular the use of the atomic bomb, was another major moment, and in the United States science fiction matured rapidly in the late 1940s and early 1950s. One could argue that American sf moved from classic to modern sf during those years, but because of the wartime limitations at home, Britain lagged behind. One of the major driving forces for the growth of science fiction was the medium of the sf magazine, and the United States had these in abundance. It was through these, especially under the guiding editorial hands of John W. Campbell, Jr. and Horace Gold, that science fiction stepped out from the shadow of the pulps and blossomed in the sunlit uplands. Writers like Robert A. Heinlein, Isaac Asimov, Theodore Sturgeon and Murray Leinster, who had served their apprenticeship in the pulps, were now producing science fiction of high quality and in turn inspired the post-war generation which included Philip K. Dick, Frederik Pohl, Robert Sheckley and many more.

Britain had no such continuous specialist market. There were writers like John Russell Fearn, John Beynon Harris (later known as John Wyndham), Arthur C. Clarke and Eric Frank Russell who had sold stories to the American pulps and were learning their trade, but the majority of writers had been blighted by the War and it was not until the early fifties that British magazines were able to establish themselves. Once that happened a new generation emerged, amongst them Brian W. Aldiss, J.G. Ballard and John Brunner, and these would start to reshape science fiction in Britain.

One factor that emerged from this was that although much adventure science fiction was relegated to the boys' magazines, what we would now classify as literary science fiction was able to flourish without having a name. You have only to look at the names of many of the authors covered here—G.K. Chesterton, E.M. Forster, Rudyard Kipling, George Bernard Shaw, Charlotte Haldane, Aldous Huxley, James Hilton, C.S. Forester, George Orwell and J.B. Priestley, to name but a few—to realize that speculation about society, science and the mysteries of time and the universe was not the preserve of a handful of cranks and crackpots, as most science-fiction devotees were regarded, with their rocket experiments and lunar dreams. Not only were none of the works of these authors labelled as science fiction, most of them are still not. It is sad to say that in literary circles science fiction was not held in high regard, because it was always judged by critics based on the lowest common denominator. If the work was good, it couldn't be science fiction.

Science fiction in Britain did itself no favours in the early 1950s when many publishers jumped on the bandwagon of its popularity and churned out poor science fiction in lurid paperbacks written mostly by writers with no idea of genuine science fiction. As a result, anyone who wrote work that would now be regarded as genuine, quality science fiction, did their utmost for their books to be treated as mainstream. It was a problem exacerbated by comic-books and by the cinema where so many awful B-movies, usually involving monsters from outer space, gave the field a dreadful reputation from which it has still not recovered.

It was in fighting against this stigma that British writers led the way, chiefly J.G. Ballard and Brian W. Aldiss, whose works were championed by Michael Moorcock. When Moorcock took over the editorship of *New Worlds* in 1964, he threw out most of the old guard writers and brought in those who could develop what became called the "new wave". This was a genuine sea change, with a noticeable shift from the traditional form of science fiction to works that were experimental, innovative and, at times, unrecognizable.

Like all such movements, the new wave eventually dissipated, but it had had its effect both in Britain and the United States and a new generation of writers (and reinvigorated older writers) shook science fiction by the scruff of the neck and gave it a new suit of clothes.

So, the period around 1964 to 1966 is a good moment to mark the end of the classic period, roughly seventy years after H.G. Wells ushered in the realm of the scientific romance. Those seventy years contain a wealth of material, some of which is well known—George Orwell's *Nineteen Eighty-Four* being the most obvious—but much of which was little known at the time, let alone remembered today. In fact the only reason some of the books I cover here are remembered at all is because they were rescued or recorded by science-fiction devotees dedicated to tracking down and listing works in their favourite field of fiction.

Those reference works listed in the bibliography to this volume were amongst my starting points in compiling these one hundred titles, alongside my own collection. I wanted a selection that explored the diversity of ideas in British sf and which were representative of some of the best of those seventy years but also some that were unusual and quirky. These books are therefore not necessarily the best, neither are they all my favourites. Lists that attempt "best" and "favourite" are based on individual tastes which can change overnight with moods and fancies. I went for books which I felt reflected the times in which they were written, but which were also innovative, original, sometimes idiosyncratic, and, with the following caveat, a pleasure to read.

It is important to note that because these books reflect their times they also betray the prejudices and attitudes of the day. Some of them present ideas or characterizations which are today recognized as outdated or offensive, especially as regards issues of race and gender. It is disappointing that there is not a black hero in science fiction until Jan Rodricks in Arthur Clarke's *Childhood's End* in 1953, and of course this is still the work of a white author. Women are frequently represented in stereotypical roles and it is only occasionally that they rise above that, most spectacularly in Susan Ertz's *Woman Alive* from 1935. These books reflect a white man's world, and male perspectives at a time when, for most of these years, the British Empire had dominion over a quarter of the globe.

Most of these books I had read many years ago and needed to revisit them to make sure I remembered them accurately (and its sobering how often I hadn't). A number, though, were new, recommended by the reference works I checked or by fellow devotees, and these were a thrill to discover. My original working list was well in excess of a hundred books, which I gradually whittled down, but I haven't lost them all together, because I refer to many in my notes about the key books. With the exception of two authors (Wells and one other) I have limited the selection to one book per author.

So, here they are. One hundred books that reflect the fascination and fear Britain felt towards the advances in science and society from the end of the Victorian period through two world wars to the start of the swinging sixties. If your interest in any of them is sparked by this book then I will have achieved my purpose, and I hope if you are able to track them down you can explore and understand the breadth of what they have to offer.

WELLS, WELLS AND WELLS AGAIN

WITH THE ARROWS ALL POINTING TO H.G. WELLS AS THE starting point for our journey through classic British science fiction, we must ask the question as to what it was about Wells that caused him to write such innovative material. Why him and not his contemporaries? Was there something about his upbringing or education that steered him in this direction?

Wells was not born with a silver spoon in his mouth. His parents had been in domestic service but they took over a cousin's china shop in Bromley in 1855 and started a family. Their fourth child, born 21 September 1866, was christened Herbert George, but was always known as "Bertie". He received a basic education which was interrupted in October 1877 when his father fell off a ladder and broke his thigh. He had earned extra money as a cricketer, but that now ceased. The reduced income plus the cost of medical bills along with the shop not being profitable meant that Bertie's mother returned into service and the young lad had to find his own employment as soon as possible. By 1880 he was apprenticed first to a draper's, and then to a chemist, but neither lasted for long. His mother's

income allowed him to go to Midhurst Grammar School where his intellectual abilities were recognized. At the same time his sense of wonder was
being encouraged by the world about him, as he studied Jupiter though a
telescope, watched the sunset in awe and marvelled that the chalk downs
upon which he walked had once been at the bottom of a Cretaceous Sea.

All this was stifled when Bertie, now 15, was whisked away to a draper's
shop in Southsea to serve another apprenticeship. This ran for three years
before he returned to Midhurst Grammar where the headteacher, recognizing Bertie's talents, ensured he won a scholarship to the Normal School of
Science (which became the Royal College of Science in 1890 and Imperial
College in 1907) in London. For his first year he studied biology and zool-
ogy under T.H. Huxley (the grandfather of Aldous Huxley) who had been
a passionate supporter of Charles Darwin. Wells was heavily influenced
by Huxley who challenged his thinking, focusing his mind on the scientific
method. Wells's later teachers for physics and geology were, by contrast,
plodding and uninspiring, but Huxley was enough to make Wells a free
thinker who could let his imagination roam through the possibilities of
science and the future. Years later Wells wrote:

> I am extravagantly obsessed by the thing that might be, and impa-
> tient with the present; I want to go ahead of Father Time with a
> scythe of my own; I have a faith in human possibilities which has
> become the core of my life…

Wells had discovered his love of books at age seven when he broke his leg
at a cricket match. He spent weeks in bed and devoured adventure books.
He continued to read whenever he could and even made attempts at writing with mock pieces for *Punch*, though with no serious intent. By his own
admission everything he scribbled was "rubbish" and he made no use of
his growing scientific knowledge and passion.

While at the Normal School, Wells began a student magazine, *Science
Schools Journal*, with the first issue in December 1886. It contained his first

published work, a brief essay on Socrates. Although he was robbed of his editorship from April 1887, he continued to contribute and his earliest speculative writings appeared here, "A Tale of the Twentieth Century" (May 1887) and "A Vision of the Past" (June 1887). It also ran the earliest draft of *The Time Machine* called "The Chronic Argonauts", of which more later.

Wells attained a teaching post in Wrexham in 1887, but a serious foul in a football match injured his kidneys. He returned home to recuperate where it was also feared he might be tubercular. He continued to read voraciously and by 1889 was able to return to teaching, finding a post at one of the early Correspondence Course schools. He also married in October 1891, though soon divorced. From the papers compiled at the Correspondence School he assembled his first book, *Text-Book of Biology* in 1893.

Wells found he could supplement his teaching income with essays and reviews for newspapers and magazines. Amongst these early works were some significant items. "The Rediscovery of the Unique" (*Fortnightly Review*, July 1891) was a further step in the direction of *The Time Machine*, as was "The Man of the Year Million" (*Pall Mall Gazette*, 6 November 1893). He compiled some of these essays as *Select Conversations with an Uncle* (1895), his second book. He was now placing articles regularly with magazines and with two published books and a third in the offing, Wells took the plunge and gave up teaching to become a full-time writer. He was working day and night on the final version of *The Time Machine* and the infant world of the scientific romance was about to change for ever.

The Time Machine   H.G. Wells

London: William Heinemann, 1895

There had been a few stories of time travel prior to *The Time Machine*, but they rather cheated at the science and were not influential. People might unaccountably slip through time into the past and equally unaccountably return to their present. In "The Clock That Went Backward" (1881) the

American writer Edward Page Mitchell sent people into the past via a clock. In *El Anacronópete* (1887), by the Spanish writer Enrique Gaspar, the time machine is only able to travel back in time by flying fast around the Earth, backwards. Neither of these were memorable at the time, and Wells was almost certainly unaware of them.

Wells went about it entirely his own way and endeavoured to explain methodically the nature of time. Through the voice of the Time Traveller— we never learn his name—Wells explains that time, or rather duration, is the fourth dimension. The first is a single point, the second a line and the third is a cube which gives height (or depth) to what is otherwise on a single plane. For a cube to exist beyond a single moment, it has to have duration, but because we all travel through time—we all age at the same rate—we tend to disregard time as a dimension. And in the same way that a balloon allows you to rise up through the third dimension and then descend, so the Time Traveller exhorts that we should be able to move ahead through time or return.

He explains this to a group gathered in his study and demonstrates it with a small model of his time machine, which his audience believe to be a trick. Nevertheless, they agree to meet again a few days hence for a full demonstration. When they reconvene, the Time Traveller puts in a sudden, dramatic appearance, dishevelled and exhausted. He had experimented with his machine and now had a tale to tell.

He reveals how after a few tentative moves of a few hours and days the Time Traveller put the machine into fast forward and watched as the world about him changed rapidly. He became so entranced with the rise and fall of buildings and changes that he scarcely watched the year counter and when he finally stopped, he discovered he was in the year 802701.

He encounters a group of humans, the Eloi, each of whom was only around four feet in height and seemed almost child-like in their understanding and awareness of the world. He finds their world idyllic and believes that at last humanity has learned to live in peace and harmony. Then he learns the truth. During the last eight hundred millennia, the human race had followed divergent evolutionary lines. Those who had once been elite, the aristocracy and artists, had evolved into the Eloi whose lives were now essentially useless. They were ruled over by the original lower-class workers who had evolved into the strong, dominant, vicious ape-like Morlocks. They live underground and herd the Eloi like cattle. The Morlocks hide the time machine in their underground lair. He has to penetrate their world in order to recover the machine.

Most of *The Time Machine* takes place in the world of the Eloi and Morlocks, but the Traveller does venture into the far future, witnessing the dying Earth and the last living thing.

Wells's fascination with the future of humanity and his belief in Darwin's theory of evolution had produced a fascinating adventure based on sound scientific speculation. It was a true scientific romance—though Wells called it a scientific fantasia—and with it he launched what we could call the true Golden Age of science fiction. It had not happened over night. Wells has worked on his time travel theory for seven years. His original story "The Chronic Argonauts" remained incomplete and bore little in common with the final work other than the nature of the machine and the theory of time travel.

Wells continued to explore his thoughts on the future of mankind in several essays. In 1894 he wrote seven articles for the *National Observer* covering the possibility of time travel, the nature of a time machine and what the future might hold. His thoughts were still developing and it was another year before he reformulated them in the advance version of *The Time Machine* serialized in the *New Review* from January to May 1895. Texts were further amended for book publication—the American edition appeared first and is closer in parts to the *New Review* version—but the British edition became Wells's final statement. A short section about a possible devolution of humankind was deleted, and later reprinted as "The Grey Man".

The reception of the book was exceptional. The *Westminster Gazette* called it "ingenious", *The Realm* called it "wonderful", whilst the *Review of Reviews* called Wells "a man of genius". It established him immediately as a name to watch. Over the next three years he published *The Wonderful*

Visit (1895), *The Island of Dr. Moreau* (1896), *The Invisible Man* (1897), and the blockbuster *The War of the Worlds*.

The War of the Worlds   H.G. Wells

Pearson's Magazine, April–December 1897; revised, London: William Heinemann, 1898

There can be few who are not aware of *The War of the Worlds*, if not from the original novel, then from any of the film or TV adaptations or Jeff Wayne's musical version. Its plot is straightforward and perhaps all the more striking for that.

Observers are aware of flashes on Mars and soon what is believed to be a meteorite strikes the Earth near Woking, south of London. An astronomer, Ogilvy, goes to inspect and discovers it is not a meteorite but a metal cylinder, which has created a huge pit. Before long the cylinder top begins to unscrew and from it emerges a being about the size of a bear that glistens like wet leather. Wells succeeds in describing a creature that is truly alien, unlike any previous Martian in literature, and is evil. The authorities send a deputation to try and communicate with the creatures but are met with instant death from some form of heat ray. This weapon keeps humans, including soldiers, away from the Martians as they con- struct their walking machines during which time further cylinders arrive. It is only a matter of days before the Martians leave their pits, their bodies encased in a tripod fighting machine, and begin their destruction of the locality and their conquest of Earth.

One reason why the novel is so readable is because it is narrated by an everyday man-in-the-street who is caught up in events and can describe them in a way to which we can all relate. It brings the horrendous invasion right to our own door. The narrator pulls together threads of accounts by other survivors and gradually pieces together a wider picture. He believes the Martians have come to Earth because theirs is a dying world and they need another for expansion and food. Often forgotten is that within their capsules are other beings brought from Mars for food. These beings, already dead upon reaching Earth, are described as "bipeds with flimsy, silicious skeletons ... and feeble musculature, standing about six feet high and having round, erect heads, and large eyes in flinty sockets." The Martians, who have no body to speak of but are essentially large heads surrounded by tentacles, feed upon humans they have killed. They suck the blood from bodies and inject it into their veins.

By making these beings so evil and repugnant Wells reduces any sympathy we might have for intelligent aliens and makes it the challenge for humans to find a weakness and so subdue them. The fact that humans do not overcome them, and that the human race survives because of the smallest bacteria to which we are immune but to which aliens are not, shows humanity is not prepared. Wells, speaking through the narrator, draws a parallel with the British colonization in Tasmania at the start of the nineteenth century which led to the almost complete annihilation of the native population. "Are we such apostles of mercy as to complain if the Martians warred in the same spirit?" he writes.

Those thoughts may have been the seed that grew into *The War of the Worlds*. Wells later recalled that he and his brother Frank were walking through the Surrey countryside when Frank remarked: "Suppose some beings from another planet were to drop out of the sky suddenly and began laying about them here!" As the story developed in Wells's mind he sought to keep everything within the bounds of possibility and to contrast their existence with the commonplace on Earth. That way he made the story realistic which is why it is still so readable over a century later.

The original magazine serial was illustrated by Warwick Goble, with almost every page depicting the Martian war machines spreading death and destruction (*see Plate 2*). Many artists have returned again and again to depicting the war machines and a statue of one by the sculptor Michael Condron has towered above the pavement in Woking since 1998.

The public and critical reaction to the novel were immediate and immense, many recognizing Wells's extraordinary imagination and its power of presentation. Wells had made some revisions to the text after the magazine serial before the book edition, mostly by way of explaining the events in more detail, which added to the realism. He also left open in his epilogue the chance that the Martians might return.

If one measure of a book's success is the number of sequels, adaptations and parodies, then *The War of the Worlds* must surely be Wells's most successful and popular book. Probably the best known adaptation was that by Orson Welles with a script by Howard Koch for his Mercury Theatre radio broadcast on 30 October 1938. Its realistic format and presentation purportedly caused panic in the locality in New Jersey where the broadcast was set. It has added to the legend of *War of the Worlds* as one of the most effective and memorable works of early science fiction.

When the Sleeper Wakes   H.G. Wells

The Graphic, 7 January–6 May 1899; London: Harper & Brothers, 1899

After *The War of the Worlds*, Wells worked on several projects, including a batch of short stories, but his health remained poor. He had an abscess on his kidney and suffered a mental breakdown after meeting again his first wife Isabel (he had remarried in 1895). It was in this feverish period during 1898 that Wells's mind turned to a man severely overworked and unable to sleep, who turned to drugs to keep functioning but who eventually fell into such a deep, catatonic sleep, that he did not awake for two hundred years.

Such was the start of *When the Sleeper Wakes*, originally serialized in *The Graphic* with many fascinating illustrations by Henri Lanos, and then issued in a slightly revised book edition. Wells later grew dissatisfied with this version and revised it for a new edition in 1910 as *The Sleeper Awakes*, but his revisions add little and I believe the original version, with his still youthful exuberance and passion and a more intimate style, is preferable.

Wells has moved on from his thoughts of the far future evolution of humans, to considering the near future socio-political and economic evolution of the capitalist West.

The name of the Sleeper is Mr. Graham. He had been befriended in Cornwall by Mr. Isbister, an artist, in whose home Graham fell asleep. Unable to wake him, Isbister takes Graham to a local surgery and from there to London where he remains in a coma, looked after by Isbister and a cousin, Warming, a solicitor. Years pass and Isbister is now an old man but Graham has not aged at all. Between them Warming and Isbister set up a trust and guardianship for Graham and bequeath their estates to him. Isbister has made a fortune by creating murals along the cliffs of southern England—perhaps a prevision of "Banksy"!

Isbister and Warming pass away and Graham sleeps on—in time the phrase "When the Sleeper Wakes" passes into the English language for "Sometime, Never". But wake he does, after two hundred years in 2100 A.D., to find himself lying naked inside a transparent bubble. He frees himself but is weak and collapses.

When he comes to, he is bewildered by his surroundings and overwhelmed when he learns he has slept for two hundred and three years. Once clothed, washed and shaved, he is taken by his "guardians" to a nearby balcony and witnesses the world beyond. He sees a city of "overwhelming architecture" with huge buildings linked by bridges, roadways and moving platforms bathed in vast globes of light. He cannot take it all in but is aware of chanting. The public has discovered he has awoken and he later learns he had become a symbol of hope in what turns out to be an oppressed, controlled world.

What Graham has yet to learn is that through the Trust established by Warming and Isbister, he is a very wealthy man. The Trust is run by a Council of Twelve who had hoped Graham would never wake, because now he endangers their domination. As Graham becomes more aware, he looks for a way to escape and is helped by a popular uprising which allows him to flee across the rooftops. He runs into the protection of Ostrog, whom he sees as a friend. In fact, Ostrog is even more ruthless than the Council of Twelve, from which he had been rejected, and is looking to become master of the world. A Civil War breaks out with Graham as a pawn. He must fight both sides, but especially Ostrog, in order to survive.

The main thrust of the novel was to depict a dystopian fascist state ruled by an elite, and the story had an obvious influence on most such fiction, especially George Orwell's *Nineteen Eighty-Four*. But as part of the story's background, Wells considered what technological advances the world will have made in two centuries, something all too often overlooked in futuristic novels of the day. Transport is almost entirely by flying machine. Most tasks were achieved by machines, including pneumatic tubes which can send items vast distances very quickly. Graham marvels at the "neat dexterity of counting and numbering machines, building machines, spinning engines, patent doorways, explosive motors, grain and water elevators, slaughter-house machines and harvesting appliances…" There are huge television screens, though Wells gave them the laborious name of kinetotelephotographs. The idea of projection by electricity, which has an inkling of the internet about it, fascinated Graham. He realizes that most small villages have disappeared. "After telephone, kinematograph and phonograph had replaced newspaper, book, schoolmaster, and letter, to live outside the range of the electric cables was to live an isolated savage." Then there are the Babble Machines, spouting propaganda, a clear forerunner of George Orwell's omnipresent Telescreens in *Nineteen Eighty-Four*. Besides mechanical advances there is the curious case of hypnotism, practised by most psychologists and which has overcome the need for drugs and anaesthetics, and advanced the brain to do rapid mathematics.

Wells was not a one-idea man. When he developed his speculation on the future he followed it as far as his imagination would go. This was recognized by the editor of the *Graphic* when serializing the novel. In a special feature he wrote: "Mr. Wells stands out as a most original and daring writer, with a brain so active in its imaginings that at times one fancies he must see the whole future of the world written on the scroll of his fancy…"

The Country of the Blind and Other Stories   H.G. Wells

London: Thomas Nelson & Sons, 1911

In addition to his many novels, historical studies and political, theological and social tracts and essays, Wells wrote almost a hundred short stories, most of which are science fiction or fantasy. Some early stories were assembled in *The Stolen Bacillus and Other Incidents* in 1895 followed by *The Plattner Story and Others* (1897) and further compilations. More recently there has been an omnibus *Complete Short Stories* compiled by J. R. Hammond and during Wells's lifetime there were similar volumes, less complete but representative. Of these *The Country of the Blind and Other Stories* brought together, as Wells stated in his introduction, "all the short stories by me that I care for anyone to read again. Except for the two series of linked incidents that make up the bulk of the book called *Tales of Space and Time*, no short story of mine of the slightest merit is excluded from this volume." His total was thirty-three, most of which are science fiction and many of which first introduced the reader to unusual concepts. Most of them date from the 1890s when the youthful exuberance of his imagination poured forth visions of wonder and speculation.

There are stories involving previously unknown flora or fauna, such as a plant that sucks blood in "The Flowering of the Strange Orchid" (1894), an unknown species of bat in "In the Avu Observatory" (1894), the discovery of a dinosaur egg that hatches in "Aepyornis Island" (1894), giant octopi in "The Sea Raiders" (1896) and particularly voracious species of spiders in "The Valley of Spiders" (1903) and ants in "The Empire of the Ants" (1905). We experience the fourth dimension not as time but as another world in "The Remarkable Case of Davidson's Eyes" (1895) and "The Plattner Story" (1896). In "The New Accelerator" (1901) a drug speeds up the body's metabolism which in effect slows down time for the observer to the point when everything around seems to have stopped.

Of the remaining scientific stories three stand out. "The Crystal Egg" (1897) can be seen as a prequel to *The War of the Worlds* with an object found in an antique shop that seems to allow anyone who peers into it to see events on Mars. In "The Star" (1897) Earth survives total destruction from a near-Earth object thanks to the Moon. And "The Country of the Blind" (1904) in which an explorer discovers a lost world high in a valley in the mountains in South America where everyone is blind and is not even aware of sight as a sense.

Perhaps the most surprising omission from the book is "The Land Ironclads" (1903), an imaginary-war story in which Wells forecasts the tank, though one with pedrail wheels rather than a caterpillar tread. In 1911 Wells clearly did not consider this story important, but when the Great War was at its height the story was reprinted in the November 1916 *Strand Magazine* with a commentary by Wells.

Despite this omission *The Country of the Blind* is an excellent compilation of most of Wells's best short fiction and demonstrates the diversity of ideas and the extent to which he established a firm foundation for science fiction.

In his early scientific romances Wells had made speculative science both exciting and respectable and he established better than those before him, many of the basic concepts of science fiction. He would continue to speculate in the later books *The First Men in the Moon* (1901), *The Sea Lady* (1902), *The Food of the Gods* (1904), *A Modern Utopia* (1905), *In the Days of the Comet* (1906) and *The War in the Air* (1908), but most of these were written from his perspective of how mankind ought to find ways of bettering itself and moving towards a World state. He almost turned his back on science fiction and moved to social and satirical fiction ranging from *Kipps* (1905) to *The History of Mr. Polly* (1910) and *Ann Veronica* (1909) to *The New Machiavelli* (1911), but whilst these and other works play their part in English literature, it was his early scientific romances that had the biggest influence.

WARS TO END ALL WARS

H.G. WELLS'S *WAR OF THE WORLDS* IS A STORY OF INVASION and fits into a category of fiction that had mushroomed during the last quarter of the nineteenth century since the anonymous publication of "The Battle of Dorking" in the May 1871 issue of *Blackwood's Magazine*. Its author was Lieut.-Col. George T. Chesney, who had served in India and been wounded at the siege of Delhi.

Chesney's story, written after the defeat of France in the Franco-Prussian War, warned how unprepared Britain was for an invasion by Prussian forces, with their technologically advanced weapons. The story had a huge effect on the British public leading to a flood of stories speculating on the invasion of Britain, either by Germany or France. These in turn led to stories and novels about future wars, with Britain enmeshed in conflict, or of the threat of terrorists who use new weapons to dominate not just Britain or Europe, but the world.

By the 1890s these novels were appearing frequently, further inspired by the works of Jules Verne. Both *Twenty Thousand Leagues under the Sea* (serialized in France in 1869–70 and published in Britain in 1872) and

Robur the Conqueror (France, 1886; UK, 1887 as *The Clipper of the Clouds*) portrayed super-scientists bent on revenge. In the first, Captain Nemo has his powerful submarine, *Nautilus*, and in the second Robur has his battleship-like helicopter, the *Albatross*. It was clear from these novels that few nations had any response to a rogue scientist with advanced sea or air power.

The main catalyst in Britain was a serial published in the weekly paper *Black and White* between January and May 1892 and set just a few months hence. It was serialized as "The Great War of 1892", but when issued in book form later that year the date was left open as *The Great War of 189—*. It was a detailed projection written by a body of experts and presented in journalistic form as a series of reports, commentaries and announcements. The experts included Rear-Admiral Philip Colomb, Colonel John F. Maurice and Captain Frederic Maude. The reportorial style and its attention to detail gave it a frightening verisimilitude. It also proved to be remarkably prescient of the First World War. Following an attempted murder of Prince Ferdinand of Bulgaria by Serbian assassins, Serbians invade Bulgaria supported by Russia and the French. The Austrians, who are supported by Germany, declare war on Serbia and the various compacts lead Germany to invade both Russia and France, attacking France via Belgium. Britain allies itself to Germany against Russia and France. The war is short-lived as the Russians capitulate after heavy defeats.

Other papers soon capitalized on its success. *Pearson's Weekly* chanced upon the abilities of one of its own employees, George Griffith. He had put together an outline called *The Angel of the Revolution* and *Pearson's* ran the first episode on 21 January 1893 before Griffith had finalized the plot. As a consequence the serial rambled on for nine months, but proved immensely popular. Griffith tidied it up for book publication later that year. War has broken out in Europe in 1903, with Russia, France and Italy on one side and Britain and Germany on the other. Britain is overwhelmed and the government turns for help to a group calling themselves the Brotherhood of Freedom. These are really anarchists who have funded a fleet of flying machines. The Brotherhood agrees to help provided they can take over the government. Once in control the Brotherhood defeat the enemy and peace is restored with the Brotherhood ruling the world. Griffith wrote a sequel set twenty-five years later, *Olga Romanoff* (1894; serialized as "The Syren of the Skies") where it is seen that the Brotherhood have become a totalitarian master-race called the Aerians, and the last of the Romanoffs seeks to destroy them with a new super-submarine and mind-controlling drugs. All plans are thwarted, however, when it is discovered a comet is heading to Earth.

Griffith threw everything into these novels to the point where they become unbalanced and unrealistic, but that did not stop them being popular and reinvigorating the future-war novel. That same year (1893) E. Douglas Fawcett produced *Hartmann the Anarchist*. Like Robur, Hartmann has an advanced airship, the *Attila*, which is held aloft by pockets of hydrogen and driven by electrically powered propellers. He plans to destroy the major governments of the world to secure peace. However, he is overcome by grief when he realizes that in his attack on London he has killed his mother and Hartmann ends it all.

The other main contributor to the future-war novel was William Le Queux (pronounced "Cue"). In *The Great War in England in 1897* (1894; serialized as "The Poisoned Bullet" in 1893–4) Le Queux repeated the reportorial approach to chronicle a threatened invasion of Britain by Russia, who are supported by the French. The Germans and the Italians ally with Britain and invade France. Because of their superior sea power, Britain defeats the enemy at sea, but the Russians have advanced weapons and almost defeat Britain on land until a climactic battle south of London.

Between them, Griffith and Le Queux had set in motion a small industry in novels of future war or terrorist anarchy.

The Outlaws of the Air   George Griffith

Short Stories, 8 September 1894–23 March 1895; London: Tower Publishing, 1895

To capitalize on the success of *The Angel of the Revolution,* Griffith reworked the basic idea at a much shorter length and with a stronger framework. It is still a slightly rambling novel—Griffith was no stylist, but he was full of ideas—and has rather too many stereotypical characters, especially the evil German scientist Franz Hartog, who talks in mock German, but the end result is more readable and accessible.

The main villain is the charismatic Max Renault, a member of the Brotherhood of the Better Life, a group of terrorists whose actions are limited by a lack of funds. They come into a fortune when one of their members dies and his father, a rich industrialist, not only donates his money but also the plans his son had made for a scientifically advanced flying ship. Renault inveigles his way into the trust of other industrialists and soon has enough money to build a fleet of flying ships and develop the Brotherhood's island haven in the Pacific which they have called Utopia. With Utopia as a base, Renault starts his bombing raids on shipping and governments. Renault also intercedes in a war between Britain and Germany on one side and France and Russia on the other, effectively crippling both sides. At one point, Renault refers to his newly designed flying machine as an aeroplane, and though this word had been in use in technical papers since 1875, Griffith's use may well be its first appearance in fiction.

There is the inevitable falling out between rogues and Renault meets his fate, but the industrialists build upon his achievements and with the Utopians under the control of the newly formed Aerial Navigation Syndicate, establish the State of Oceana which, with its flying ships, now rules the world. Griffith introduces as co-founder and chairman of the Syndicate, the historical character Hiram S. Maxim. He was an American inventor, at odds with Edison over the invention of the lightbulb, and best remembered today as the inventor of the first portable fully automatic machine gun. Maxim had experimented with heavier-than-air flight and in July 1894, after he had settled in Britain, succeeded in flying an aeroplane for a few yards, but it was tethered for safety reasons. Maxim's name was in the news at exactly the time Griffith incorporated him in his novel.

It is clear that Griffith had not only reworked his own earlier plot but borrowed heavily from Jules Verne, with both flying ships like Robur's *Albatross* and an advanced submarine called the *Nautilus*. But unlike those novels, where Verne's vengeful scientists meet their ends and the world returns to normal, Griffith carries it through to achieve a super-state which ensures world peace.

Griffith continued to mine the mother-lode producing less inventive imaginary war novels such as *The Great Pirate Syndicate* (1899), *The Lake of Gold* (1903), *The World Masters* (1903), *The World Peril of 1910* (1907) and finally *The Lord of Labour* (1911) which he dictated as he was dying. But Griffith was not a one-horse writer and there was more to him than is first apparent. Until H.G. Wells established himself in the late 1890s, Griffith was regarded as the leading purveyor of pseudo-scientific fiction. Wells recognized this and, when he came to write his own future-war novel, *The War in the Air* (1908), his lead character (and former bicycle-repair man!) Bert Smallways, is inspired to experiment with building flying machines after reading Griffith's *The Outlaws of the Air*.

In his youth George Griffith (1857–1906) worked hard to obtain the necessary diplomas to teach but did not enjoy the experience and quit the profession in 1887. He secured a position with publisher C. Arthur Pearson and his talent and knowledge was put to good use answering questions in *Pearson's Weekly*'s "What Can We Tell You?" column. Griffith had served briefly as an apprentice on a merchant ship travelling between England and Australia, and he still delighted in travel. In March 1894, as a publicity stunt, Pearson challenged him to beat the previous record of 74 days for travelling round the world. Griffith achieved it in 65 days. At the same time he was working on "The Syren of the Skies".

Because he was so busy, it is no surprise that he borrowed ideas from others. For example, *Valdar the Oft-Born* (1897), a story of resurrection through the ages, owes much to *The Wonderful Adventures of Phra the Phoenician* (1890) by Edwin Lester Arnold. But he had moments of originality. "The Great Crellin Comet" (1897) is the first story where a giant gun is used to fire a projectile at and destroy a comet which would otherwise collide with Earth. *A Honeymoon in Space* (1901) follows Lord Redgrave and his new wife on their tour of the solar system in an airship powered by antigravity. They explore most of the worlds protected by space-suits.

Unfortunately, perhaps because of overwork, Griffith's health suffered and he turned to drink. He died from cirrhosis of the liver in June 1906 aged only forty-eight. By then his science-fiction achievements had long been overshadowed by those of H.G. Wells.

The Invasion of 1910   William Le Queux

Daily Mail, 14 March–4 July 1906; London: Eveleigh Nash, 1906

Building upon the success of his *The Great War in England in 1897*, but after detailed research and with more realism and atmosphere, Le Queux's *The Invasion of 1910* was also something of a publicity stunt. Lord Northcliffe, publisher of the *Daily Mail*, commissioned Le Queux to explore the consequences of Britain's lack of preparedness for any military invasion. Ahead of the newspaper serialization, Northcliffe published a map (*see Plate 3*) showing the German advance through England and ran a quote from Lord Roberts, who had been Commander-in-Chief of the British forces at the start of the Boer War, warning the public "what would be the condition of Great Britain if it were to lose its wealth, its power, its position."

Le Queux follows, in reportorial style, complete with maps, notices and proclamations, the surprise attack by German forces along the east coast of England and their rapid advance inland. The story covered events at many local villages and towns—thereby adding to sales of the *Daily Mail*—and showed the inadequacy of British troops. It is only when an army of volunteers comes together as the League of Defenders, that the Germans are outnumbered and defeated. But this is not before much of England is in ruins, many civilians killed and the economy in ruins. At one point, in acknowledgement of Lord Roberts's original demands, Le Queux wrote: "If Lord Roberts's scheme of universal training in 1906 had been adopted, the enemy would certainly never have been suffered to approach our capital."

The serial obtained further publicity at the start when Le Queux objected to the Prime Minister, Sir Henry Campbell-Bannerman, criticizing the invasion map as scaremongering. Le Queux took exception to the comment that "...it might conceivably alarm the more ignorant public at home." He countered by saying that the British public were as well educated and intelligent as those in any Continental country and he was disturbed that the British Prime Minister would cast such aspersions on his countrymen.

The book is only borderline science fiction, because it contains little by way of advanced military technology. Much of it reads as if someone was providing a running commentary, as would happen today on radio or television. There are moments of disturbing prescience, such as the attack on the British Museum, which came true in the Second World War during the Blitz when a total of six bombs caused considerable damage. The final bomb in May 1941 destroyed some 250,000 books. Thirty-five years earlier Le Queux had written:

As though to complete the disaster ... there came one of those terrible shells filled with petrol, which, bursting inside the manuscript room, set the whole place ablaze. In a dozen different places the building seemed to be now alight, especially the library, and thus the finest collection of books, manuscripts, Greek and Roman and Egyptian antiques, coins, medals, and prehistoric relics, lay at the mercy of the flames.

The serial and book were immensely popular. It is claimed the book sold over a million copies. Certainly the *Daily Mail* stated it had been read by millions, but that probably referred to the paper's circulation. The book's first edition of 130,000 copies sold out within days and over the next year it saw twenty-seven translations and was even popular in Germany.

Not surprisingly, a book of such popularity was lampooned, the best example being *The Swoop! Or How Clarence Saved England* (1909) by P. G. Wodehouse. The British are far too interested in the cricket results to pay much attention to an invasion. Not only had the Germans landed in Essex but eight other nations had taken the opportunity to invade. "There was barely standing room," Wodehouse noted. Britain is ill prepared. There was no regular army, and both the Territorials and the Legion of Frontiersmen had disbanded leaving only the Boy Scouts. When the enemy do untold damage to cricket pitches, golf courses and croquet lawns action must be taken and the Scouts, armed with catapults and hockey sticks and led by the redoutable Clarence, step up to the challenge.

William Le Queux (1864–1927) was a prolific writer with almost two hundred books to his credit, mostly detective thrillers or spy novels—he is regarded by some as the father of spy fiction. Besides his future-war fiction, or such warning stories as *The Terror of the Air* (1920), only a few of his works are classifiable as science fiction such as the lost-race novel *The Eye of Istar* (1897) and *The Unknown Tomorrow* (1910), about social change in Britain in 1935, which leads to mob rule (the British Museum is attacked again!). Le Queux was a radio pioneer claiming to be the first wireless experimenter to broadcast from his station in Guildford in 1920, but then Le Queux claimed many things and in his autobiography, *Things I Know* (1923), he enjoyed embellishing the truth.

When William Came   Saki (H.H. Munro)
London: John Lane, 1914 [1913]

Rather than spend time on military matters and explain how the Germans managed to invade and defeat Britain in a matter of days, Saki concentrated on what came after and how the British come to terms with living under German domination.

It's a rather carefree novel, so very different to the works of Griffith or Le Queux, and all the more refreshing for that. We discover the changes in society through the eyes of Murrey Yeovil, who had been unwell while in Finland and has only recently returned to England to discover the extent of the changes. He finds his wife Cicely has reconciled herself to the new regime as a *fait accompli* and is learning how to take advantage of it, but Yeovil is disgusted by how much of the upper class has been ingratiating itself with the German hierarchy.

We learn that the royal family and many landed gentry has left Britain for the colonies, particularly India. The German presence is primarily in London and the Germans have sought to respect the English culture and lifestyle. Whilst they realize that the current generation will have their axes to grind, for the Germans to succeed they need to win the hearts and minds of the younger generation, and that may not be so easy. Perhaps as a nod to Wodehouse's spoof, at the end of the novel a planned march-past by the Boy Scouts on the Kaiser's birthday doesn't happen, and the Germans keep waiting.

The novel is really a comedy-of-manners with a dark undertone, but written in Saki's deceptively light style, not unlike that of Oscar Wilde, with clever *bon mots* and social attitude. It is in stark contrast to some of the later novels where Nazi Germany occupies Britain, such as Brown and Serpell's *Loss of Eden*, discussed later.

Hector Hugh Munro (1870–1916), who wrote under the alias Saki, was a British journalist, born in Burma, who spent six years as a foreign correspondent in Russia and the Balkans. He was renowned as a short-story writer, many first collected in *The Chronicles of Clovis* (1911) and *Beasts and Super-Beasts* (1914). Munro was in Serbia at the time of the assassination of the Archduke Ferdinand and narrowly avoided death in the bloodshed that followed. He did not need to sign up to serve in the War because of his age, but he chose to. Alas, he was killed at the

Battle of Ancre in November 1916 by a sniper's bullet while sheltering in a crater.

The Struggle for Empire   Robert W. Cole
London: Elliot Stock, 1900

Although this book was published well before the previous two, I have placed it after them because it is so out of its time that considering it at its publication date affects our sequence of thinking. For although *The Struggle for Empire* is a future-war novel, it's not set in the years before the First World War but in the year 2236, and it's not set in Europe, or even on Earth, but in the depths of space beyond our solar system.

The author provides a quick future history. There had been a great European War early in the twentieth century when Great Britain, Germany and the United States allied against France, Russia, Turkey and other states. Britain and her allies were victorious and, between them, carved up the rest of Europe (Africa, Asia and the Pacific aren't mentioned). Britain became so dominant, that she and the United States were reunited and, with Germany, held sway over the rest of the world in an Anglo-Saxon Empire, with its capital in London. The French and Turkish races "died out".

Under British dominance education priorities changed, focusing on mathematics and science with the result that great scientific geniuses emerged. New forces were discovered—Dynogen, Pralian and Ednogen—which could be drawn almost limitlessly from the depths of space. These lead to astonishing engineering projects, including shifting the tilt of the Earth to bring a more tropical climate to Europe—regardless of its impact elsewhere! Scientists developed anti-gravity, enabling huge airships to travel to the other planets. The inner planets were not inhabited, and the natives of the outer giants were harmless.

The Anglo-Saxon Empire ruled all the planets and sought to reach further. The territorial gains beyond the solar system mirror the many

land-grabs on Earth during the Victorian era, especially in Africa. A problem arose when they came up against an equally powerful Empire based
on the planet Kairet orbiting the star Sirius. The Anglo-Saxon and Sirian
races were not only equally powerful, but equally greedy. It is at this point
the story starts, with a struggle for Empire on a galactic scale.

We are introduced to Lieutenant Alec Brandon of the interstellar
warship *Lightning*, his girlfriend Flora Houghton, daughter of the great
scientist Dr. Houghton, and their acquaintance James Tarrant who, at the
start, is absorbed on a scientific challenge of which we know nothing but
which he believes will make him Master of the Universe.

Events escalate when the Sirians discover that the Anglo-Saxons are
plundering the riches of a planet near the Sirian Empire. The two forces
clash with deaths on both sides. The Sirians send a Declaration of War to
London. Both sides develop their fleet. Earth's fleet consists of over 3000
vessels, the biggest of which are three-hundred yards long. This armada
leaves for the outer base on Neptune. En route two battleships collide with
their complete destruction and bodies hurled into space. Cole's description
is graphic, but as nothing compared to his account of the battle between
the two enemy forces. The Anglo-Saxon fleet is outnumbered and almost
destroyed. The Sirians advance on Earth, annihilating all in its path and
laying London to waste.

At that point James Tarrant perfects the invention he has been struggling
with and we learn that he has devised a way of countering the anti-gravity
drive of the Sirians. With a new fleet the Empire defeats the enemy and
drives them out of the solar system. The scale of the battle has corrupted
the fabric of space creating a warp that works back through the ether and
causes two of Jupiter's satellites to collide.

The ensuing treaty is harsh on the Sirians who have to pay huge repa-
rations. For his part in the victory Tarrant is given his own planet and
becomes Prince of Kairet. He marries Flora Houghton. Alec Brandon
also survived the war and marries the girl who had rescued him after the
destruction of his battleship.

The Struggle for Empire is a remarkable work on a cosmic scale. Although humanity still seems to have Victorian manners and attitudes, Cole tries his best to describe a future super-scientific world. No other work of British science fiction would envisage such galactic endeavours for another thirty years, and it was almost twenty years before the American pulp writers Homer Eon Flint, Edmond Hamilton and E.E. Smith wrote anything on an equivalent scale. SF historian E.F. Bleiler called it one of the "great missed opportunities in the history of science fiction", noting that had it had the same recognition as Wells's *The War of the Worlds*, science fiction may have advanced significantly.

There is little in the life of Robert William Cole (1869–1937) to explain how he came to write such an astonishing work. He was born into the landed gentry and was intended for the bar, but gave up law for literature and photography. He wrote two other novels of interest. *His Other Self* (1906), a humorous novel of a man possessed by his alter ego and *The Death Trap* (1907) which saw his return to the future-war theme. This time Britain and Germany fight to their economic self-destruction and the United States becomes the new power.

DOOM AND DISASTER

H UMANS HAVE COPED WITH SO MANY DISASTERS OVER THE
centuries—floods, earthquakes, plagues, drought, volcanic eruption
and comets from space—that it's not surprising stories about catastrophes
have been a regular part of science fiction.

Leaving aside the Apocalypse, the first disaster novel published in
Britain was *The Last Man* (1826) by Mary Shelley, the author of *Frankenstein*.
Europe, including Britain, is ravaged by plague. The last few survivors try
to reach Switzerland, but all but one die in the attempt. Lionel Verney,
the eponymous Last Man, makes it to Rome but decides he will wander
ceaselessly across Europe and Africa.

Mary Shelley had experienced the Year without a Summer in 1816.
That had been caused by the explosive eruption of Mount Tambora in
Indonesia in April 1815, the effects of which spread far beyond Asia. The
sun was obscured for most of the year. Rain was incessant, temperatures
plummeted and crops failed, leading to the worst famine in Europe in living
memory. At the same time a cholera epidemic had started in India in 1817
and spread throughout Asia and east Africa, halted, albeit temporarily, in

1824, but threatening Europe. Soon after the fear spread that Biela's comet would collide with Earth in 1832.

Thus, in just over sixteen years much of the civilized world was facing destruction by famine, climate change, plague and cosmic collision. And, as the nineteenth century progressed a further problem arose from industrial pollution. The Thames in London was polluted, as were the water we drank and the air we breathed. The average life expectancy in London in the 1850s was reported as 37. Killer smogs were known in London well into the early 1950s and were not abolished until the introduction of the Clean Air Act in 1956. One author who reflected upon the pollution in London was William Delisle Hay who, in *The Doom of the Great City* (1880) describes a London littered with corpses and a huge exodus because of excessive smog.

It was against this background that Richard Jefferies wrote the seminal book *After London* (1885). This is set over a century after some unexplained disaster had cataclysmic effects upon the Earth, tilting the planet on its axis, changing the climate and causing a psychological impact upon humanity. The result is an almost desolate, overgrown England, much altered, with a central lake and a deeply polluted area that was once London. Jefferies was one of a growing number who, horrified at the pollution inflicted upon England by factories and over-industrialization, looked back to more bucolic times.

As if natural disasters were not enough, those created by man also became a focus for writers who considered the power of the atom. And that is where we start.

The Crack of Doom   Robert Cromie

London: Digby, Long & Co., 1895

One of the earliest novels to consider the destructive power of the atom. As the megalomaniac scientist Herbert Brande comments near the start of this story, "...you will find that one grain of matter contains sufficient energy, if etherised, to raise a hundred thousand tons nearly two miles." Brande intends to put that power to use, but he does not reveal his hand straight away.

The narrator of the story, Arthur Marcel, trained as a doctor but never qualified because of an inheritance, and instead drifts around the world. He meets Herbert Brande upon a ship returning to Britain and becomes fascinated by Brande's eccentric, bombastic comments, such as "The Universe is a mistake!" He is even more entranced by Brande's sister Natalie and her friend Edith Metford, both of whom are modern girls, who dress like men, speak their minds and defy convention. Marcel is initially horrified by this and seeks to remedy their thinking, which he has little hope of achieving and, as the book progresses, he accepts their ways and subsequently finds he owes them much for his own survival.

It is his pursuit of Natalie that causes Marcel to meet Brande again and learn of his experiments with the atom. Brande has established a secret society, *Cui Bono?* (Latin for "who benefits?") which Marcel joins, after wrestling with his conscience, even though he knows there is danger. Brande, and a colleague Edward Grey, can exert telepathic influence over those in the Society even to the point of causing their death if they choose to leave or expose the society's plans. Brande also has telepathic control over his sister who knows far more about his plans than Marcel at first believes.

Brande plans to use atomic power to destroy the Earth in the belief that over aeons of time it will be reformed in its pure, virgin state. Brande believes that the release of atomic power has to be controlled. An attempt to reform a planet millennia ago led to that planet's destruction and the formation of what is now the asteroid belt. Brande thus plans a series of controlled atomic experiments culminating in the appalling destructive finale set to happen on the last day of the nineteenth century. Marcel has to find a way of stopping him and rescuing Natalie, despite the telepathic control.

Whilst the novel is uneven, the story propels the reader through the gathering events to the climax, where Cromie pulls few punches. It is especially interesting in presenting the image of the new woman, which was emerging in the 1890s, and seeing how Marcel comes to terms with these innovations, which he initially finds indecent.

Robert Cromie (1855–1907) was a proud Ulsterman, born and bred in County Down, into a large, prosperous, much respected family. He followed his brother into a career in banking, but found this too restrictive, and turned to journalism. He produced nine novels and three collections of stories in addition to many newspaper articles, often on engineering subjects or nature. His first book, *For England's Sake* (1889), described Britain's prowess in an imaginary future war between England and Russia in northern India and Afghanistan, and proved extremely popular, even being adapted for the stage. *The Next Crusade* (1896) was a sequel. His most imaginative work, *A Plunge Into Space* (1890), which led to him being compared with Jules Verne, tells of the eventful journey in a closed sphere to Mars and the adventures amongst the scientifically advanced Martians. The sphere was powered by an atomic force which created antigravity, and it seems that Cromie's thinking along these lines sowed the seeds for *The Crack of Doom*, which was his bestselling work. Unfortunately for science fiction, Cromie's other novels are primarily romances and did not sell so well, although the dramatic *The Lost Liner* (1898) about the fate of a supposedly unsinkable super-liner, caught the public imagination, and is eerily prescient of the *Titanic* disaster. Cromie died suddenly at his lodgings in Belfast aged only 51, from chronic nephritis, or what was then called Bright's disease.

The Violet Flame   Fred T. Jane
London: Ward, Lock, 1899

As in Cromie's novel, we meet a mad scientist, though one not so self-destructive as Herbert Brande. But, like Brande, Jane's Professor Mirzarbeau has harnessed the power of the atom which he can use to disintegrate matter by everything reverting to hydrogen. Mirzarbeau, known colloquially as the Beast, seeks no less than world domination which he rapidly achieves by his destruction of Waterloo Station and the Albert Hall. He savagely puts down any social unrest and ensures the execution of leading officials. He manifest a protective circle about him which no one can penetrate without their own destruction. The only way through is to wear a protective green disc which the Professor hands out cautiously to his apparent friends and supporters. These include Mr. Lester, the story's narrator, and a rich American lady, Landry S. Baker, with whom the Professor is infatuated. The Professor also has a secret society, with the rather transparent name of *Finis Mundi*, but it is not his plan to destroy the world, even though that is within his capabilities. Quite the opposite.

We discover that the solar system is sentient, with the Earth as the central brain. Mirzarbeau has tapped into the energy of the Earth to harness his destructive power. But the Earth is using the Professor for its own ends. It has tired of humankind and its endless wars. At the start of the novel, which is set only a decade or two in the future, Jane describes a global war, which is not a physical one, like the Great War, but an economic one. It is hoped that countries have recognized the destructive cost of war and will become more co-operative. How much of this came about naturally or was manipulated by the Earth is not explained. But although the Earth is in control of the Professor, there is some uncertainty over the Earth's plans. Mirzarbeau reveals, "The Earth is still bent on suicide, and millions of miles away in the depths of space a body of flaming violet is growing to do the deed…" Mirzarbeau uses his machines to control this comet and hold it at bay, but everyone believes that the Professor is controlling the comet to destroy Earth.

The novel thus has two dooms hanging over civilization, and it seems that only Lester, Miss Baker and a few others can overcome Mirzarbeau, but at what cost? This explains the novel's subtitle, "A Story of Armageddon and After." Jane has some powerful scenes as the comet approaches the

Earth and although the ending is now regarded as clichéd, Jane was amongst the first to use it in fiction.

John Frederick Thomas Jane (1865–1916) is best remembered for his series of books studying the world's navies, later called *Jane's Fighting Ships*, which first appeared in 1898 and to which he added *All the World's Airships* in 1909. He had long been a noted press artist and illustrator of naval events—living in Portsmouth, this world was on his doorstep. He illustrated many novels involving the sea and ships, as well as several sf novels where he used his imagination to create ships and aircraft of the future. This included the works of George Griffith, starting with *The Angel of the Revolution* and E. Douglas Fawcett with *Hartmann the Anarchist*, both in 1893. He soon turned to writing his own novels starting, not surprisingly, with a near-future imaginary war adventure, *Blake of the "Rattlesnake", or the Man Who Saved England* (1895). His later novels were something of a surprise as he moved away from his trusted territory, but they are no less ground-breaking. *The Incubated Girl* (1896) describes the creation of a human by chemical means, from an ancient Egyptian scroll. *To Venus in Five Seconds* (1897) is the first novel to suggest matter transmission as a means of visiting the planets. *The Violet Flame* was his last before he became committed to his naval and airship reference books and developing his Naval War Game scenario. He died suddenly at his home in Southsea aged only fifty.

The Purple Cloud   M.P. Shiel

The Royal Magazine, January–June 1901; revised, London: Chatto & Windus, 1901

On the surface, *The Purple Cloud* seems a straightforward last-man-on-Earth novel, yet it is anything but straightforward because Shiel wraps it in wreathes of mystical, cosmological and psychological shadows.

The basic story concerns Adam Jeffson who, through the machinations of his fiancée, joins an Arctic expedition. A millionaire has bequeathed $175 million to the first man to reach the North Pole. At the time Shiel wrote the novel, no one had reached the Pole, so Shiel could give free vent to his imagination. The expedition progresses only so far and it is left to four men to make the final push. Two die from exposure, and Jeffson kills another in an absurd duel, so reaches the Pole alone, discovering a pillar of ice in a lake perhaps a mile across. This provides one of those mystical moments for Jeffson, as he imagines the pillar has carved on it a name and a date, and fancies that the lake, which churns and splashes with the Earth's rotation, is alive.

As Jeffson returns to his ship he notices on the horizon a purple cloud and tastes in the air the flavour of peach. He encounters several dead animals and birds and, when he reaches his ship, his fellow explorers are also dead. Single-handedly he sails the ship back to England, landing in Dover, where he finds all are dead, including many from Asia. This puzzles him until he discovers that the death of humanity was caused by the eruption of a volcano in the Pacific which poured forth clouds of poisonous gas and dust. People had fled west away from the eruption and a few made it to Britain, but they could not escape the cloud.

Jeffson uses whatever means of travel he can find, including a steam train, to journey the length and breadth of Britain. The first sign of his later madness is when he comes across a sign outside a mansion saying "Trespassers Will be Prosecuted" and laughs hysterically. In his travels he comes to the house of Arthur Machen, and not only describes Machen in death but also an erotically-charged image of Machen's dead wife—a liberty that could be taken only by a close friend. Jeffson takes Machen's note pad and it is in this that he writes the account we are reading.

Jeffson's mental state deteriorates. He had already shown signs of paranoia and schizophrenia. He believed the universe is a battleground between Black (Evil) and White (Good) which are never quite in balance. Black seeks to destroy the human race and White to improve it. Jeffson wonders if he is an agent for Black but is being sustained by White. He dresses like a sultan and has delusions of grandeur, deciding he will build himself a palace. He becomes obsessive, wondering whether, if he did meet another, he might kill them. His actions towards the corpses become disturbing.

I have taken a dead girl with wild huggings to my bosom; and I have
touched the corrupted lip, and spat upon her face, and tossed her
down, and crushed her teeth with my heel, and jumped and jumped
upon her breast, like the snake-stamping zebra, mad, mad...!

He decides to destroy London through a series of explosions and leaves
England for France. He writes nothing in his journal for fourteen months
and is now clearly unstable. After briefly returning to England he records
nothing for seventeen years.

His later record reveals he had attempted to get to China where he
was convinced someone was alive, but was unable to approach the Pacific
as poison still lingered. He builds his palace on the island of Imbros near
Turkey and leads a decadent and delirious life. He has also been destroying cities and considers destroying Constantinople, which he had spared
because it was his main source of supplies, but cannot bring himself to
do it. Wandering the city in a state of madness he discovers a human foot-
print and following it stumbles upon a young girl, barely twenty. His first
reaction is to kill her for food and the belief he could no longer share the
world with anyone. After a long period of indecision between rejecting
or accepting her, he realizes he cannot live without her. He calls her Leda
rather than Eve, as he believes that absurd, but he recognizes that they are
indeed the new Father and Mother of mankind.

Matthew Phipps Shiel (1865–1947) is a difficult author to discuss. He
was at one and the same time a remarkably gifted writer of florid, exotic
prose, and a racist and paedophile. The latter caught up with him in
1914 when he served sixteen months for having sexual relations with the
12-year-old daughter of a woman with whom Shiel was living. It is difficult, knowing this, to read some of the passages in *The Purple Cloud* where
Shiel refers to young girls. One can't help but wonder whether some of
the anguish and hatred expressed by Jefferson in the novel represents Shiel's
own self-loathing. He never acknowledged that his conviction related to
a crime under English law because he saw neither himself nor the girl as

English. He had been born in Montserrat in the West Indies. His father, a ship-owner and lay minister was of Irish descent, and his mother was almost certainly black. Shiel hid that side of his ancestry admitting only to his Irish blood. He has been called anti-semitic chiefly because of the portrayal of the main Jewish character in *The Lord of the Sea* (1901), though this was not significantly at variance to the prevailing attitude in Britain at the time, much like his anti-oriental attitude in *The Yellow Danger* (1898). Although Shiel did not invent the phrase "yellow peril"—it had been used by the press since 1895 describing the threat of Eastern forces to the West after the Sino-Japanese War of 1894–5—he used it flagrantly in both *The Yellow Danger* and *The Dragon* (1913; itself reprinted as *The Yellow Peril* in 1929). It was these future-war novels along with *The Purple Cloud* that established Shiel's reputation, though his most effective and less prejudiced writing was his short fiction, much in the style of Edgar Allan Poe and more exotic, collected in *Shapes in the Fire* (1896), *The Pale Ape* (1911) and others.

The Machine Stops   E.M. Forster

The Oxford and Cambridge Review, Michaelmas 1909.
First collected in The Eternal Moment and Other Stories, London: Sidgwick and Jackson, 1928

"The Machine Stops" was first published in magazine form in 1909 and did not appear in any book until included in Forster's collection *The Eternal Moment* in 1928 and his *Collected Short Stories* in 1947. In either of those later years it would still seem remarkably prescient, but to appreciate the sheer vision of this story its original publication date should be noted.

The story is set in a distant future when much of humanity lives underground, and that is all they know of the world. They exist in small cells which they seldom leave and though they can travel they rarely do. It is their belief that the outside world is uninhabitable and would be instant death. Their whole life is cared for by the Machine, which provides food, communication, entertainment and rears their children. Most people love the Machine, almost worship it.

The story concentrates on the relationship between Vashti, who lives somewhere under what was Sumatra, and her son Kuno, who lives beneath what was England. Vashti is totally controlled by the Machine and is happy with the *status quo*, but Kuno has challenged his existence. He implores his mother to visit him, which she does reluctantly, because he does not wish to relay his story via the Machine. He tells her face to face that he has visited the outside world and that it is beautiful. He believes that the Machine is malfunctioning and will soon cease to operate.

The inevitable happens with the resultant chaos and the deaths of most, if not all of those underground. But, as Kuno had discovered, humans do exist on the surface and it is not the end of mankind.

Forster wrote the story against an over reliance on industrialization and in response to the future imagined by H.G. Wells in *The Time Machine*. Rather than the effete Eloi being controlled by the troglodyte Morlocks, Forster saw technology as controlling society. The story is also an allegory of totalitarianism, where the Machine represents the State and humans are manipulated as slaves. Yet Forster's image of the Machine is a remarkable forecast of much that is provided today by the internet and such applications as Skype, Wikipedia, video conferencing and, of course, television and radio, none of which was available when the story was written.

Edward Morgan Forster (1879–1970) is best known for his novels *A Room With a View* (1908), *Howard's End* (1910) and *Passage to India* (1924), none of which would prepare you for "The Machine Stops". He wrote no other works classifiable as science fiction, though the allegorical "The Celestial Omnibus" (1908) is a scathing comment upon intellectual snobbery and social ignorance.

FUTURES NEAR AND FAR

M OST OF THE BOOKS ALREADY DISCUSSED ARE SET IN THE future, usually because it's a way of warning of things to come, especially war or catastrophes. But the future allows for other opportunities such as satirizing the present, showing how society may change, considering new inventions or reminding us of the fate of the Earth and its inhabitants.

The following group of stories do all those things, but before discussing them it is interesting to consider when or why we started to think about the future at all.

The future was once the domain of prophets usually forecasting the end days of Earth and the Second Coming. Leaving aside religious prophets and turning to secular ones, the best known is surely Nostradamus, or Michel de Nostradame (1503–1566) whose *Les Prophéties*, dating from 1555, are claimed to have forecast many events in the twentieth century from the rise of Adolf Hitler to the death of Lady Diana. Of course, it's so much easier to fit events retrospectively into a vague and ambiguous text. What's more it has become clear that some of the prophecies attributed to Nostradamus were added by others in later printings. The same applies to the prophecies of the English seer, Mother Shipton (c. 1488–1561).

Amongst the English who looked to the future and dabbled in "speculative science" was Roger Bacon, who studied at Oxford in the thirteenth century. One work attributed to him, *Epistola de Secretis Operibus*, written around 1260, is a letter to a certain William of Paris, which says, in part, in a translation by Michael S. Mahoney:

> Now an instrument for sailing without oarsmen can be produced such that the largest ships, both riverboats and seagoing vessels, can be moved under the direction of a single man at a greater velocity than if they were filled with men. A chariot can be made that moves at an unimaginable speed without horses; such we think to have been the scythe-bearing chariots with which men fought in antiquity. And an instrument for flying can be made, such that a man sits in the middle of it, turning some sort of device by which artificially constructed wings beat the air in the way a flying bird does.

It's fairly certain this was written by Bacon and not a later commentator, because similar thoughts, alongside other expressed in the letter, resurface in Bacon's principal work, the *Opus Majus*, completed around 1267 and of which a copy, sent to the Vatican, survives. Bacon firmly believed in his "speculative science" because it gave an idea of something to strive for. He was way ahead of his time because later similar visionaries fell foul of the Catholic church and were imprisoned and even executed as heretics.

Even when we encounter a work of fiction looking ahead to the end of the twentieth century—*Memoirs of the Twentieth Century* (1733) by the Irish writer Samuel Madden—it was immediately suppressed and most copies destroyed. The reason for its suppression was not clear, but the book is violently anti-Catholic. Madden was Protestant, and though it was published anonymously, it was probably fear there could be a Catholic backlash.

Most of the occasional futurist texts of the eighteenth century are political in nature, but in the nineteenth century more attention was paid to scientific progress, especially in *The Mummy!* (1827), again published anonymously, but written by the nineteen-year-old Jane Webb. The book so intrigued the horticulturist John Loudon that he sought out the author and their friendship blossomed into marriage in 1830. Set in the year 2126 the novel forecasts many scientific achievements including weather control, steam-driven robot lawyers, an automaton steam surgeon, and post sent by steam-cannon. Many of these inventions are the ideas of the Queen and she is also advanced in the role and fashion of women—ladies in her court wear trousers.

Scientific progress nevertheless took a back seat to political and social changes in most future fiction and it was not until the speculations of Jules Verne and H.G. Wells that full consideration was given to how science will affect future generations.

The following examples show the diversity of how the future could be portrayed.

The Napoleon of Notting Hill G.K. Chesterton

London: The Bodley Head, 1904

This eccentric novel, which at its heart is a political satire, qualifies as science fiction not just because it is set in Chesterton's future—it starts in the iconic year of 1984—but it looks at the nature of progress and change.

Chesterton begins the novel by arguing that prophets are never right because society is driven by human nature which can be fickle. After citing several so-called prophets of his time, including H.G. Wells, Edward Carpenter and Sidney Webb, Chesterton reveals that over the next eighty years nothing has changed. He sees no World Wars or scientific advances, but there are nevertheless changes. The Royal Family has gone. Britain is governed by a despot, still called a King, but who is selected like a juryman from an official rotation list. One of the characters, Barker, argues that Britain is now "the purest democracy."

Early in the novel three characters, Barker, Lambert and Quin have a discussion with the ex-President of Nicaragua. Nicaragua has been taken over by the United States but, as the former President notes, "Nicaragua is not dead. Nicaragua is an idea."

This discussion resonates with one of the characters, Auberon Quin, who is regarded by others as a half-wit despite being well read and seemingly intelligent. Quin is fascinated by what constitutes humour and how people react to jokes. Barker and Lambert tire of him and are thus horrified when Quin, whilst bent double and talking backwards looking through his legs, is selected as the next King.

Quin's mind follows weird loops of logic which few understand but in most cases he is simply ruling by humour. One of his whims is to return London to a form of medieval government so that every borough is independent, with its own city walls and rules. Each borough is governed by a Provost and the Provost of Notting Hill, Adam Wayne, the eponymous Napoleon, who is only nineteen and had grown up admiring the King, took it seriously. He becomes very protective of the Borough and, when there are plans by the other boroughs to build a road through Notting Hill, he rebels.

A war breaks out between Notting Hill and the boroughs but Notting Hill not only acquires superior forces but a superior strategy because one of its number is a toy merchant who specializes in war games. Notting Hill wins and remains the dominant borough for the next thirty years until England tires of them. At the end, Wayne and Quin realize they should never have been at odds because they are just two parts of what constitute human needs—love and laughter, the fanatic and the satirist. These two opposing but complementary souls are needed in times of stress to guide humanity through its problems.

The novel was well received upon publication, all of the press making their own interpretations of Chesterton's intent and recognizing he was not only upholding the views of the little man against the mighty, but also supporting local patriotism over globalization. The latter has caused commentators to resurrect the novel from time to time. In 1974 Bernard Levin quoted it when considering the inevitable fate of the Soviet Union and its break-up into constituent republics, which of course happened in 1991. Michael Gove quoted it in 2008 when he wrote about the growing gang culture in London and how their territories are dictated by post-code areas. And its been quoted again with regard to the European Union and Brexit, or the possible break up of the United Kingdom into its separate nations. Whose to say that Chesterton's whimsy, based on his understanding of human nature, may yet come to pass.

G.K. Chesterton (1874–1936) is today best remembered for his series featuring Father Brown, the intellectual local priest who has a better understanding of crime and criminals than the police. These stories, which began appearing in 1910, are, to some extent, a natural extension of *The Napoleon of Notting Hill*, because Father Brown is the lord of his parish and understands it better than anyone. Several of Chesterton's later works are set in an England either threatened from within by its own underworld, as in *The Man Who Was Thursday* (1908), or threatened from without by other cultures, as in *The Flying Inn* (1914). A love of a pre-industrial past reappears in *The Return of Don Quixote* (1927). Chesterton was a political and literary polymath, able to turn his hands and mind to almost any subject and always in a challenging way. It's why his work is as relevant today as it was a century ago.

With the Night Mail   Rudyard Kipling

The Windsor Magazine, December 1905; slightly revised, New York: Doubleday, Page & Co., 1909

When this short story was first published in Britain in *The Windsor Magazine* in 1905, it was accompanied by several striking black-and-white illustrations of future transport by Henry Reuterdahl and Henry Seppings Wright.

In 1909 it was published separately in the USA as a small book with the illustrations in colour, including several not used before and, unusually, an appendix of invented advertisements and material relating to the Aerial Board of Control. It sported a wonderful cover by Frank Leyendecker, and beautifully illustrated end-boards, making the book a delightful treasure and one of the early science-fiction collectibles (*see Plate 4*).

The story is set in the year 2000, though *The Windsor Magazine* dated it as 2147. At the time it was written the aeroplane was in its infancy and Kipling envisaged a future where the airship was still master of the skies. The Aerial Board of Control, based in London, has offices throughout the world. It controls all air and related traffic and the transport of mail. Over time, it has become the major global corporation oiling the wheels of the world, and effectively running the planet.

The story tells of a mail ship transporting its contents from London to Quebec, across the Atlantic. Bearing in mind that the first successful Atlantic crossings did not happen until 1919, Kipling was way ahead of his time and describes the process in fine technical detail. He has invented something called Fleury's Ray which controls the phasing of Fleury's Gas through the turbines and powers the dirigible. The airships follow appointed lanes with Mark Ships en route to monitor progress. Although there is no national radio, the airships operate a worldwide network of radio services with weather forecasts, problem alerts, landing priorities and so on which Kipling calls "flying control" decades before that came into being.

The primary drama of the story, apart from describing a transatlantic journey through violent weather, is when they rescue the crew of a private airship, which allows for some vivid descriptions. Otherwise the story is about the technology. That makes it strained reading today, but it was eye-opening in 1905. The accompanying adverts and notices in the book edition, whilst adding to the technical data on guide-light changes and comparative notes on the advantages of dirigibles over planes, also add a sense of time and place making "With the Night Mail" a remarkable piece of science fiction.

Kipling slips certain background facts into the story. Nationalism has disappeared and with it war. We learn more in the sequel "As Easy as A.B.C.", published in *The London Magazine* for March and April 1912. We discover that population growth has been reversed, and that people are healthier and generally stronger—the average height for men is now 6 feet 8 inches (two metres).

Kipling apparently wrote the first draft in 1907 but was not satisfied with it at the time, perhaps partly because of the developments in the aeroplane over the airship. The first printing takes place in 2065, sixty-five years after "With the Night Mail", but the final printing sets the year at 2150, only three years after the revised prequel.

Kipling concentrates on the personal and social implications of the Aerial Board of Control which has robbed the world of its privacy. Individuals want to recover their personal identity. Officials of the A.B.C. learn that the North Illinois district has cut itself off from the communication network. They fly there in an efficient new aeroplane to meet the Controller but he has gone to Chicago and they meet his daughter. She immobilizes them with a system of ground-circuits, an intriguing prediction of a force-field. When the officials reach Chicago, they discover that the working-class, or "Serviles", are the root of the problem. The Serviles demand the return of democracy and the vote, but it is clear that in Kipling's future most of the public are happy to be left to their own devices and let the A.B.C. run everything. Kipling could almost be describing how the world of E.M. Forster's "The Machine Stops" came about, because both societies have relinquished the democratic rights for universal control.

Most people do not support the Serviles and are afraid of the crowds that have formed. It was likely that the Serviles would have been killed, so the A.B.C. captures them and takes them to London where they can be watched, perhaps in a music-hall "freak show".

When "As Easy as A.B.C." was first collected in *A Diversity of Creatures* (1917) one reviewer called it "Perhaps the finest short story of the future that has ever been written." Both stories have been reprinted many times since.

Rudyard Kipling (1865–1936) is so closely associated with his *Jungle Books* and *Just So* stories, and his novel *Kim*, that many are surprised that he would dabble with science fiction. But he was fascinated with new technology and explored it in several stories. In "The Ship That Found Herself" (1895), a new freighter is so well equipped that it develops its own personality. In "Wireless" (1902) he speculates that a new wireless set (still in its infancy) seems to be picking up the voice of the poet John Keats, who had died eighty years before. John Brunner assembled a selection of these stories in 1992 as *Kipling's Science Fiction*.

The Night Land   William Hope Hodgson
London: Eveleigh Nash, 1912

This work is of such towering imagination that if the author hadn't chosen to relate it in a pseudo-archaic form of English, I would unhesitatingly classify it as the most remarkable work of science fiction ever written, rivalled only by Olaf Stapledon's *Star Maker*. Alas, you must acclimatize yourself to the language, which requires such perseverance that it is all too easy to give up, and so miss a work unequalled elsewhere in the field.

The novel's framework is almost irrelevant and is another barrier to breach. A man of the seventeenth century, mourning the loss of his Lady Mirdath, forges a mental link with a young man living in the Last Redoubt on Earth, millions of years in the future. The story that follows is that of the young man.

The Last Redoubt is the final refuge of humanity, which is about a million souls. It is a huge pyramid over seven miles high and almost six miles wide on each side. Both within and under the pyramid are tunnels and chambers. The Redoubt is protected from the outside world by the Earth Current. In this far future the Sun has died and the only light comes from volcanoes and the glow of the Earth Current. Beyond the Redoubt are strange creatures which are happy to spend millennia waiting for the

Redoubt to fall. These are The Watchers, based at each of the four corners of the pyramid. The largest of these is the Watcher of the South which is immeasurably old. The narrator tells us:

A million years gone, as I have told, came it out from the blackness of the South, and grew steadily nearer through twenty thousand years; but so slow that in no one year could a man perceive that it had moved. Yet it had movement, and had come thus far upon its road to the Redoubt, when the Glowing Dome rose out of the ground before it—growing slowly. And this had stayed the way of the Monster; so that through an eternity it had looked towards the Pyramid across the pale glare of the Dome, and seeming to have no power to advance nearer.

Locations beyond the Redoubt have such evocative names as The Place Where the Silent Ones Kill, the Valley of the Hounds, The Country Whence Comes to Great Laughter, the Place of the Ab-Humans and the Headland From Which Strange Things Peer. These places and creatures were the result of irresponsible scientific experimentation in the distant past, but which is still our far future.

The narrator is telepathic and he picks up a message from beyond the Last Redoubt, another refuge, the Lesser Redoubt, which had been built millennia before but of which all had been forgotten. The message is from a young girl, Naani, who the narrator believes is a reincarnation of his Lady Mirdath. Naani reveals that the Earth Current protecting the Lesser Redoubt is fading and that they are at the mercy of the preying monsters.

An expedition is brought together to rescue the survivors but this meets a horrendous fate at the House of Silence. The narrator decides he must go it alone, and though others in the Last Redoubt try to dissuade him, he is determined to rescue Naani.

From then on *The Night Land* becomes a quest as the narrator battles to elude the horrors of the world beyond the Redoubt. He is armed only with a *diskos*, a rotating blade powered by the Earth Current. His only way of knowing where he's going is through his telepathic contact with Naani whom he suddenly stumbles across. The Lesser Redoubt had fallen and she alone had escaped. Now the narrator and Naani must make their way back to safety.

Once you attune to the language, which though a genuine barrier, does gradually add to the atmosphere, the adventure in the Night Land is as exhilarating as it is formidable.

When it was published most reviewers were perplexed. The critic in the *Pall Mall Gazette*, whilst recognizing Hodgson's vivid imagination, confessed he was baffled but added: "We can heartily recommend it to those whose mental teeth and temper are strong enough to worry contentedly a bone of truly adamantine quality." But over time the book acquired a cult following which was bolstered by H.P. Lovecraft's comment that it was "one of the most potent pieces of macabre imagination ever written."

William Hope Hodgson (1875–1918) had already established himself as a first-class writer of weird tales of the sea—he had served as a merchant seaman for most of the 1890s—and had some success with his stories of the occult detective Carnacki, which had first appeared in 1910 and were collected as *Carnacki the Ghost-Finder* in 1913. His first published novel, *The Boats of the 'Glen Carrig'* (1907) was also written in an arcane language but is more approachable. It is the story of a boat trapped in the weeds of the Sargasso Sea and of the horrendous creatures the survivors encounter. Evidence suggests that *The Night Land* may have been written earlier but was only published once his other books had established a market. *The House on the Borderland* (1908) is another work with a cosmic vision quite probably influenced by H.G. Wells's *The Time Machine*. Hodgson was killed in the First World War, at Ypres, aged only forty, and a tremendous talent was lost.

The Elixir of Life or 2905 AD   Herbert Gubbins

London: Henry J. Drane, 1914

This is more like a catalogue than a novel, but a fascinating one for all that. It's really an excuse for imagining what the world a thousand years hence might be like. A scientist, Sir Thomas Browne, realizes that through the use of radium, from which he derives a substance called electrum, he can prolong his life by suspended animation and rejuvenate his body. He hides in an ancient catacomb, from which after two centuries his body is discovered and removed to a university which is where he awakens, as planned. Thereafter the book is a series of scientific revelations and wonders.

Before understanding the technology of the future, Browne learns that there is no longer a royal family in Britain. England and the United States amalgamated as a Limited Company. The major nation is Japan which had merged with China and overpowered parts of Russia. Gubbins accurately predicts the Russian Revolution and the murder of the Czar. There have been no more wars in recent centuries—the final war had been between remote-controlled machines. There now exists a post called the Defender of the Peace of the World which decides problems between nations through a code of international law.

The sun's energy is harnessed in two ways: by way of mirrors which act as a crude form of solar panel, and by way of "sun-blocks" where energy is stored and used as fuel. Gubbins proposes that electricity circuits the Earth above the atmosphere which is utilized via a magnet tethered in orbit. Streets are lit by lamps with luminescent bacteria.

Local communication is by way of thought projection or telepathy which works by a highly developed use of "ethereal vibrations". Adepts have developed the power of the mind to controlling human actions.

For communication over longer distances there is a form of television, called the unisophone, which transmits images of events around the world. Newspapers are produced by the same means. Travel is fast—a journey from India to England takes two hours and ships can voyage round the globe in two days. To avoid collisions there is something like radar.

Page after page reveals new scientific wonders. Servants are automatons powered by a form of static electricity. There are moving walkways of various speeds through cities. Trains have been superseded by electric balls which move at four hundred miles per hour. Some cities are encased in glass domes, and many buildings are made entirely of glass. Food, providing all the nutrition required, are concentrated into chewable "tabloids", something Browne did not get used to.

Not everything has advanced. It does not appear that women have equality with men though they are more sexually liberated and it is expected that women will propose marriage, not men. Women can fly using sun-powered wings.

Browne spends time working with the scientists of the day who, though they have managed to create suspended animation as Browne had, they did not have the marvel of his electrum which rejuvenated the body.

The catalogue of inventions moves on to become a travelogue as Sir Thomas travels around the world witnessing marvel after marvel.

Browne discovers that there is an impending disaster. He learns that Earth is in regular communication with Mars and the Martians, who are even more scientifically advanced than humans, have discovered a dark planetoid heading towards the sun which will trigger a nova, destroying life on Earth. Underground shelters are being built but may not be sufficient. An adept tells Browne he should be able to send him back to his own time.

At that point Browne wakes up in Rome and discovers that it has all been a dream—a most disappointing conclusion. The suspended animation had not worked but his rejuvenating electrum had.

Newspaper reviewers were impressed at Gubbins's imagination, especially for someone aged only twenty-six and apparently sales were good. It is perhaps surprising, therefore, that he appears to have written nothing else. Research suggests that in 1919 Herbert Gubbins (1887–1950) became an assistant master at Ardingly College and, from 1924, a senior English

master at Beddingham College, but it also appears that after his father's
death in 1933 Gubbins returned home to look after his father's farm.

The Elixir of Life is one of those astonishing feats of scientific imagination that would later become the hallmark of the type of science fiction
developed in the United States by Hugo Gernsback, in the hope of encouraging enterprise and invention.

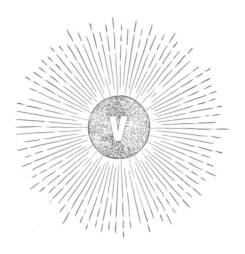

THE OLD AND THE NEW

ONE OF THE OLDEST THEMES IN SCIENCE FICTION, PERHAPS the oldest, is the discovery of lost or unknown worlds. It is not that surprising, because in the ancient world, sailors were unable to undertake long voyages or expeditions, and much of the world remained undiscovered, at least to western civilization. Humanity had, of course, expanded around most of the globe in the centuries after the end of the last Ice Age, but many islands, particularly in the Pacific Ocean, remained undiscovered and uninhabited. Hawaii was not settled by humans until around 300AD, Easter Island some time in the 1100s, whilst New Zealand was not inhabited until around 1250. The Antarctic continent was not even sighted until 1820.

So for centuries the world was wide open for writers to imagine unusual civilizations and creatures. If ever there was a book that encouraged an interest in exploration it was *Il Milione*, better known as *The Travels of Marco Polo*, written down around 1300, and telling of Polo's travels through Asia. It had a popular imitation in *The Travels of Sir John Mandeville* which was circulating by the late 1350s.

With the discovery of the Americas in 1492 the fictional travelogue expanded. Thomas More's *Utopia* (1516) is set on an island off the coast of South America. Francis Bacon's Bensalem in *New Atlantis* (1626) is an island somewhere in the Pacific, west of Peru. Jonathan Swift describes many unknown islands in *Gulliver's Travels* (1726). The list of such places and discoveries grows at an alarming rate during the eighteenth century as the globe itself is explored and blank areas on the map gradually filled. The spirit of exploring the unknown was no better stated than by Samuel Taylor Coleridge in *The Rime of the Ancient Mariner* (1798) where, after the ship is accursed by the killing of the albatross, it drifts through fog and mist until:

> *The fair breeze blew, the white foam flew,*
> *The furrow followed free:*
> *We were the first that ever burst*
> *Into that silent sea.*

As the map shrank so writers looked to more remote places to hide their forgotten lands. They might be underground as in Bulwer Lytton's *The Coming Race* (1871), or in Africa, as in *King Solomon's Mines* (1885), or the Antarctic in *The Great South Wall* (1899) by Frank Savile, or the Arctic in *The Mystery of the North Pole* (1908) by C.A. Scrymsour Nichol. Or, of course, South America, in probably the best known of all such novels, *The Lost World* (1912) by Sir Arthur Conan Doyle, discussed here. It wasn't the last lost world adventure—two more are discussed later—but they were becoming fewer and authors turned more to outer space or other dimensions to discover worlds.

As old themes faded so new ideas blossomed, one of which was of the superhuman. In some ways it was another old theme, because so many of the ancient heroes of legend, especially Greek legends, had been super-heroes, such as Herakles, Perseus and Atlas. But their strength owed much to what gifts they had been granted by the gods and it has no scientific basis. The idea that a being of enhanced physical or mental powers might be bred or engineered in some way is a far more recent idea.

The German philosopher Friedrich Nietzsche had suggested that if humanity continues to evolve in the far future humans might become what he calls
übermensch in *Thus Spoke Zarathustra* (1883). His word, properly translated as
"beyond man", was more commonly read as "superman" and it was in this
context that George Bernard Shaw used it in his play *Man and Superman* in
1903. H.G. Wells also pursued the idea in *The Food of the Gods* (1904), where
scientists develop a food which when fed to children (and animals) causes
them to grow into giants. Wells's novel, however, did not consider the
mental advance of the children or how this development in growth might
be inherited genetically. It was down to J.D. Beresford in *The Hampdenshire
Wonder* (1911) to consider the effects of mental advance by natural selection.

The Hampdenshire Wonder   J.D. Beresford

London: Sidgwick & Jackson, 1911

This is regarded as the first important novel about the next step in evolution in terms of human intelligence. Although it still feels Edwardian in its
mores and attitudes, it sets a challenge in how society copes with enhanced
intelligence on an intellectual, moral and religious level.

It is the story of Victor Stott, the son of a professional cricketer, who
for a while was England's most famous sportsman until he loses a finger
in an accident and is forced to retire. He vows he will raise a son who will
be even more famous but is horrified when the child is born with a macro-
cephalic head and is regarded, in the parlance of the day, as a "freak". The
father cannot cope with being near the child and leaves the family and the
mother raises the child on her own.

The narrator first meets the child, then a little over a year old, on a train
and is disturbed by the infant's almost malevolent stare. He seems able to
control the actions or minds of others with his eyes. It is seven years before
the narrator meets the child again and we learn that in the meantime a
benefactor has entered the boy's life in the shape of the local squire, Henry

Challis, who becomes aware of the child's superior intelligence. He moves them to a house nearer his own and allows the boy access to his library. He is astonished to see the boy methodically read every book, starting with a dictionary and the *Encyclopaedia Britannica*, but soon working through every volume, including those in other languages which he manages to teach himself. The boy seldom speaks and when he does, struggles to use a language which is clearly insufficient for the thoughts and concepts he wishes to express.

Young Victor has made an enemy in the local rector, Percy Crashaw who, despite a scientific training, is blinkered by his religious views. When Victor is five he has an altercation with Crashaw over religion, and although we do not know what the boy said, Crashaw regarded it as vile blasphemy. Although Challis has taken on the role of helping the child's education, Crashaw insists the child should be at a state school and Challis's victory over this makes an even greater enemy of the priest.

The narrative uses words and phrases which are politically incorrect these days but were in regular use in Edwardian England. Victor is frequently referred to as an "idiot" or, more specifically, a "hydrocephalic idiot", because of his enlarged head. At the time the definition of an idiot was of someone who had a very low intellectual ability, but as we discover this is far from the truth because young Stott has a greater intellectual capacity than anybody. Challis suspects that his mental capacity is a thousand years or more beyond others. Victor is aware of how different he is to others and by reading he hoped to better understand himself. More than once he asks Challis, "Is there none of my kind?"

The narrator looks for other child prodigies comparable to Victor and finds a historical reference to Christian Heinecken, dubbed "the infant scholar of Lübeck", who lived in the 1720s but died at the age of four. However, Heinecken's superior learning came from reading books, whereas Stott's mental capacity and influence was evident from the start, years before he had access to books.

Stott is contrasted with the village "idiot", a young lad called Harrison, who clearly does have learning difficulties and who frightens Stott, because he is the one person he cannot control with his eyes. Harrison wants to befriend Stott because, so the narrator feels, the boy is the only one like him. Unfortunately, Harrison is not in control of his actions and when he tries to be friendly it is interpreted as a prelude to violence.

The world is not ready for the likes of young Victor. Even those who befriend him—or as close as he allows them—find it uncomfortable. The narrator wonders whether as the child ages he will look less alien, because as the body grows so the head looks less out of proportion. Alas, fate intervenes and Stott does not have the chance to fulfil whatever his potential might have been.

When musing over the child, Challis pities him because he suspects that if Stott was the next step in human mental evolution, then Challis had "glimpsed a finality", a future robbed of mystery because all questions have been answered. While reflecting on this Challis states the driving force of humans which encourages our scientific imagination. The following statement, I feel, also highlights the role of science fiction in expanding our mind.

Is not mystery the first and greatest joy of life? Beyond the gate there is unexplored mystery for us in our childhood. When that is explored, there are new and wonderful possibilities beyond the hills, then beyond the seas, beyond the known world, in the everyday chances and movements of the unknown life in which we are circumstanced.

John Davys Beresford (1873–1947) was heavily influenced by H.G. Wells, about whom he wrote a critical study in 1915. But seeds had been sewn in Beresford's mind when young. He suffered from polio and was thus confined, spending long hours reading, just as young Stott does. He rebelled against his clergyman father's strict religious views and, for many years, was an avowed agnostic. Beresford's vision was always towards a better world but recognized that hurdles could not be overcome without some cataclysm. In *Goslings* (1913) a plague wipes out most men in Europe and

Asia and humanity has to rediscover the basics to rebuild the world. In *Revolution* (1921) the social and political upheaval in a post-war England leads to famine and a breakdown in society which only a revolution resolves. In *A Common Enemy* (1942) a series of earthquakes puts an end to the Second World War and eventually brings mankind to its senses. It concludes, rather like *A Hampdenshire Wonder*, in speculating on a new race of humans.

Beresford wrote many other works of science fiction and the fantastic but *A Hampdenshire Wonder* remained his favourite, partly because it almost wrote itself, and was completed in under four months. Amongst his literary friends were H.G. Wells, Walter de la Mare, George Bernard Shaw, D.H. Lawrence and Cecil Day-Lewis, and the literary spirit continued through his children, notably Elisabeth, the creator of the Wombles.

The Lost World　Arthur Conan Doyle

The Strand Magazine, April–November 1912; London: Hodder & Stoughton, 1912

By 1911 Sir Arthur Conan Doyle had accepted he would have to write more stories featuring Sherlock Holmes. He did not like the idea, but it was favourable for his bank balance. But he was always on the lookout for new and exciting ideas.

He had become interested in the fossils of dinosaurs, especially when some were found in a quarry near his home at Windlesham in Surrey. In February 1911 Doyle attended a lecture given by Colonel Percy Fawcett who was mapping the Amazon basin. Doyle showed interest in Fawcett's description of the flat-topped plateau of the Ricardo Franco Hills in the Mato Grosso, now known as the Huanchaca Plateau, in Bolivia's north-east border with Brazil.

Doyle brought together the two threads and wrote *The Lost World* in just three months. In the process he created another memorable character, Professor George Challenger, a man with total belief in his profound knowledge and infallibility. Doyle had based him partly on his old anatomy professor at Edinburgh University, William Rutherford, who was short, had an enormous chest, a voluminous beard and a booming voice.

Challenger was convinced that prehistoric creatures may still survive on an isolated plateau in South America. He assembles a team of four, including himself, journalist Edward Malone, explorer Lord John Roxton, and Professor Sumerlee, the token sceptic.

Using a map Challenger had acquired from a former explorer, the four reach the base of the plateau but find the only access route had been blocked by a rockfall. Instead they climb an adjacent pillar of rock and fell a tree to cover the chasm between them and the plateau. Unfortunately, once on the plateau two of the native bearers dislodge the tree removing the only escape route, so the explorers must find a way to survive. They discover a variety of dinosaurs, are captured by ape-men, rescued by cavemen and eventually find another way off the plateau.

At the end of the novel, we discover that the party has smuggled back to England a pterodactyl's egg, which has hatched. When Challenger gives a lecture about their adventures to a highly sceptical audience he releases the pterodactyl, causing much havoc before it flies away across the London rooftops heading back to South America.

When the novel was serialized in *The Strand Magazine*, the artist Harry Rountree provided over forty illustrations including several of dinosaurs such as pterodactyls, an iguanodon, a stegosaurus and an allosaurus (*see Plate 5*). It would have been an innovative introduction for many readers to the monsters of the prehistoric world.

There is a dark element in the serial. With the help of the explorers, who are armed with guns, the cavemen defeat and destroy the entire race of ape-men. It reflects Doyle's view of the authority of superior races over the inferior. He concludes the extermination of a race with the following chilling summary.

All the feuds of countless generations, all the hatreds and cruelties of their narrow history, all the memories of ill-usage and persecution were to be purged that day. At last man was to be supreme and the man-beast to find for ever his allotted place.

Challenger's attitude towards this is unforgiveable, especially for a scientist. The world was itself edging closer to a global war where the fate of millions was decided. Challenger's soliloquy is a reminder of Doyle's belief in Britain's imperialist superiority.

Arthur Conan Doyle (1859–1930) scarcely needs an introduction as the creator of the world's most famous fictional detective, Sherlock Holmes. Although his preference was for historical novels such as *The White Company* (1891) and *Sir Nigel* (1906) he wrote several science-fiction stories and novels. These include further Professor Challenger adventures. In *The Poison Belt* (1913) Challenger believes all life on Earth will be destroyed when the Earth passes through a toxic realm in space and takes the necessary precautions. In "When the World Screamed" (1928) he believes the Earth is sentient and proves it by drilling down through the crust. In "The Disintegration Machine" (1929) Challenger shows his ruthlessness by destroying the inventor of a machine that can disintegrate and then reintegrate matter. "The Land of Mist" (1926) is an investigation into spiritualism, of which Doyle was himself a true believer. Perhaps Doyle's most original sf story is "The Death Voyage" (1929) where he portrays an alternative ending to the First World War.

Doyle admitted that *The Lost World* was the closest he came to writing a boys' adventure novel. Indeed, had Doyle not been the author, that is probably how it would have been regarded. *The Devil-Tree of El Dorado* (1896) by Frank Atkins (writing as Frank Aubrey) has a similar setting, on the plateau of Roraima on the border of Venezuela and British Guiana. Atkins was best known for his lost-world stories in boys' magazines under the name Fenton Ash. The success of *The Lost World* helped blur the boundaries between adult and juvenile speculative fiction.

ESCAPE OR REALITY?

THE HUNDREDS OF FUTURE-WAR STORIES AND NOVELS THAT had appeared since 1871 did nothing to prepare people for the reality and horrors of the real conflict after Britain declared war on Germany on 4 August 1914.

Novels about war continued, of course, many as propaganda. Cyril Ranger Gull, who also wrote as Guy Thorne, produced several novels in which our hero manages to defeat the Germans with some wonderful new invention, such as *The Secret Sea-Plane* and *The Cruiser on Wheels* (both 1915), the last featuring an armoured-car not too different from a tank. Likewise, William Le Queux kept his hand in developing new technologies to combat dastardly plots (and vice versa) in such titles as *The Mystery of the Green Ray* (1915) and *The Zeppelin Destroyer* (1916).

Edgar Wallace, then best known for his novel *The Four Just Men* and his stories featuring Sanders of the River in colonial West Africa, made an uneasy foray into future war with *1925: The Story of a Fatal Peace* (1915). Though the War ended in 1915, the enemy were not to be trusted and at a tenth anniversary peace celebration the Germans start new hostilities.

Rather surprisingly the British publisher John Long decided to print a translation of a bestselling German novel by Paul Muench as *Hindenburg's March Into London* (1916). Some commentators welcomed the translation as it highlighted the vile plans Germany had once England was conquered. The book was promoted as "no better incentive for enlisting."

In the hopes of alleviating some of the distress of the War, publishers issued works of hope and escapism. The American author Edgar Rice Burroughs had considerable success with his novels featuring Tarzan, the powerful jungle hero whose adventures had first appeared in the pulp magazines in 1912 and in book form in 1914. The British publisher Methuen issued the first book, *Tarzan of the Apes*, in 1917, just ahead of the first movie adaptation. The books sold well and Methuen continued with more Tarzan books and with Burroughs's other series featuring John Carter on Mars, starting with *A Princess of Mars* issued in Britain in early 1919. This type of escapist fiction was, at the time, more American in style than British. Britain's answer was—aside from P. G. Wodehouse starting his Jeeves and Wooster stories to raise British spirits—such light-hearted fantasies as *Upsidonia* from Archibald Marshall and J. Storer Clouston's version of Jekyll and Hyde, *Two's Two* (1916) where the individual's split personalities get in each other's way.

But there were also plenty of warning stories and concerns about how the war might develop. There was an unusual example in Arthur Machen's *The Terror*, discussed below, which suggested that if humanity cannot look after the planet maybe animals should.

There were also thoughts for what might happen after the War and what society could emerge. Two of these I discuss below, *The New Moon* by Oliver Onions being the more positive, and *Meccania* by Owen Gregory, the more bleak, but two others are worth noting.

1920. Dips into the Political Future (1918) is a political satire, credited to "Lucian", the alias of economist John A. Hobson. It was serialized during 1917, when the War was still raging. According to the narrative the War is *still* raging in 1920 and Britain is forced to take drastic measures. All those over sixty-five are called up for war service but then killed to alleviate the food shortages. With a low birth-rate polygamy is legalized and divorces are encouraged as are fixed-term marriages. A Laboratory of War-Truth issues statements of "fake news", or, as one of the technicians expresses it: "It is our duty to compose the sort of news which it is good for the respective parties to receive, and to mould the sentiments and opinions it is good for them to hold." Hobson shows how during a War society is manipulated by the state to its benefit and the public's detriment.

As that was being serialized in Britain, *The Messiah of the Cylinder* was appearing in the United States, and it was issued in Britain as *The Apostle of the Cylinder* in December 1918. The author, Victor Rousseau, was English but had settled in America and became a prolific writer. It's a "sleeper-awakes" style novel where our hero, Pennell, is put into suspended animation and reawakens in 2015 where a World-State is governed by two individuals. One of these, Dr. Sanson (who was the evil genius who sent Pennell into the future), is a rabid eugenicist and in his world people are divided into normals and defectives, based on cranial data. The defectives are allowed to live so long as they are useful. Everyone is monitored closely, almost to the point of the Thought Police.

The degree of totalitarianism in both these books, in each case inspired by the horrors of the Great War, shows the fear the public had for what post-War Britain or Europe might become. As one reviewer of Rousseau's book remarked, "We really shall have to be most tremendously careful during the period of reconstruction."

A Drop in Infinity   Gerald Grogan
London: John Lane the Bodley Head, 1915

The idea that there may be another world alongside ours, separated by our limited perception of three dimensions, has been a theme of fantasy for centuries. A popular example was "The Elves" (1812) by Ludwig Tieck, translated into English in 1827. A mother warns her children not to cross a stream and enter the wood for they will be in another world. Of course the children disobey and find themselves in the entrancing world of the Elves. They return home after a day and a night to discover they have been away for seven years.

The writer who promoted the idea of other dimensions was Charles H. Hinton whose essay "What is the Fourth Dimension?" (1880) was included with other speculations on time and space in *Scientific Romances* (1884). That volume intrigued H.G. Wells and encouraged his thoughts on other dimensions developed in *The Time Machine* and several short stories.

There were also occult and spiritualist beliefs in another dimension or astral plane, or a world separated from us by vibrations. Algernon Blackwood made use of this in such stories as "A Victim of Higher Space" (1914, but written before 1908), but no one set a whole novel in a parallel world until Gerald Grogan completed *A Drop in Infinity*. As a result, it is on the one hand a daring and experimental novel, but on the other hand somewhat naïve and underdeveloped. Grogan clearly wanted to explore how a young couple might survive in an uninhabited, pure world, going one step further than H. De Vere Stacpoole had in *The Blue Lagoon* (1908), where two children are shipwrecked on a desert island.

Jack Thorpe, having been sacked from his job but having inherited a small sum from a great aunt, takes himself to Cornwall where, by a stroke of fortune, he meets his former girlfriend, Marjorie, on a cliff path. She is now engaged to Angus Crawley, who is after her money. While on the path, Jack and Marjorie fall into the clutches of a mad scientist, whose name we only learn later, but whom they call Hubble-Bubble because it's a phrase he mutters. He lures them to a remote cave in which he has built his laboratory which includes a machine that uses electricity to set up waves that create an entrance into other dimensions. He has explored several, most of which were dangerous, and it is these adventures that have driven him crazy. He has found one safe world which is uninhabited and which he now wants to people. He had thought Jack and Marjorie were married, and his plans are further thwarted when Angus Crawley turns up to rescue his betrothed. But the scientist has duped Marjorie into passing through the portal and he will allow only one of the men to follow her. Angus reveals his true craving self and is killed, whilst Jack enters another world.

Once Jack and Marjorie come to terms with their predicament and, with due Edwardian propriety, they go through a marriage ceremony, construct a dwelling, and adapt what they have to hand for fishing, making an axe, and over time domesticating animals, especially a cow and a calf. Marjorie takes the lead on many of these developments saying that she is the boss because she's more intelligent than Jack. This world becomes called Marjorie-land.

On one of his trips, Jack encounters a plesiosaur, suggesting that Marjorie-land might be somewhere in Earth's ancient past, but since this world also has cattle and bears and other mammals, that is unlikely.

Much of the novel is an exercise in primitivism which had been a popular theme in recent years. H.G. Wells had explored ancient humans in "A Story of the Stone Age" (1897), the American writer Stanley Waterloo had success with *A Story of Ab* (1897), likewise Jack London with *Before Adam* (1907) and the Canadian Charles G.D. Roberts with *In the Morning in Time* (1919). In Grogan's case, though, he is exploring how modern humans could cope with having to revive Stone-Age skills.

At one point, Hubble-Bubble's machine malfunctions and Jack is whisked back to Cornwall. He tracks down the Professor and returns to Marjorie-land, but not before Jack learns that, when he was sent into another dimension, an alter ego was created back home. Tension builds in Marjorie-land when Hubble-Bubble sends through other groups and conflict erupts with one fellow, Michael Quelch, who tries to seduce Marjorie while Jack is away. Most of the novel's drama is the conflict between Jack and Quelch.

The Professor continues to contact Jack occasionally, sending through items that might help them. On one occasion they discuss the nature of other dimensions and speculate on whether there is an infinite number of worlds separated by an infinitely small distance. This is the first proposal in fiction of what later became termed the Multiverse by Michael Moorcock (see *The Sundered Worlds*).

The remaining individuals have families and develop into a society. At the time Jack is writing his account he notes that his son, Bill, is fifty-five. It is evident, by the end of the book that the group has prospered and will continue to grow.

In one discussion with Hubble-Bubble Jack learns that war has broken out in Europe. Grogan (1884–1918) was writing this book during the build-up to the Great War in 1914 and by the time it was published, just before Christmas 1914, Grogan was already fighting in the trenches in France. Grogan was born in Scotland but his father was Irish. He had hoped to be a soldier but short sight put paid to that. He trained as a doctor but disliking pathology switched to being a mining engineer. This knowledge proved invaluable during the war, when he joined the Royal Engineers for tunnelling work. Grogan's younger brother James was killed at Gallipoli in June 1915 and Gerald died at Ypres in January 1918 when a shell exploded directly overhead. Some of the stories collected posthumously in *William Pollok and Other Tales* (1918) are also science fiction.

As a final note it is interesting that a year after *A Drop in Infinity* was published the humorist Archibald Marshall published *Upsidonia* (1915) where a man walks through a cave into an alternate world where everything in society is topsy-turvy. Did Marshall read Grogan's book, I wonder.

The Terror   Arthur Machen

The Evening News, 16–31 October 1916; London: Duckworth, 1917

After some moderate success with *The Great God Pan* (1894), *The Three Impostors* (1895) and *The House of Souls* (1906), which still contain some of his best writings of the fantastic, Machen's work rather languished for the next decade before he had a surprise resurgence with the public's fascination with his story "The Bowmen". Printed in *The Evening News* for 29 September 1914, many people believed the account of a vision during a retreat at the Battle of Mons, where a soldier believed he saw the British troops supported by a ghostly army of Agincourt archers, was true. The rumour mill soon gathered pace and before long the legend of the Angel of Mons was born.

Machen regretted that his story had started such a belief, but it also provided hope to many at the start of the War, and it is a legend that lives to this day. Machen was intrigued how, the more wartime censorship was imposed, the more rumour spread as it had no firm anchor in truth. As a result all kinds of beliefs and interpretations of events could develop. He used this as the basis for his short novel, *The Terror*, which also appeared in *The Evening News*.

A series of strange events starts across Britain but because of wartime censorship few knew that it was so widespread and regarded them as localized. People are found dead in mysterious circumstances and no one can explain how these deaths occur. The narrator, who had been elsewhere in England, had witnessed first-hand some of the events, such as the plane that crashed after it encountered a flock of birds that seemed to fly straight at it. And an explosion in a factory where the faces of the dead had been bitten to pieces. Other incidents include a girl stung to death by a swarm of bees, a woman found dead in a quarry alongside a sheep, soldiers trampled to death by horses, and a farmer killed by his pet dog. Most mysterious of all was a tree that grew visibly before the witness's eyes.

Speculation is rife with some believing a homicidal maniac is on the loose, others believing German soldiers have invaded, yet others believing the Germans have perfected a ray that turns susceptible people into maniacs and drives animals crazy.

Eventually the plague of deaths ceases and, because of censorship, no explanation is given. The narrator, though, suspects that because mankind was despoiling the planet through its mechanized warfare that mankind had thus abdicated its role as the responsible dominant creature on the planet

and that the animals had decided all of humanity should die. Machen does
not go so far as to state what we now call the Gaia principle, after James
Lovelock, that the Earth is self-regulating and that, in the story, the Earth
would shift the hierarchical balance from humans to animals, but that idea
is implied. Although there was no answer to what happened, the story's
conclusion makes it a form of metaphysical science fiction.

Interestingly, in 1925 Violet Murray used a similar idea in *The Rule of
the Beasts*, where a plague has almost wiped out mankind and the animals, who have developed an enhanced intelligence, decide to monitor
the regrowth of mankind to ensure that humans are in closer harmony
with the planet.

Arthur Machen (1863–1947) is regarded as one of the major writers of
supernatural fiction but at the core of his work, certainly his early writing,
is an idea that is firmly in the field of science fiction. As background for
stories such as "The Inmost Light" and "The Shining Pyramid" Machen
considers that the beings regarded as the Little People are in fact a degenerate
form of a separate race of humans that once dominated Britain. Machen
was a serious student of the occult, and a member of the Hermetic Order
of the Golden Dawn, alongside Algernon Blackwood, Aleister Crowley
and W.B. Yeats.

The New Moon   Oliver Onions

London: Hodder & Stoughton, 1918

Those who have read anything by Oliver Onions—and he is best known for
his supernatural stories—know that he was a no-nonsense Yorkshireman
who expects the characters in his books to get on with life regardless. Of
course, the First World War was a considerable hill to climb compared to
the hummocks of most daily life, but Onions still expects his characters to
cope. And that is the message at the heart of *The New Moon*, one of hope
and determination. Subtitled "A Romance of Reconstruction", Onions

considers how Britain will rebuild itself after the War. His attitude is summed up in one paragraph:

It was in the spirit not of cynicism but of goodwill, that departmentalists and trades union men, mechanics and soldiers, statesmen and farmers, and business men and parsons, had spent their days and nights in deliberation, not what to do (they knew that) but the best way to do it.

Onions writes from the viewpoint of the soldier. He had himself served in the Royal Engineers and most of this book was written during his few periods of leave. Thus his narrator, Dick Helme, also served as an engineer in the War—or the Bloodletting as it's called here—and his skills are used in reinvigorating the old canals for transportation. Additional small railways are built. Wherever possible the armed forces are brought back to Britain to serve in the Peace Service and the Imperial Emergency Service spread throughout Britain to rebuild and regenerate the country.

Onions starts with a mood of hope. Helme is transporting materials and en route picks up a young woman, Elizabeth Lygarde, who is also trying to move goods. Their journey takes three hours by which time they have fallen in love and Helme has proposed marriage. This might seem preposterous, but Onions wanted to emphasize a feel-good factor from the start. This is a story of hope, new beginnings, and achievement.

The only drawback, if drawback it is, is that all of this recovery must be rigidly organized and the State becomes authoritarian in order to achieve its ends. But those who want such results, looking forward to a utopia, serve willingly. In Onions's eyes this rigour and determination overcame the more likely debilitation that struck those returning home, "a home fit for heroes" that was announced but which did not eventuate. Other writers, as we shall see, could only see social strife after the War, but Onions had a plan. "You may not agree with the plan," the promotion for the book announced, "but you ought to study it…"

The end of the book jolts us back to reality. We discover that Helme is still in the trenches in the Great War, and his vision of the future has been no more than a dream. Normally the tired "only a dream" ending spoils most stories, but here it works, because it reminds us of what those serving in the War were fighting for and that if we don't have a dream, what do we have? The message of *The New Moon* is every bit as relevant today, in a divided Britain with an uncertain future, as it was a century ago.

Oliver Onions (1873–1961), who later changed his name to George Oliver, is remembered today almost solely for his supernatural stories, most of which are to be found in the omnibus *The Collected Ghost Stories* (1935). He wrote over forty books, mostly social and historical novels, including some very strange works, notably *The Hand of Kornelius Voyt* (1939) about an orphan's increasing isolation and alienation from his carer. An earlier work, *The Tower of Oblivion* (1921) explores further alienation, this time of a man who believes that as he reached middle age his location in time reversed and he is living his life backwards. Onions is not always an easy writer to read—there can be unrelenting misery in some books—but he is one we should never forget, and *The New Moon* was one of his few visions of hope.

Meccania, the Super State   Owen Gregory

London: Methuen, 1918

Meccania was published in early December 1918, less than a month after Armistice Day and the end of the Great War. The book was therefore written without knowing the outcome of the War and is intended as a warning against the consequences should Germany be victorious. Although the world *kultur* does not appear in the book, nor for that matter is Germany mentioned, there is no doubt that the totalitarian, future state of Meccania is Germany. In the promotional advertising for the book the connection is made. It was announced as "A satire on 'Kultur' in the 20th century.

Meccania is the Super State, Germany, seen from a new angle of vision by an unprejudiced observer."

The book may have been encouraged by a speech Rudyard Kipling gave in Folkestone on 15 February 1918 where he spoke about Germany's *kultur* as a religion to be imposed upon the world. He ended his speech by saying "But be sure of this: Nothing—nothing we may have endured now will weigh one featherweight compared with what we shall most certainly have to suffer if for any cause we fail of victory." *Meccania* is one such vision.

The book is presented as an account written by a Chinese visitor to Europe, Mr. Ming, who claimed he had visited Meccania in 1970. The date is challenged as a mistake for 1917, and it is evident that there is no time travel and that the date is a device to consider what Germany may become on the hundredth anniversary of its existence—the German Empire came into being on 1 January 1871.

Ming is warned about visiting Meccania, saying that if he returns he will be viewed with suspicion and will likewise be suspect while in Meccania. Ming still goes and from the moment he reaches the border he realizes how controlled is every aspect of life. His passport is not enough to allow him in, he has to have an additional permit. While he waits in No-Man's Land he asks if he might read a newspaper, which is frowned upon and he is questioned about what he wants to read. Before entering Meccania he has to have a disinfectant bath so as not to bring in germs, and once he's in the country he has to have another disinfectant bath to avoid contracting an illness.

Ming is allotted a guide to take him on a tour. Although Ming has letters of introduction to certain citizens he is advised that that will not happen until formal authorization is issued. He learns the city is planned in a series of concentric rings with the superior residents at the centre and the menial serviles in the outer ring. Those in the outer rings are only allowed to shop on certain days and can only visit the same supplier for each foodstuff, e.g. always the same baker for bread. There is no choice. Everything is controlled by the state, monitored and regulated. Weekly budgets and expenditure for these lower classes are checked weekly by the state to ensure no excesses. All individuals are prescribed a model diet which may only be amended if an individual is ill and their diet is changed to improve their health—surprisingly this is one of the few things in Meccania which might have some merit!

"Uniformity is the law of all organic life" is one of the pronouncements of the State and all Meccanians have been institutionalized to believe this and conform. Any who don't are imprisoned in an insane asylum and if they continue to rebel are sent to concentration camps.

Although Ming is forbidden to meet other foreign visitors, he makes the acquaintance of two, an Englishman and a fellow Chinese man. The latter, Kwang, has been in Meccania for fifteen years and acquired certain privileges and insider information. Ming learns that Meccania practices eugenics with a breeding programme amongst the elite which, over time, should produce a master race of unquestioning dedication, almost a Hive Mind. He also learns that Meccania has been developing plans for a possible chemical war.

There is much experimentation on animals and humans in what we might now call genetic engineering, especially with developing medicines or vaccines. "People do not always know when they are being experimented upon," remarks Ming's guide.

The tour of Meccania and its disturbing revelations begin to pall after a while as it is unleavened by any humour. At the end Ming is allowed to leave (after a medical) and rather hopes he will forget about Meccania, but reflects, "It seemed not impossible that the nightmare I had escaped from was a doom impending over the whole world." Though the author had concentrated on Germany's *kultur* as it was during the Great War, his vision of a super-state foresaw much that would emerge in Stalinist Russia and Hitler's Nazi Germany. The book is chilling in its matter-of-factness.

The identity of Owen Gregory is not known. The name is presumed to be a pseudonym but no one ever claimed it.

When the World Shook   H. Rider Haggard

The Quiver, November 1918–April 1919; London: Cassell, 1919

Rider Haggard (1856–1925) is best remembered for *King Solomon's Mines* (1885) closely followed by *She* (1887) which gave us the character of Ayesha, or "She Who Must be Obeyed." Haggard was the godfather of the lost-race novel and perhaps also to science fiction by opening the public's eyes to the wondrous possibilities of the unknown. That he was still producing material of this kind for nearly forty years is a measure of his popularity but for the most part he added little that was new with many of his novels simply variations on a theme. That makes *When the World Shook* something of a turning point.

During the War Haggard had become depressed that the Government had not put any work his way so he was delighted when the Royal Colonial Institute agreed to send him on a world mission to the Empire to obtain statements of help from colonial governments to provide post-war settlement for soldiers and sailors. This took place between February and July 1916, a hazardous undertaking during such a conflict, but it was successful. It was while crossing the Pacific, and feeling lonely, that Haggard started work on *Ora*, which became *The Glittering Lady* and finally *When the World Shook*, so it was written during the very midst of the war. It was not finished until March 1917 as Haggard needed to undertake further research once he was back home, including consulting a learned astronomer about the positions of the stars over 250,000 years. The end result was a romance, all too typical of Haggard, but with strong scientific passages, which was unusual, and a warning that man's control over science must not be misused.

The story begins with a voyage across the Pacific. Humphrey Arbuthnot—adventurers never have such names as that these days—has recently lost his wife, Natalie, but she had told him to take a voyage as they may meet again. He is accompanied by two friends, Basil Bastin, a religious individual, who is described as "incredibly simple" but "painfully good", and Bickley, a no-nonsense unimaginative medical man. They also take Tommy the dog.

Somewhere near Samoa they encounter a hurricane and by a miracle a tidal wave carries their ship on to the shores of an unknown island. Their shipmates have been killed, but Bastin, Bickley, Arbuthnot and Tommy survive. The native islanders are cannibals and might have killed the adventurers but they were frightened by the dog, the like of which they had never seen before—and they are even more overwhelmed when a man whom Tommy bites dies in convulsions. They were also overawed by how the travellers had arrived. Bastin can speak Polynesian, and tries to teach them Christianity, to no avail, but he learns they worship the god Oro. Stupidly, Bastin chooses to destroy their idol of Oro, and the adventurers have to flee for their lives.

They take refuge on a sacred island in a lake, which the natives will not approach. They had learned that during the recent hurricane a small mountain had risen on the island and upon approaching the mountain they discover a cave entrance, which had been sealed when the mountain had previously sunk beneath the island. On entering the cave, which proves to be enormous, they are astonished to discover a fleet of aeroplanes, untarnished, despite their age. Beyond the planes is a large statue guarding two crystal coffins inside which are an aged man and a young woman.

Upon opening the coffins they discover that both man and woman are in suspended animation, supported by some form of radioactivity. Thanks to Bickley's medicinal skills they revive the two humans. It transpires they are Oro, the original of the native's god and his beautiful daughter, Yva, the Glittering Lady of the original title. There is an immediate rapport between Yva and Arbuthnot and it appears that during her long sleep, Yva's spirit had been incarnated in other bodies, including that of Natalie.

We learn that Oro was head of the Sons of Wisdom and had ruled the world two hundred and fifty thousand years ago—the men speculate whether this may have been Atlantis. Oro had powerful psychic abilities and was also a scientist of great learning, but he ruled viciously. There was a rebellion in which many died and the Sons of Wisdom withdrew to their underground city. Oro decides to wipe the surface of the Earth clean of all humans. He is able to control a giant gyroscope at the centre of the Earth which keeps the world spinning on its axis. Through his abnormal powers, Oro shifts the gyroscope causing the Earth to tilt on its axis, resulting in catastrophic destruction on the planet's surface—that was "when the World shook". Oro and Yva go into suspended animation, the period of which is calculated on the position of the stars.

Oro dislikes the men and would have killed them but recognizes the attraction of souls between Yva and Arbuthnot, who also turns out to be a reincarnation of an ambassador in the Old World whom Yva had loved. Through astral travel (or mind control) Oro takes Arbuthnot on a journey around the world, and whilst he approves of developments in India and Japan, and marvels at the ocean-going ships, he is horrified at the images of war in France and Belgium. He decides that the world is no better than it had been a quarter of a million years before and decides once more to destroy human life. He takes the men, with Yva, down to the core of the world where they witness the giant gyroscope. Haggard's description of this wheel of fire is amongst his best writing and is reminiscent of his work thirty years before. When Rudyard Kipling read the completed manuscript he was overwhelmed by it, saying it was as "fresh and as convincing as the work of a boy of 25." Haggard was 62.

Oro's plans to shift the gyroscope are thwarted by Yva and she dies as a result. Distraught, Oro triggers the mechanism to lower the mountain beneath the island again, suggesting he would return to suspended animation, but his fate is not known. The three men and the dog find their way back to the surface. They salvage the lifeboat from their crashed ship and leave.

When Oro was witnessing the devastation of the Great War in Europe he remarked to Arbuthnot, "What goes around, comes around," which was one of the messages Haggard wanted to stress in this novel. Man never learns from war. And, of course, the Second World War came just twenty-one years after the First, though Haggard mercifully did not live to see it. What is pertinent is that to get his message across Haggard had turned to science rather than the supernatural to demonstrate the advance of mankind and its inherent dangers.

It is also worth noting that at the same time that *When the World Shook* was being serialized—in, of all places, the quasi-religious magazine *The Quiver*—the American author, Abraham Merritt, had published "The Moon Pool" and its sequel in the pulp magazine *All-Story Weekly*. Merritt had not copied Haggard, as "The Moon Pool" appeared first, but the setting, a remote Polynesian island, along with a cave and a passage underground to a being of light, the Dweller, bears comparison. Merritt became one of the most popular writers of science fantasy in the United States in the 1920s and was a strong influence on early writers. It is as if with this novel, Haggard had handed the baton to Merritt to continue the tales of wonder. Haggard also continued to write till his death in 1925, but his later works are little more than revamps of earlier titles. *When the World Shook* saw the old guard recognizing the power of science and handing the flame to the next generation.

A Voyage to Arcturus   David Lindsay

London: Methuen, 1920

Like *When the World Shook, A Voyage to Arcturus* might be considered fantasy by many. I would classify it is a philosophical fantasy that uses the trappings of science fiction. But it is because it poses as science fiction, that it is one of the cornerstone books of the genre. It sold poorly on first publication but is one of those books that refuses to be ignored, and has developed a significant cult following over the decades.

To describe it simplistically does it no favours, but the more you excavate into the lower levels the more complicated it becomes. Lindsay wanted to create a strange other world, which he could manipulate to explore an inner self. That world could have been anywhere but the more remote the better, so he takes us beyond our solar system to a planet orbiting the star Arcturus, or rather stars, as Arcturus turns out to be a double sun.

The story begins at a séance which is visited by Maskull and his companion Nightspore. The session is interrupted during a spirit manifestation by a youth who bursts into the room and destroys the spirit. The youth is Krag who, once outside the house, tells Maskull that he has come for him, something he had planned with Nightspore. If Maskull wants to understand more he must follow Surtur to Tormance, the planet orbiting Arcturus.

Krag arranges to meet them again at the old observatory of Starkness in north-east Scotland. Maskull and Nightspore arrive before Krag. When Maskull attempts to climb up into the observatory he finds himself getting heavier and hears a voice hinting that there is some duality between him and Nightspore. Returning to the ground, Maskull meets Krag who tells him that the increased weight was what he would experience on Tormance. He cuts Maskull's skin with a knife and spits on it, relieving the pressure.

The voyage to Arcturus is made in a forty-foot long crystal ship, the shape of a torpedo. It is powered by "back rays"—light that returns to its source. There are bottles of Arcturan back rays which will transport them to the star at the speed of thought rather than light. Maskull falls asleep and knows nothing of the journey.

He awakens on a plain, and discovers he has grown additional sensory organs: a third eye, knobs on each side of his neck, and a tentacle from near his heart. He is approached by a woman, Joiwind, who gives him clothes and performs a blood transfusion to allow him to cope with Tormance's gravity. If it was not already clear it is evident by now that the name Tormance is an allegory for "torments", and it is as if we are experiencing a modern version of John Bunyan's *Pilgrim's Progress*.

From here on Maskull has many experiences too numerous to mention. As he proceeds he learns about the world and about himself, and is horrified when he discovers that, despite his initial refusal, he manages to strangle a woman's husband at her request. He is told that he will atone for this and that comes in a bizarre fashion. At a point when he believes he is dying he finds himself back at the séance but as the spirit that first appeared, and is killed by Krag. He immediately returns to Tormance but rejuvenated from his vision and even more keen to find Krag and solve the mystery of Surtur.

Maskull learns that Surtur, also known as Crystalman, purports to be the God of Tormance, and many revere him as kind and benevolent, but as his travels continue Maskull suspects that Surtur is evil. The original of Surtur had come from Muspel, a name that Maskull keeps hearing, and we discover that Muspel, an island, is all that remains of Tormance that has not been corrupted.

It is only at the end of the book (which I will not reveal) that Maskull—who is also Nightspore—discovers the identities of Krag and Surtur and their relationship to Earth and what role he may need to play.

A Voyage to Arcturus is a complicated, demanding and frequently frustrating book, but it is also compelling and requires more than one reading. I have read it at least four times across a span of over fifty years, and always find something new, and confess I still don't understand it all, but each time something sparks in my mind which provides further clues.

Although the first edition did not sell well it did receive some good reviews. Ralph Straus, writing in *The Bystander*, called it "daring" and that Lindsay's unusual philosophy of life "invests it not only with a strange dignity of its own, but also with a particular interest for those who may have studied the sub-conscious mind and its symbols." J.B. Priestley, who discovered the book in 1932, called it "a grand piece of wild imagining." Colin Wilson, who was perhaps the greatest champion of David Lindsay, called it "one of the greatest books of the twentieth century."

The reviewer in the *Yorkshire Post* said it reminded him of the works of Dante, Samuel Butler, William Blake and even Lewis Carroll, and there is doubtless more source inspiration. Lindsay (1876–1945) had enjoyed the works of George Macdonald, and there is some similarity of vision with *Phantastes* and *Lilith*. Lindsay was also inspired by Rider Haggard, and

I wonder whether he had also read *The Night Land*, as there is much of Hodgson's apocalyptic imagination here.

But despite all these possible influences, Lindsay's approach is unique. He struggled for years to succeed as a writer but sales and finances were poor despite five books published in his lifetime and two others (one unfinished) published long after his death. All are worth reading, especially *The Haunted Woman* (1922), *Sphinx* (1923) and *Devil's Tor* (1932). His lack of success took its toll on his health and his marriage, and he would be astonished to discover that his books, and especially *A Voyage to Arcturus*, continue to be read by generations of new admirers. Even though it is not pure science fiction, all sf devotees will draw much from it.

BRAVE NEW WORLDS

THE GREAT WAR LEFT THE BRITISH ECONOMY DEVASTATED AND ill equipped to cope with the return of combatants from Europe, or with the loss of so many. The Government reported a figure of 743,702 military personnel killed or missing during the war, plus another 16,829 civilian deaths. No sooner had the War ended than a flu epidemic claimed a further 228,000 lives, so there were close to a million deaths over and above those from natural causes. By 1921 the unemployment rate was over 11% of the adult population. The 1920s was a period of social strife, resulting in the General Strike of 1926.

This was reflected in fiction. Whilst there was initially some hope once the War ended, as Oliver Onions had suggested in *The New Moon*, this soon gave way to concern over the nation's social status, reflected vividly in Edward Shanks's *The People of the Ruins*, and fears of another war. Following the Russian revolution there was also fear of further political unrest and the infiltration of society by terrorists or anarchists, often called Bolshevists as a general term. Alongside this was an increasing number of stories of criminal masterminds with access to super-scientific weapons or facilities. The best known prototype was Dr. Fu Manchu created by Sax Rohmer in *The Mystery of Dr. Fu Manchu* in 1913. Although not science fiction it established many concepts that would reappear in both crime and science fiction. For instance, Fu Manchu's desire to create a body of expert scientists at his command reappears in Eden Phillpotts's *Number 87*. Even Agatha Christie succumbed to the international criminal mastermind theme in *The Big Four* (1927) where Madame Oliver, a nuclear physicist, has perfected a lethal weapon based on gamma rays emitted from radium.

The dramatic increase in technology during the War made the public realize for the first time that science could produce super-weapons and the fear grew that if someone mastered atomic energy the world would be at their mercy. The phrase "atomic energy" had been coined by Ernest Rutherford in 1903 during his studies of the disintegration of elements and the power within the atom was later expressed by Albert Einstein in his famous equation, $E=mc^2$. We have already seen that Robert Cromie had considered the power of atomic disintegration in *The Crack of Doom* in 1895, and the idea of atomic weapons had been used by George Griffith in *The Lord of Labour* (1911) and H.G. Wells in *The World Set Free* (1914). Post-war fiction made frequent reference to harnessing atomic energy to provide the ultimate power—not in terms of powering industry or our homes but in terms of weapons of mass destruction.

Another post-war concern was what might become of human beings, either by natural evolution or genetic manipulation—not that gene technology was understood then, but the idea of creating or adapting other forms of humans was already appearing in fiction. I shall explore that in section VIII.

These fears were neatly encapsulated in the first two books in what became the series *To-day and To-morrow* published from 1924 to 1931. These were non-fiction, usually extended essays or studies looking at different aspects of society. The first two had a significant impact—*Daedalus: or Science and the Future* by J.B.S. Haldane and *Icarus: or the Future of Science* by Bertrand Russell. Haldane's book raised such issues as the need for wind-power in the future as fossil fuels decline, synthetic food, eugenics and, most startling of all, test-tube babies, which he called "ectogenesis". Russell's predictions were more bleak, as he saw the darker side of the scientific revolution, such as birth control resulting in a form of "race suicide", the rise of despotism and dystopia, and the loss of a free press.

These two books in particular, along with much of the rest of the series (not all of which were about the future), influenced many writers of this period. The following, all of which appeared in the decade or so after the War, voice concerns over social strife, warfare, plagues and other disasters. Very few saw science as a saviour. I'll first consider those that foresaw the impact of science on society leading, most likely, to chaos and catastrophe.

The People of the Ruins   Edward Shanks

Land and Water, 16 October 1919–12 February 1920; London: William Collins, 1920

More or less forgotten today, in his lifetime Edward Shanks was a popular poet, journalist and critic. He won the first Hawthornden Prize in 1919 for his collection of poetry *The Queen of China* (1919). In presenting the Prize, Edmund Gosse remarked that it was a book "which awakened hope for the future" in that first year after the Great War.

The People of the Ruins also awakened hope with one hand, but dashed it with the other, leaving the reader quite numbed, especially with the final few paragraphs.

The book starts in 1924 on the first day of the General Strike. Shanks was two years out, as the historical General Strike began in 1926. Jeremy Tuft had promised to visit his friend Trehanoc in Whitechapel, who wanted to demonstrate an experiment. Annoyed to find no buses are running, he has to walk. He witnesses the rising tide of unrest of the workers against the "boorjwar" and by the time he reaches Trehanoc, things are turning nasty.

Trehanoc attempts to demonstrate a new ray which he knew did something but wasn't sure what. Both he and Tuft are intrigued by a dead rat which had run in front of the ray some weeks earlier and though it looked dead, was perfectly preserved. Trehanoc's warehouse is then broken into and he, and another friend, are killed. Tuft is caught in a bomb blast and is bathed in Trehanoc's mystery ray. He passes out. When he comes to, he discovers that where he had been protected under a collapsed table, was now covered by soil and turf. He guesses he must have slept for quite some time into the future but is naturally shaken when he is told the year is 2074.

He learns that the unrest escalated into a series of civil wars, not just in Britain but throughout the world, which persisted for fifty years, a period called "the Troubles". During those years and the century since people have lost the ability to use technology, which has fallen into disrepair apart from a few ancient steam trains. Most buildings are in ruins and much of the population live in huts or hovels. Yet Tuft senses a degree of peace and tranquillity and an acceptance of the circumstances. There are those who do not believe that the world before the Troubles had been scientifically advanced and that stories of flights to America were myths. (At the time Shanks wrote this book, the first transatlantic flights by airship had only just happened.)

Britain is governed by The Speaker who runs the Treasury. No other form of government exists although there are regional bases in the North, at Bradford, and in Wales. When the Speaker discovers the existence of Tuft, and is convinced of his story, he realizes Tuft's experiences in the Great War as an artillery officer could be put to good use. The Speaker hopes to renovate some ancient breech-loading guns, but no one has the knowledge or skills. Tuft is put to work repairing them. The inevitable happens when the governor of the North sends an ultimatum that he will no longer pay local taxes to London. If that is not granted, there will be war. The Speaker, relying on his guns, calls their bluff. In the ensuing battle Tuft, more by chance than design, delivers a killer blow with his guns, destroying the enemy's ammunition, and the Speaker proclaims victory. The celebrations are short-lived, however, because the Welsh are now marching on London. The Speaker's forces are betrayed and this time they lose. London is overrun and the Speaker flees. Tuft also flees with the Speaker's daughter, Eva, with whom he has fallen in love.

Let not her name fool you. This is no new Adam and Eve and there is no happy ending. Tuft realizes that mankind never learns. Although civilization had collapsed after the Troubles, the existing life is tolerable, and a new civilization could have been reborn, but the usual human traits of greed, stubbornness and power once again deliver disaster.

During the story Tuft learns that the League of Nations still operates, attempting reconciliation. One of the character's remarks resonate today: "...they sit at Geneva and tell everyone how to manage their own affairs. We take no notice of them, except that we send them a contribution every year." Shanks was topical because although there had been much talk of a League of Nations towards the end of the War, it had only been established on 10 January 1920, when the novel was being serialized. Shanks also makes the final conflict as much about religion as politics. The Speaker notes that in the south they are mostly Catholic, the Welsh are Methodists and the North are all Spiritualists!

Edward Shanks (1892–1953) had, like Tuft, served in the Great War but was invalided out in 1915 and served in the War Office. He wrote no other work of science fiction. *The Old Indispensables* (1922) is an impish satire on the war at Whitehall whilst *Queer Street* (1932) and *The Enchanted Village* (1933) both explore similar social issues to *The People of the Ruins*, finding humour and despair in how disparate groups of people exist side by side. Shanks had a keen eye for humanity's faults and foibles.

The Secret Power   Marie Corelli

London: Methuen, 1921

Marie Corelli (1855–1924), who was as much her own creation as any of her books, was the bestselling novelist of her generation. She tapped into a vein of mystical romance which she imbued with a vivid passion, her narrative drive developing larger-than-life characters and visions both audacious and vivacious, that they glossed over any inconsistencies or impossibilities in the plot. None of that bothered Corelli, because she recreated herself in every book and lived those lives in her imagination.

Her first book, *A Romance of Two Worlds* (1886), written when she was thirty though she claimed she was seventeen, was a form of occult scientific romance which had been growing in the late nineteenth century with the rise of interest in spiritualism. Corelli explored how individuals could overcome physical and mental illness through spiritual enhancement bringing you closer to God. Corelli's was also entranced by advances in science and her books considered how the spiritual and the scientific might meld. Part of the novel includes astral travel to the planets. Jupiter is scientifically advanced with everything powered by electricity.

Critics hated the book but it caught the public's attention and thereafter Corelli had an ever growing readership. She had spectacular success with *Barabbas: A Dream of the World's Tragedy* (1893), set at the time of the Crucifixion, and *The Sorrows of Satan* (1895), a deal-with-the-devil story which reflected the soul of the decadent 1890s.

Corelli continued to write almost up to her death and her books remained popular. Despite her increasingly poor health she never lost her passion as she recreated herself as the heroine of each volume. *The Young Diana* (1918), for example, has a scientist creating an elixir of rejuvenation, a "soul fluid", and the woman who serves as a guinea-pig to test it is not only made young and beautiful but becomes a superior being, heartless and inhuman.

The Secret Power was her last novel and reads as if Corelli had two ideas too short for separate novels and brought them together in an uneasy mix. She manages to blend the lost-race adventure with the atomic age—though she never uses the word "atomic".

Her heroine is Morgana Royal who has inherited a fortune and is fascinated with the potential power that the new sciences promise. She has discovered an etheric force (in fact radioactivity) which she harnesses to power her new airship, the *White Eagle*, which has retractable wings that flap. It can travel at least three hundred miles per hour. With this she plans to discover the legendary Brazen City as told in the *Arabian Nights*. With the usual good fortune of fiction they discover it on the airship's maiden flight, or rather the City discovers them. The City is surrounded by an etheric force field which destroys anything that encounters it, so the airship is trapped in a force beam. The men on board become unconscious but Morgana receives a message from the City via a "Sound Ray" along with images via a "Light Ray". The humans she sees are clad in tunics like Greek heroes. Morgana learns that the City has existed for thousands of years deliberately set apart from the world but waiting for that day when they are called forth to a new age. The Voice speaking to Morgana tells her that she is a woman of the future and that provided she comes alone she will be admitted to the City but cannot leave, until she is part of the New World.

Parallel to Morgana's adventure is the story of Roger Seaton, who lives in California, and has discovered how to harness atomic energy or, in Corelli's words, "the condensation of radioactivity." Obsessed with the carnage of the Great War, Seaton has created bombs which he hopes to sell to the United States on condition they will use them to control world peace—even if it means bombing and killing millions. Seaton had been in love with Morgana, a love that was not returned as Morgana had no interest in physical passion. In fact, Seaton is loved by the woman who looks after him, Manella, whom he treats badly and is unaware of her feelings. One day, when Seaton is conveying his box of bombs to its hiding place in a cave, Manella confronts him. He slips and in his fall the bombs are detonated. The devastation is reported as an earthquake. When Morgana hears of the disaster, she takes her airship to California and finds the bodies of Seaton and Manella. Although they are dead Morgana revives them using a radioactive potion. Seaton is seriously brain damaged and remains a vegetable, his secret now lost. Via the Sound Ray, Morgana hears a summons from the Brazen City and realizes her moment has come.

The book again proved popular and went through four editions in as many weeks. The public enjoyed Morgana's message that the devastating power of radioactivity could also be harnessed for good and that with the Brazen City monitoring the world, there was hope for mankind. The role of the City is much like Shangri La in James Hilton's *Lost Horizon*, which is discussed later.

Theodore Savage   Cicely Hamilton

London: Leonard Parsons, 1922

This is a bleak, uncompromising but at heart, an honest book. Its roots lay in the First World War when Miss Hamilton worked at a hospital near the Front and witnessed the horrors first hand. When a bomb dropped from an aeroplane exploded an ammunition dump with frightening devastation, she formed the view that science is a menace to mankind, not a saviour, and favoured the Biblical belief that mankind should not eat of the Tree of Knowledge.

Theodore Savage is the eponymous hero of this book, though hero is not the right word—survivor is more accurate. The surname is significant because, as the result of a new World War, even more destructive than the last because of new weapons of mass destruction, the few who survive revert to primitive savagery. At the start we see Theodore as a mundane, unexceptional, pen-pushing clerk who falls in love with Phillida, and looks set to lead a routine life. War breaks out when a country called Karthania, perhaps in the Balkans, is dissatisfied when its claims (we don't know the details) are rejected. Hamilton provides almost no background detail other than that once hostilities start, they spread rapidly and Britain is soon involved.

There are new tactics. Cities are bombed and destroyed forcing people into the countryside where few can survive. It seems that this is happening worldwide, but no one really knows. Theodore is sent to a depot in York to help distribute food and goods and witnesses the rapid decline of civilization. Only a few survive a bombing raid and he is left to live by his wits and by chance.

Somehow he does, and in time meets a woman called Ada, who is more a parasite than a help, as she expects Theodore to look after her. He does, albeit reluctantly, and it is many months before they grow close together. After a couple of years, on one of his exploratory trips, Theodore is caught by men from a settlement and though he is distrusted at first, they accept him and allow him and Ada to live in the group. They have a family, years pass, Ada dies, Theodore grows old and, in relative terms, rich with the land he has tilled and the flocks he tends.

For years both Theodore and Ada hope that somewhere there must still be civilization, even if not in Britain, and that eventually they will be discovered, but they are not. They have to accept that the old world has died. The tribe into which Theodore has been accepted have a code which forbids any thoughts or attempts to revive the "devil's knowledge"—an understanding of science and technology. It was pursuing science that led to the end of civilization. In that sense this book is anti-science fiction, as its message forbids scientific progress. At length, in his final days, Theodore becomes the oldest survivor of the days before the Fall, and as such is both revered and shunned, as he alone remembers the perils of science. Hamilton's message is powerful, if depressing.

It is perhaps surprising that although Cicely Hamilton (1872–1952) was a devout feminist—and had served as a suffragette before the Great War—she seems content to portray women in a subordinate role in the book. Women do all the cooking, mending and look after the men, who do the hunting, husbandry and other "tough" jobs. No women are presented in a strong light, and none rise above their station. Ada is portrayed as a weak woman who hates what life has dealt her and constantly whines for the pleasures and fashions of the Old World.

Hamilton was born Cicely Hammill. She changed her name when she took to acting on the stage. She also wrote plays including several about the suffrage movement, notably *A Pageant of Great Women* (1909).

She experienced the World War close at hand and wrote her best known novel, *William—an Englishman* (1919) surrounded by the sound of guns and shells. It tells of a newly married couple who find themselves in the midst of war while on honeymoon in Belgium. *Theodore Savage* is almost a thematic sequel. Certainly the horror of warfare stayed with Hamilton as she reissued *Theodore Savage* as *Lest Ye Die* in 1928. Most critics found both editions too bleak to contemplate. They wanted more uplifting stories in the 1920s, but Hamilton's message has become more powerful over the years. And the author experienced the horrors of a second World War, proving that mankind never learns.

Number 87   Harrington Hext (Eden Phillpotts)

London: Thornton Butterworth, 1922

This is essentially a mystery book with a series of high-profile murders by a seemingly impossible assailant, who becomes known as "The Bat". Somewhat bizarrely, there is no indication of how the police are investigating these murders, especially as the victims include the Prime Minister and the favoured future President of the United States. Throughout the book the discussion about these crimes centres on a group of individuals who call themselves the Club of Friends. One of them, Ernest Granger, who becomes the only one to learn the full story, tells the narrative.

It begins with the murder of Alexander Skeat who had been one of the Club and only a few days earlier had been arguing with new member Paul Strossmayer over whether science or the arts are more important. Skeat is found to have been injected by something that left barely a mark on the skin. Death is instantaneous, and the sole witness thought he saw a bat-like shape that vanished into the air leaving behind a potent stench.

Further murders occur over the next year in Britain and abroad, all following the same pattern and all involving leading individuals. There is much speculation over the perpetrator, some believing it is a recently disturbed prehistoric monster or an alien being. There are also inexplicable acts of destruction. The Albert Memorial is the first, disintegrated to dust in seconds.

The speculation takes up most of the book and goes on for rather too long. Suspicion falls on Paul Strossmayer, who is recruiting scientists from Britain to help build the new state of Jugo-Slavia. Amongst his discoveries is a talented scientist, Ian Noble, whom we don't meet until near the end of the book but from whom we learn much that might explain the events. Noble has, for instance, isolated the element with the atomic number of 85 and is striving to isolate number 87.

I shall not spoil it by revealing the perpetrator of the crimes, but he has isolated element 87, which is radioactive and is able to produce astonishing power when harnessed. Not only is it this element which kills the victims and destroys buildings, but it powers a machine capable of flying at 180,000 miles per hour, possibly more, though it has only been put to the test once at that speed. Its inventor calls it a rocket, which is one of the earliest such references in a work of British science fiction.

The scientist had started on his killing spree to rid the world of those who would do most harm should they also harness the power of element 87. He had planned to use it for the benefit of mankind, but soon found that he had become overwhelmed by his power. The book is one of the first to consider how atomic power can be used in rocket flight. The scientist had not yet used it to travel beyond Earth's gravity, though plans were in place to visit Venus.

It may seem surprising that its author was Eden Phillpotts (1862–1960), best known for his novels of Dartmoor life. He was President of the Dartmoor Preservation Association and a close friend of Agatha Christie. Indeed, his advice had encouraged her to write.

Phillpotts had a remarkably long writing career—his first poem was published in 1880, his last book in 1959—and amongst his 200 or so books are several that qualify as science fiction such as *Saurus* (1938) about an alien reptile and *Address Unknown* (1949) where an alien observer tries to improve human life on Earth.

The idea behind *Number 87* suffered when element 87 was discovered by Marguerite Perey in 1939 and called Francium. It is yet to prove useful in any way, as it has a half-life of only twenty-two minutes. Such is the predictive quality of science fiction.

Nordenholt's Million J.J. Connington
London: Constable, 1923

This is another bleak story exploring how humanity might survive a world-wide catastrophe, and it isn't by help-thy-neighbour. It's a ruthless answer which might well be the real one if such an event happened.

Connington, under his real name, Alfred Walter Stewart (1880–1947), was a Professor of Chemistry, which is evident in the opening chapter of this, his only science-fiction novel, though he went on to establish a solid reputation as a writer of detective fiction. The story is narrated by Jack Flint, a mechanical engineer and car manufacturer, who is visiting his friend Wotherspoon, a dabbler in scientific matters. He does no original research himself but builds upon the work of others. Wotherspoon explains to Flint the nature of plants which depend upon nitrogen in the soil for their growth. He has in his "sanctum" several incubators in which are cultures of both nitrifying and denitrifying bacteria. There is a thunderstorm outside and Wothspoon's room is struck by a fireball, which destroys the incubators full of the denitrifying bacteria.

The story is set in a future where air travel is common place. Unknown to Flint or Wotherspoon this bacteria is carried on the winds and the air currents created by the planes and within weeks is attacking plants and the soil. This is called the Blight. All vegetation is dying and food will soon be in very short supply.

The British government vacillates and into the breach steps ruthless business tycoon Stanley Nordenholt. He proposes that a sealed area be established where research into the Blight can be undertaken and where food and people can be held. He proposes the Clyde Valley because there is access to minerals, raw materials and good agricultural land. Roughly a thousand square miles between the Clyde and Forth estuaries, it becomes dubbed the Nitrogen Area. It was established with military precision. Ships were brought up the estuaries which were then sealed off with mines. Planes patrolled the air and troops the boundary. Into this colony were transported five million volunteers, some to undertake research but most to work the land. All available nitrogenous supplies were taken there.

The obvious consequence of this is that the rest of Britain was sacrificed. The Royal Family chose not to go, believing they should meet the same fate as their subjects. Although a partial government was transferred to Glasgow, Nordenholt was effectively in charge of the colony, and was soon carrying out his ruthless plans to enhance and protect the colony. Ireland is raided for food, especially cattle, and left to its fate. Nordenholt implements a plan to destroy the rest of Britain's population so as to safeguard the Colony from raids or civil unrest. Early on Flint is sent to London to study the situation. He discovers the city is already dying, peopled by the starving who are prepared to pay eight pounds for a rat. Fighting had taken place between communities and many non-English, especially Germans, were killed. This part of the novel is difficult for modern readers because of the flippant racist comments.

Flint finds the experience mortifying and is lucky to survive the mobs, but returning to the Colony, he is driven by a determination to succeed and reconstruct Britain. He serves as Nordenholt's deputy and successor and plans to marry his daughter Elsa, though she distances herself from Flint and her father when she learns the truth about what is happening.

The work in the Colony is fruitful. The bacillus appears to have weakened and the research will allow the land to be planted and revived. However many of the volunteers have been affected by their isolation and have established religious cults. They rebel, destroying the mines. However, one of the researchers in the Colony, who goes by the superbly English name of Henley-Davenport, finds he has solved the mystery of atomic power. His work results in a violent explosion in which he is killed, but his meticulous notes allow others to build upon his discovery. Although the radioactivity kills others. they eventually harness the power and atomic power plants are constructed.

At this moment of triumph Nordenholt dies. Flint assumes the responsibility of rehabilitation and reconstruction. It takes ten years before they are able to repopulate Britain. Exploration by plane reveals that apart from two colonies in the United States and one in Japan the rest of the Earth's population has perished. Africa has become one vast desert. As the book closes we are left with a vision of near total devastation but with vegetation gradually being restored. Just how the world would be rebuilt is left to the imagination.

There was scope for Connington/Stewart to write a sequel but he chose not to. His success as a writer of detective fiction and his continuing work as a lecturer in chemistry at Queen's University, Belfast, kept him more than busy.

Ultimatum   Victor MacClure

London: George G. Harrap, 1924; retitled *The Ark of the Covenant*, New York: Harper & Brothers, 1924

This novel is a throwback to the future-war novels of George Griffith and William Le Queux in which scientific masterminds seek to rule the world, or impose peace, through control of the air. The theme had been reinvigorated following the Great War because of the advances in air travel and the promise of greater scientific achievements. MacClure's novel introduces further new themes and has a bibliographic element of interest.

First the plot. Three banks in New York are robbed of millions in gold and securities and in their place is left the equivalent value of radium. During the robberies everyone in the vicinity is put to sleep. James Boon, son of the president of one of the banks, and who is something of an inventor, having perfected the fastest seaplane in the world, the *Merlin*, decides he must investigate the crime. There are further robberies and Boon, with his scientist friend Lamont, believe the robberies have been made from an advanced airship using a powerful sleeping gas. While investigating, Boon is asked if he will take his seaplane over the Atlantic and collect Lord Almeric Pluscarden, deputy governor of the Bank of England, who has been returning from America on the *Parnassic*, but wants to reach his destination quicker. When Boon reaches the ship he finds everyone asleep and a fortune in gold bullion has been stolen.

Bringing Pluscarden home they discover the Bank of England has been robbed as have the central banks in Germany and France. Returning to the United States, Boon meets with the President who commissions Boon to find the perpetrators. Boon also meets a high-ranking British naval official, Commander Sholto Seton.

Boon's hunt for the villains eventually leads him to South America where they trace the super airship, the *Ark of the Covenant*, on a remote plateau near the Brazil/Venezuelan border. He also meets again Sholto Seton. It transpires that years before, whilst exploring South America, Seton encountered a scientist, known only as The Master, who had plans for world peace. His base is a major source of radium, and he has developed atomic energy. In addition to his sleeping gas he has also created a method of transmuting metals. His plan is to disrupt the world economies and then, by controlling the skies, demand world peace. The Master operates a form of benevolent terrorism in that he wants no deaths. However, whilst many nations are prepared to submit, the United States plans to fight. The Master had already won over Seton and now both Boon and Lamont sign up to his plans. With two airships they invade the USA, defeat the military and take over the White House. The Master has achieved his aims and allows countries to retain their sovereignty but they have to relinquish their armed forces other than for local protection. The Master, who is dying, returns to South America, and destroys his base and secrets.

Although the plot seems naïve today, it was popular in the 1920s with many such novels in both Britain and the USA. MacClure, whose real name was Thom MacWalter (1887–1963), was better known in Britain for his detective novels and thrillers and this was his only work of science fiction, or what we call a techno-thriller today. His hatred of War was almost certainly following his serious injuries at Gallipoli. The book was published in the United States as *The Ark of the Covenant* later in 1924 and was selected by publisher Hugo Gernsback for serialization in his magazine *The Experimenter*. I shall return to Hugo Gernsback later, but suffice it to say that Gernsback was the publisher of the first all-sf magazine, *Amazing Stories*, which began in April 1926. Before then he had published several technical magazines that also ran short fiction designed to encourage people to experiment with science and technology. Apart from one reprint by H.G. Wells, MacClure's novel was the first by a British writer to feature in one of these technical magazines. It was later serialized in Gernsback's *Air Wonder Stories* from its first issue in July 1929 giving MacClure a prominence amongst science-fiction readers in America, that he never had in Britain. He continued to write novels and for the cinema into the early 1940s.

Menace from the Moon   Bohun Lynch

London: Jarrolds, 1925

This book is a delight to read because even though it is based upon a preposterous premise, its central idea would appeal to all conspiracy theorists.

Imagine that in the seventeenth century the scientist and inventor Cornelius Drebbel, who is credited with creating the first submarine, succeeded in building an engine capable of taking him and others, including women, to the Moon. Now, three centuries later, the existence of their descendants has become perilous and they are appealing to Earth for help.

It's a fun idea which Lynch backs up with some intriguing facts. But first the story. It starts on Dartmoor where the narrator, Frank Bassett, is staying with friends. He goes for a walk on the Moor and becomes lost when a mist descends. In the mist he sees flashing lights and fancies he can make out a face. He tells his friend, James White, and learns that another local out on the Moor had also seen something. White takes Bassett to where his wartime friend, Peter Pawl, is helping construct a new aeroplane. Pawl had been flying over the Moor the previous night and also saw the lights and the face. A further flight over the Moor by all three showed that the face was projected on to a cloud bank and was accompanied by some form of exotic writing. There are similar sightings elsewhere across England.

The story gets into the press and one bumptious scientist interprets it as a message from Mars, but has no idea what the writing means. Another scientist, younger but more qualified, Lancelot Downey, does recognize the writing. He consults Bassett and the others and is taken on a plane flight where he makes a better copy of the writing. He realizes the script is based on a universal language invented by John Wilkins, a real person who lived in the seventeenth century. He set down his "philosophical language" in a book in 1668, but it is believed he had created the language at least twenty years before. Though an Anglican clergyman and brother-in-law to Oliver Cromwell, Wilkins was an enthusiast for the pursuit of science and while at Oxford had established the Oxford Philosophical Club in 1649 to which many eminent scientists of the period belonged. Wilkins, who became one of the founders of the Royal Society in 1660, was interested in how we might travel beyond the Earth and explored the idea in *The Discovery of a World in the Moone* (1638) and later books.

According to Downey, Cornelius Drebbel, inspired by Wilkins, invented a machine capable of travelling to the moon and ventured there with Richard Kitto of Cornwall and Pietro Paoloni of Italy, and their wives. The date of their journey is given as 1654 (misprinted on first reference as 1634, the year after Drebbel's reported death). I cannot find details for Richard Kitto (presumably of the Kitto family of Bodmin) or Pietro Paoloni (an alumni of the University of Rome), but both were living in the early seventeenth century. Downey suggests that Drebbel feigned his death and spent the next twenty years creating his machine.

Further messages are received showing that the lunar colony is becoming desperate. They no longer have the plans to recreate the space machine, but they have developed a heat ray and threaten the Earth that unless help is forthcoming, they will start to destroy the Earth. They prove their ability by destroying the port of Nantes, boiling the sea off Italy, and blasting a circle of fire around London.

Meanwhile, Bassett and friends conduct a frantic search for the original engine plans in places where they believed Drebbel, Kitto and Paoloni had lived but without success. Earth is at the mercy of the dying moon colony. Although a message is displayed for the lunar survivors to read, there is no response. Time passes. There are no further attacks upon Earth and the suspicion grows that the colony no longer survives. Downey believes they had died before the original messages reached Earth. The first to be translated noted that it had been sent by "direct parallel length light" which made no sense to Downey until he realized it was sent by gravitational rather than light waves. Although even in Lynch's day it was suspected these waves travelled at the speed of light, it had not been proven. Downey suggests they travel much slower and that the messages had been sent much earlier. A Brazilian astronomer had noticed a flash of light on the moon a year before. It was now believed that that was when the colony died, destroyed by the very heat ray they had focused on Earth.

Despite the naïvety of this idea, it was an ingenious one for 1925 and since Lynch acknowledged the help of Professor da Costa Andrade, who was a colleague of Ernest Rutherford, the book seemed to have some authenticity. The fact that it's pretty much hokum does not detract from enjoying it today, as one of the true novelty items of classic British sf.

John Gilbert Bohun Lynch (1884–1928) was less of an expert on the Moon than he was on boxing, writing several books on the subject. Of Irish parentage he was born in London and educated at Oxford where he studied medicine and took up boxing, but his poor health stopped both pursuits and he turned to journalism and art—he was a clever caricaturist. His last book was *A History of Caricature* (1927). He was also an authority on ghost stories compiling *A Muster of Ghosts* (1924).

Man's World   Charlotte Haldane
London: Chatto & Windus, 1926

Charlotte Haldane was the wife of the renowned scientist J.B.S. Haldane. They had met in 1924 when she interviewed him for the *Daily Express*. They shared an interest in "ectogenesis", a term J.B.S. Haldane had coined in his book *Daedalus*. She hoped Haldane would help with ideas for her novel, which became *Man's World*. The two soon became lovers but it was not until she obtained a divorce from her first husband that they were able to marry, in April 1926. *Man's World* followed seven months later.

Haldane later wrote that the seed behind *Man's World* was to imagine how society might change if people could choose the sex of their child. This core idea grew into developing a society with eugenic control over the breeding of children and one where a woman has a choice. She can either become a mother or choose not to have children, in which case she is sterilized and becomes an "entertainer". Marriages are approved by a Council and society is monitored to ensure there is no deviation from these basic choices. Any human deviation is bred out of the child through the eugenic process. Marriage and family is abolished with children raised by the state.

The book is set in an unspecified future but starts with the death (by euthanisation) of the geneticist Mensch at the age of 113. He had developed a vision for mankind fifty-seven years before, sometime after the First World War, around the time of a Second World War. There is no date for this, but it would seem to have been in the 1940s so the events of the novel must be at the start of the twenty-first century. Haldane describes this second War as one of "unbounded destruction", which gave impetus to the need for change, for science to be controlled and work for the benefit of mankind.

The first third of the book is an exposition about how this society came about. It was clearly influenced by J.B.S. Haldane's thinking in *Daedalus* in the *To-day and To-morrow* series but also quotes from Bertrand Russell's *Icarus*, highlighting the potential conflict between the direction in which science is taking society and the desires of individuals. The slightest deviation upsets the overall balance.

Much of this development is disturbing. Mensch created a eugenic community called the Nucleus with carefully selected and reared children developed to become the superior race—all white. One chemist had developed a toxin called Thanatil which attacks the enzyme in the skin of the black races causing paralysis and death. There is discussion about whether something similar can be developed for the Oriental races. This is a horrifying vision by Haldane presaging the Nazi Holocaust a decade later—Haldane even uses the world "holocaust" (page 22) but she does not mean a Jewish holocaust. Haldane was Jewish (Franken was her maiden name) as was her visionary scientist, Mensch. The rise of white supremacy was not Mensch's intention, but as a natural consequence of his research.

This future world is devoid of religion which has been outlawed, though not eradicated. The title *Man's World* is not meant to imply it has been created by Man for Man but that it is no longer God's World, implying that this society is a fall from grace.

The story set within this future is relatively simple but far-reaching. It focuses on young Christopher, his sister Nicolette, and their acquaintances in the Nucleus and nearby communes. Christopher feels a void in his life which he believes can only be filled by a religious faith. He undertakes a pilgrimage into the countryside to commune with nature and to understand the world about him. He meets Lois, an "entertainer", who has a similar love of nature and birds, but the few weeks he spends with her only underlines his love for his sister and his desire for a faith. He returns to the Nucleus where he discovers a rift has grown between Nicolette and her prospective mate, Raymond. Nicolette has become attached to Bruce, a strong, charismatic figure whom everyone looks up to.

Christopher comes to believe that religion has been pressed out of people's lives by the suffocating regimentation of society. Nicolette wants a child which she can rear herself and not give up to the state. She decides to be sterilized but has found a way to neutralize the injection so when she and Bruce have sex she becomes pregnant. What neither Nicolette nor Christopher realize is that Bruce is a spy who has been monitoring the group and has betrayed them to the authorities. Christopher, who is ultra-sensitive and feels robbed of his dreams, takes his own life.

There is much philosophical discussion throughout the story on this society and its relationship with the past. An architect, for whom Nicolette goes to work, is in charge of Reconstruction, where copies of ancient cities are recreated for people to visit and relive the past, experiencing the problems.

When Charlotte showed her future husband the synopsis for *Man's World* he remarked, "You will not easily persuade me that man's future will be less surprising and tragic than his past." That encapsulates the essence of the novel. All societies of whatever age have their problems which, for some, are insurmountable. What is a utopia for one is hell for another.

The life of Charlotte Haldane (1898–1969) is one of pioneering science and crusades against political and social injustice. She was a strong feminist although many argued that neither *Man's World* nor her next book *Marriage and its Enemies* (1928) showed such traits. She was of the view that women should embrace motherhood, and science and society should help women to be mothers and to contribute to society. Her many thoughts on the subject along with communism, fascism and the Soviet Union are explored in her autobiography *Truth Will Out* (1949).

To-morrow   Alfred Ollivant

London: Alston Rivers, 1927

After so many post-war dystopias Ollivant presents a fully fledged utopia, and for those who imagine that an apparently perfect world cannot contain sufficient conflict for an interesting story, then *To-morrow* is the exception to the rule. It is a beautiful, charming book.

We are in an unspecified future, at least three centuries hence, with the setting mostly southern England. We meet Mary who has just completed her obligatory ten years of service, a requirement that everyone must provide between the ages of eighteen and twenty-eight. It ensures equality as during those years everyone undertakes all the menial tasks rather than them being imposed upon a working-class. Once that is completed, they have a year's sabbatical during which they may mate (which is not the same as marry) and confirm what employment they want to pursue. There are two types of work. People can be either an Aspirant, who is in effect a scientist who works to enlarge the dominion of mankind over Nature; or a Content, who works in agriculture or shops.

Mary mates with Mark, who has also completed his ten years' service. To satisfy the local Council, which administer all affairs, they undergo a series of mild eugenic tests to prove good health and compatibility. In this future, women are larger and stronger than men. Nudity is the accepted norm, though simple tunics are worn at times. Because bodies are exposed to the sun, they absorb more light and part of the eugenic test is to measure the level of "Light" within the body. If a body has been corrupted in any way, such as through smoking or eating meat, the body will appear blurred. We later learn that it is exposure to Light that had allowed the mystical scientist Zed to create this new world and make himself something of a messiah.

Society has returned to a pre-industrial bucolic life. There is no heavy industry except in specified zones. There are no roads or railways. All transport is by air, from great liners to individual two-seater air-canoes. Weather is controlled by a dissipator, invented by Zed. Most people have developed mental skills to control their health and wellbeing and, thanks to Zed, many are telepathic—that is their thoughts are transmitted via a small mobile communicator.

The exceptions are those living on the Isle of Wight, where the rebellious Diehards prefer the old way of life. Mainlanders are depicted as Free (once they've served their ten years) and happy, whilst the Islanders are bitter and angry. Mary and Mark plan to visit Wight but first they travel to the New Forest. This has been left to return to nature, with no weather control. At this point we discover that both Mark and Mary have an affinity with nature and an empathy for animals and plants. Mary endures considerable pain when a tree is felled.

On the Isle of Wight Mary is horrified by the society, with illness prevailing and no fresh air. To the reader it feels as if it has regressed to Victorian times with the aristocracy taxing everyone and keeping the money for themselves. Little of the land is used for produce but is kept for hunting. Most Islanders are poor and starving. The island is patrolled by a fascist police. Mark and Mary are arrested for sunbathing naked and imprisoned, but soon released. There are public executions, though these are usually contrived affairs. An execution is aborted when there is a revolt amongst the crowd. Mary and Mark escape but are caught up in a hunt where a convict is released for sport and chased by hounds. Mark, Mary and the convict are rescued by an air-boat and returned home.

Mark and Mary visit Zed, whom Mary had long admired, in the hope of employment. We learn that he is extremely old, having witnessed the end of the old era. He calls his ability to draw power from Light and Nature "at-one-ment". At one time this power was immense and allowed him to walk on water, but an accident to a colleague and the ensuing punishment meant his powers declined and are only gradually returning. By becoming "at one" with Nature Zed believes he can fly but he tries too soon, and it is left to Mark and Mary to conquer the air. The final chapters of this book in which the two seek to fly are genuinely uplifting. It is a book with a New Age spirit. Throughout *To-morrow* Ollivant explores the future of science but recognizes that the strength to progress comes from within us, and that if we develop our psychic abilities we can master the world.

The book ends on a highly spiritual, religious note, perhaps not surprisingly as Ollivant completed it just before his death at the age of fifty-two.

There is an earnest hope in Mary's words to one of the Council that, "...
we are standing at last on the threshold of Eternal Life."

Alfred Ollivant (1874–1927) was born and raised in the Sussex Downs,
which is the setting for the novel, but soon after he entered the army in
1893 he fell from a horse and injured his spine. He spent most of the next
four years in bed during which time he wrote his first book, *Owd Bob*
(1898). The book was a sleeper but over time it became a bestseller, with
over 700,000 copies in various editions. He never had such success again,
but people were so endeared to *Owd Bob*, that they bought Ollivant's later
books anyway. Knowing that Ollivant spent most of his adult life as an
invalid makes *To-morrow* even more poignant in his hope for an England
full of health and pleasure, and the hope to fly.

Concrete   Aelfrida Tillyard

London: Hutchinson, 1930

Sub-titled "A Story of Two Hundred Years Hence", a period called the "Age
of Reason", this novel explores an apparent utopia which has been created
following a period of revolution, war and plague which wiped out nearly
80% of the world's population. The utopia is maintained by a strict regime
of eugenics, allowing mating between only the top classified individuals,
and by the ruthless elimination of religion. Any who deviate from the rules
are euthanized. The result is a society which whilst superficially happy is
increasingly bored with the population in rapid decline. Elsewhere in the
world is similar dissatisfaction. In Russia is the emergence of a group who
favour euthanasia and refuse to have children.

The story is seen through the eyes of Alaric, son of the President of
Britain and the Empire, who is a perfect A+ example of manhood, and his
future mate Eleuthera, a beautiful, strong-willed girl who is a near-perfect
A. Alaric is head of the Ministry of Aesthetics for which at the start of the
book he has a passion, believing everyone benefits from an appreciation

of the beauty in the world. Eleuthera is a teacher of children and follows the principles of aesthetics, teaching children to admire Nature and art.

Amongst Eleuthera's class is six-year-old Jimmy, who is of poor health and is less academically endowed than the others. He does not understand the world in the way other children do, but he clearly has a sense of the divine in how he observes Nature. This generates in Eleuthera feelings for something beyond the physical world but any mention of God or a religious belief is punishable by death and Alaric insists that she does not explore the subject. However, she is given by her great-grandfather what may be the last surviving copy of the *Book of Common Prayer* and although it takes Eleuthera a while to understand it, the book opens up a world of faith and hope which is missing from society. She finds comfort in the book, especially after Jimmy is condemned to death for being sub-normal. Eleuthera pleas unsuccessfully on his behalf and, in what is the most moving chapter in this novel, she decides she will administer the toxin that puts him to sleep, after having read him a series of stories about the wonder in the world.

Alaric is friends with Manlius, head of the Ministry of Reason who is also known as Big Brother. Manlius has no time for aesthetics and believes Alaric should work for him. This Ministry monitors everybody, including other countries, and Manlius tells Alaric of the growing deprivation elsewhere in the world. He also warns Alaric that Eleuthera has the prayer-book which Alaric destroys. This causes a rift between them, but such is their love that Alaric and Eleuthera go through with the mating ceremony and settle down to a life raising children. Alaric does not believe either of his children will live up to his standards and he begins to doubt his enthusiasm for aesthetics, so grabs the chance to accompany Manlius to the League of Nations in Geneva. The President, who has recently gained a new lease of life having been cured of a fatal disease, has decided that to counter the growing lassitude in Britain the law needs to change, not only allowing mating to take place earlier than thirty, and for there to be more children, but also that mating should now be allowed between white and black races, hitherto forbidden. The President believes that the black races possess a greater joy of life and he hopes this will raise public morale in Britain.

The chapters covering Alaric and Manlius's time at the League of Nations is an uncomfortable read today because it reveals the prejudices of white people against all other races in Tillyard's day, which she projected into the future. Whilst there are some positive comments and the desire for greater integration, that fact that in those two hundred years Tillyard believed all black people would still be regarded as "backward" is difficult to read.

While Alaric was away, Eleuthera takes the children for a walk and finds the ruins of a church where she conducts an impromptu religious ceremony. Unfortunately, she was followed by her neighbour, Miguel, who gets her to confess her actions, thus condemning her to euthanasia. Alaric arrives home in time to save her and whisks her and the children away in his small plane. They land on a remote, hitherto unknown tropical island which, by rather good fortune, had been occupied two centuries before by a religious group from Cambridge. The islanders welcome them but although Eleuthera fits instantly into the island society Alaric is uncomfortable, even angry. He despairs and tries to commit suicide, but slowly Alaric recognizes how religion helps the islanders. Following his own religious experience, Alaric is prepared to accept the existence of God.

The islanders help distil fuel for the plane and Alaric returns to Britain alone. He confronts his father, the President, whom he sees as a tyrant, and they have a debate about which is more important—the President or God. At one point the President remarks, "the world is not big enough for me and God. One of us has got to go." Manlius is to decide and, we are left with a wonderfully clever "lady or the tiger" ending.

The book's title is not explained, but evidently Tillyard sees the "Age of Reason" as unreasonable and inflexible, its system set in concrete.

There is much in *Concrete* that might have influenced both Aldous Huxley in *Brave New World* and George Orwell in *Nineteen Eighty-Four*, and the novel is every bit as memorable as those and unjustifiably overlooked.

Aelfrida Catherine Wetenhall Tillyard (1883–1959), was part of a liberal minded, affluent and well-educated family. She became a Sunday School teacher at sixteen, and helped teach undergraduates at Cambridge. She married in 1904 but though they had two children the marriage was not happy and they divorced in 1921. She poured her energy into writing, compiling an anthology, *Cambridge Poets 1900–1913* (1913), and producing several mystical and religious books, such as *The Making of a Mystic* (1917), books for children and several novels. These included another work of science fiction, *The Approaching Storm* (1932), a vision of a future communist Britain. Throughout her life she explored various religions and doctrines, including Buddhism, and practised for a while as a Quaker and then a Christian Scientist before she entered a convent in 1934 as Sister Placida.

SUPER, SUB OR NON-HUMAN?

A LTHOUGH WE ASSOCIATE THE THEORY OF EVOLUTION WITH
Charles Darwin and his landmark text *On the Origin of Species* (1859)
there had been others before him who speculated on the diversity of life
on Earth and questioned how much was due to creationism and how much
might be a process of adaptation. As early as 1735, the Swedish botanist and
zoologist Carl Linnaeus had introduced his system of classifying plants,
recognizing the many similarities and how some may have been adaptations of earlier plants. Further ideas were proposed by Pierre-Louis de
Maupertuis who, in 1751, suggested that such variations in animals might
be transmitted by sperm, and most notably by Jean-Baptiste de Lamarck
who, in several volumes starting with *Systèmes des animaux sans vertèbres*
in 1801, demonstrated the theory of animals evolving from a lesser to a
higher species through a process of adaptation.

Writers of fiction found it difficult to pursue such theories in a world
dominated by the Church but the occasional renegade talent appeared, not
surprisingly in France. In 1781 Restif de la Bretonne published *La découverte
australe par un homme-volant*, where his exploratory flying man investigates

remote islands in the southern hemisphere and finds creatures that seem to be vying with each other in evolutionary terms amongst them an intelligent human-like ape. The idea of intelligent apes, even before Darwin, allowed for cutting satire as in Thomas Love Peacock's *Melincourt* (1817) where an intelligent orang-outan is elected to Parliament. The American author James Fenimore Cooper, best known for *The Last of the Mohicans* (1826), envisaged an intelligent monkey society on hitherto unknown islands near Antarctica in *The Monikins* (1835).

Closely associated with the theory of evolution is that of eugenics, a term coined by Francis Galton in 1883 to cover the idea of selective breeding in humans to encourage the best traits, to the point of sterilizing those deemed unfit to breed. This notorious idea was soon subjected to the science-fiction treatment in "A Child of the Phalanstery" (1884) by Grant Allen in which a future society destroys any deformed children to protect a divine humanity. The most notable early novel of eugenics was *The Demigod* (1886) by American educator Edward Payson Jackson. He depicts a programme of selective breeding that had started in the seventeenth century and by the late nineteenth had produced a superman of astonishing intellect and prowess. Fellow American Luther Marshall depicted a superman in *Thomas Boobig* (1895), whose abilities develop from birth, rather than through breeding,.

These were the starting points for what became a significant branch of science fiction either envisaging super-beings—and we live in a comic-book world of superheroes today—or the evolution of humans into either vastly intelligent societies or one-off individuals with unusual talents. We have already encountered one such in Beresford's *The Hampdenshire Wonder* and we will encounter others, such as in Muriel Jaeger's *The Man With Six Senses*.

One champion of Darwinism was H.G. Wells who, as a trained biologist, was fascinated with the potential for human development. We have seen this in *The Time Machine*, where he showed the disparate evolution of the Eloi and the Morlocks based on the worlds in which their antecedents existed, and this Wellsian social evolution features in several books covered here, such as *The Collapse of Homo Sapiens* by P. Anderson Graham and *The Last of My Race* by John Lionel Tayler.

Wells also considered how humans, or animals, might be helped on their way by manipulation, what we now call genetic engineering. The creation of a human being can be traced back to Mary Shelley's *Frankenstein* (1818) but this was not trying to improve or develop a human, rather to take on the godlike power of creating man. In *The Island of Dr. Moreau* (1896), Wells portrayed a scientist who attempts to rebuild animals as humans, even to the point of them obeying strict laws. Julian Huxley wrote a similar story in "The Tissue-Culture King" (1926) where a scientist adapts blood cells in cultures from which he is able to produce giants, dwarves and other physical abnormalities.

In *The Food of the Gods* (1904), Wells considered how the growth of creatures might be chemically enhanced by creating a wonder diet. This food creates not only giant humans but animals and leads inevitably to a breakdown in society and the threat of war.

One idea that Wells did not pursue was that of a human enhanced by machines. The American writer and editor Edward Page Mitchell had considered this in "The Ablest Man in the World" (1879) when a man of limited intelligence becomes a genius when a calculating machine is installed in his head. This is clearly the forerunner of the cyborg, though that word was not coined until 1971. An example discussed here is *The Clockwork Man* by E.V. Odle.

Cyborgs differ from robots in that they are essentially human with various skills enhanced through machines. Robots are entirely mechanical. The term robot made its appearance in Karel Čapek's play *R. U. R.* (1920). The title translates as *Rossum's Universal Robots*. First performed in Prague in January 1921, it made it to the American stage in October 1922 and Britain in April 1923. It took a while for the word robot to catch on. Hitherto the usual word for a mechanical man was an automaton, and to make it even more complicated, Čapek's robots are grown in vats using chemicals, and are really what are called androids. We will see an increasing number of automata, robots and androids in science fiction as we progress.

Finally there was the question of enhancing human lifespan, certainly beyond the allotted threescore-years-and-ten but even perhaps to immortality. We have already encountered it in Henry Gubbins's bizarre *The Elixir of Life*, and the idea of an elixir dates back to such gothic fantasies as *St. Leon* (1799) by William Godwin. His daughter, Mary Shelley, explored the theme in "The Mortal Immortal" (1833). Walter Besant's *The Inner House* (1888) portrayed immortality as a curse leading not only to rivalry between young and old but a stagnation in society. It was a problem further explored by Martin Swayne in *The Blue Germ*, which is the starting point for this section.

The Blue Germ   Martin Swayne
London: Hodder & Stoughton, 1918

After falling over his cat and lying unconscious for three days, Richard Harden, a Harley Street specialist, has a sudden brain wave about how bacteria might be adapted (what we would now call genetically engineered) for human benefit. Sharing his thoughts with the eccentric Russian scientist, Professor Sarakoff, the latter puts Harden's ideas into practice and come up with a new bacillus which he believes will cure mankind of all its physical ailments and possibly confer immortality. So convinced are they of the benefits of this new "germ" as they think of it, which is effectively a super-antibiotic (and remember that penicillin was not discovered until 1928), that they empty a supply of it into the water supply for Birmingham and await the results.

The first visible effect is that those infected have a bluish tinge to their skin and eyes making them highly visible and consequently shunned. These individuals soon find themselves free of any colds or diseases they had and a feeling of abundant vitality. The two scientists feel vindicated in their actions but when Sarakoff reveals this to the press there is a backlash. Not only are the government horrified that they should have taken such actions on their own—one official treats them as terrorists—but when the scientists declare their belief that people will become immortal, there is an unexpected response amongst the public. The poor and the needy see nothing ahead of them but endless poverty. Those who might be happily married now wonder how long love will last. And those who had hoped to inherit or benefit from the deaths of others now feel robbed of their heritage.

Although the germ seems to cure those affected by illness, it does not protect them from accidents. As a result there is an outbreak of hostilities by the young against the old, the young believing they have been robbed of all privileges. The possibility of death by accident leads to an uncontrollable fear of injury. The prospect not of dying, but living with some physical injury, like losing a limb, for the rest of eternity causes panic attacks.

Alongside this is a growing lethargy. If life everlasting is stretching ahead for everyone, then why rush things. People drift into a feeling of tranquillity and calm and finally a deep sleep. All ambition and progress seems to have been lost.

The sleep lasts little more than a week and as people awake they discover the blue tinge in their skin and eyes has gone and their vitality has returned. Have the effects of the blue germ been dissipated? Are people still cured of all physical ills? Is everyone immortal or not—a question which might take a long time to answer. The author leaves these questions open and ends the book with the reader pondering on the human condition and what motivates us.

The book was well received. The renowned critic, A. St. John Adcock said that it was "one of the most curiously fascinating things of the kind I have read for a long while."

That was a response the author had hoped for. Martin Swayne was, in real life, the Scottish psychologist Henry Maurice Nicoll (1884–1953), son

of the church minister and journalist William Robertson Nicoll, editor
of the nonconformist newspaper the *British Weekly*. Maurice Nicoll had
adopted the Swayne alias for his non-psychological books, although *The
Blue Germ* was really an exploration of ideas he had developed in *Dream
Psychology* (1918). Nicoll was fascinated in what drives people to do what
they do, and believed that individuals' actions might be spurred on by
subconscious thoughts beyond the five senses. In *The Blue Germ* he questions whether people would continue to achieve greatness if all of life's ills
were solved. Mankind needs challenges to progress. Nicoll was aware that
the Great War had damaged people both psychologically and spiritually,
through such mental states as what was called shell shock or, these days,
post-traumatic stress disorder, which he incorporates in the novel in the
panic reactions to danger. To progress, Nicoll believed humanity had to
be aware of the unsteady balance between striving for new achievements
and the perils they may bring.

Back to Methuselah   George Bernard Shaw
London: Constable, 1921

The subtitle of this play is *A Metabiological Pentateuch*, a mouthful that
tells us it's a sequence of five interrelated plays about longevity. It is rarely
performed because the sequence takes up to twelve hours. It was first
performed in New York at the end of February 1922 and its first British
performance was in Birmingham in October 1923 over consecutive nights.
There have been several radio adaptations by the BBC but generally it's a
play that few will have seen or heard.

Shaw wrote a lengthy preface to discuss his thoughts on the inadequacy
of humans. Simply expressed, he believed that humans did not live long
enough to cope with the world about them. His thoughts had coalesced
with the First World War. Writing in 1920, Shaw wondered if civilization
will survive. He questioned "whether the human animal, as he exists at

present, is capable of solving the social problems raised by his own aggre-
gation, or, as he calls it, his civilization."

Shaw considered the impact of Darwinian evolution and suggested
that there ought to be a form of Creative Evolution, meaning that humans
should be able to determine their existence through their own willpower,
based on faith and hope, rather than relying solely on natural selection.
Despair brings discouragement and mental/physical decline. If humans
could extend their lifespan from threescore-and-ten years to three hundred
or even three thousand it would mean civilization would not need to keep
relearning each generation and could progress faster. The five connected
plays explore this idea.

The first play sows the seed. "In the Beginning" is set in the Garden of
Eden and shows Adam and Eve becoming increasingly bored with eternal
life and no progress. The Serpent beguiles Eve with the idea that "imagination is the beginning of creation. You imagine what you desire; you will
what you imagine; and at last you create what you will." Encouraged by
the Earth Mother Lilith, Eve is convinced that to progress and leave behind
something of importance, they need to create other humans. Thus are
born Cain and Abel, but Cain sullies life by killing Abel. Adam and Eve
create more children and the generations grow but none lives as long. Eve
observes, "...most of our grandchildren die before they have sense enough
to know how to live."

The second part, "The Gospel of the Brothers Barnabas", is set in the
present. Two brothers, and others who arrive at their house during the
discussion, including the local rector and the parlour-maid, consider the
benefits and otherwise of longevity, stating the points Shaw had raised in
his preface. One individual assumed the Brothers had a special elixir and
is surprised that they were talking about willpower alone. Pointedly the
Brothers state that unless humans can achieve something other than self-
destruction, the time will come when they will be superseded by something
superior. "The force behind evolution, call it what you will, is determined
to solve the problem of civilization; and if it cannot do it through us, it

will produce some more capable agents." For its own survival mankind must progress and so humans must live longer. The Brothers felt that three hundred years was appropriate.

The next play, "The Thing Happens" is set in the year 2170. By now there are several long-lifers including the rector in the previous play, who has become the Archbishop of York, and the parlour-maid, who is now a government minister. It is discovered that the Archbishop has kept feigning his own death because the world was not ready to accept his longevity, and because he always looked too young to retire. It is suspected that there are other long-lifers in hiding. The play opens depicting a room with one wall filled by a videophone screen. Most government officials are either black Africans or Chinese, because they mature quicker. The long-lifers, or those who believe they may be, become cautious and take fewer risks as they don't want to develop any health problems with which they will have to live for a long time. The Chief Secretary, a Chinese man called Confucius, congratulates a minister who feared getting rheumatism because of an assignation at sea, saying that he has shown the first stages of maturity: "...you are a sensible coward, almost a grown-up man."

The fourth play, "Tragedy of an Elderly Gentleman" shows us the world of 3000AD. Society has changed considerably. The long-lifers are categorized by their age: those in their first century bear a number 1, those in their second a 2, and the oldest a 3. The mature long-lifers have developed a mental acuity and can converse almost telepathically aided by an instrument like a tuning fork. English remains the predominant language but it has changed. In the British Isles, including Ireland, where most long-lifers live, language is precise with no metaphors or idioms. The British Empire is governed from Baghdad and an "elderly" visitor from there, whose son-in-law is the Prime Minister, becomes frustrated over problems communicating. There is also present the Emperor of Turania, from Central Asia. He and the Elderly Gentleman wish to consult the Oracle, a veiled woman. She tells them that if they wish to stay, they will likely die of discouragement. It becomes apparent that those in their second or third century are tired of those who live short life spans (only seventy years) and find ways to exterminate them with their mental powers.

The final play, "As Far as Thought Can Reach", takes us to 31910AD. All short-lifers are extinct and long-lifers are almost immortal, barring accidents. The fear of accidental death causes the ancients to wish they could become pure thought. A scientist called Pygmalion has created artificial beings, or homunculi, but he is accidentally killed by one at the Festival of the Artists. New humans are born in eggs and emerge fully formed and intellectually advanced. The Ancients and the "children" seldom communicate.

As the play ends the ghosts of Adam, Eve, Cain, the Serpent and Lilith emerge in the darkness and give their views on human evolution. Adam does not understand the nature of progress, but Eve can see that the intelligent and artistic have furthered life. Lilith, who started the whole process, has the final word, glad to know that what she set in motion continues and that the next phase of human evolution is near.

George Bernard Shaw (1856–1950) must have practised what he preached to some degree, since he lived to be 94. A lifelong socialist and one of the founding members of the Fabian Society, Shaw expressed his views in many plays, novels and essays, and amongst his works are several that fall within the ambit of science fiction. He had already used his idea of Creative Evolution in *Man and Superman* (1903) whilst *Heartbreak House* (1919) considered the catastrophe of the World War upon humanity. Several plays are set in the near future—*Press Cuttings* (1909) about women's rights, *On the Rocks* (1933), about an emerging dystopia, and *The Millionairess* (1936), a satire on eugenics. With his huge body of thought-provoking work it is perhaps a shame that the play he's best known for is *Pygmalion* (1913), and then chiefly because of the musical adaptation as *My Fair Lady*. Yet, the central idea in *Pygmalion*—how it should be possible to improve one's status in life through education, manners and language—shows some of the thoughts about extending life Shaw returned to in *Back to Methuselah*.

The Cheetah Girl   Christopher Blayre (Edward Heron-Allen)

London: privately issued, 1923; later issued in a limited edition, Heathfield: Tartarus Press, 1998

This mildly erotic novelette long remained a mystery. In April 1921 the publisher Philip Allan released *The Purple Sapphire and Other Posthumous Papers* by Christopher Blayre. It purported to be a selection of material chosen by Blayre, in his role as Registrar at the University of Cosmopoli, from papers donated to the archives by those at the university who did not want their work published until after their death. Blayre's "Antescript" is dated January 1952 suggesting that the authors of the nine papers might have been dead by then (other than Blayre himself, who contributed one item), but were almost certainly still alive in 1921. By a clever literary conceit Blayre is taking us into his confidence and allowing us to read material which would not otherwise be released for another thirty years.

But, the final story listed on the contents page, "The Cheetah Girl", wasn't there. Instead a simple note from the publisher stated that he was unable to publish it. When *The Purple Sapphire* was reprinted in 1932 as *The Strange Papers of Dr. Blayre*, a few additional stories were included, but not "The Cheetah Girl". Collectors of the strange and fantastic were puzzled. In fact "The Cheetah Girl" had been published, but privately, early in 1923, in a limited edition of only twenty copies for private circulation. It transpired that the publisher, Philip Allan, was horrified to find how sexually explicit the story was and fearing he would fall foul of the country's obscenity laws, cut it.

By today's standards the story is only mildly explicit and certainly not pornographic. Events are told by Rex Magley, Professor of Physiology at the University and successor to Paul Barrowdale. Barrowdale had introduced Magley to Mrs. Clayton. After Barrowdale's death, when Magley visits her regarding her legacy, he meets her daughter, Uniqua. The result is explosive. Uniqua is sexually aroused and had her mother not returned, matters would have gone too far. But Uniqua cannot be stopped. She visits

Magley and when Mrs. Clayton finds them, the situation is way beyond compromising. Magley apologizes but says he wants to marry Uniqua and though Mrs. Clayton will have none of it, within days Magley and Uniqua have eloped and married under special licence. They retreat to Paris.

Horrified, Mrs. Clayton kills herself and Magley is summoned home where he is presented with a manuscript written by Professor Barrowdale to be given to anyone who plans to marry Uniqua. It is a little too late as Uniqua is pregnant.

As Magley reads the manuscript he discovers that Uniqua is only half human. Barrowdale had conducted experiments in cross-breeding and though most failed, he succeeded when he found Menagerie Sal, a prostitute regarded as the lowest of the low. She was prepared to do anything. Barrowdale takes care of her and introduces her to a young male cheetah whom he had been raising. After manipulating their blood cells, he let nature take its course. He suspected the offspring would be a monster, but it turned out to be a perfectly formed little girl, human in all respects except for being covered in a light fur-like down.

When Magley realizes what Uniqua is he cannot bear to imagine what their child will be like, but when he tries to talk her into having an abortion, she becomes the protective mother. Magley resolves he must kill her, despite being obsessively in love with her. A footnote at the end of the manuscript reveals both her and his fate.

It's a powerful, emotionally charged story. Barrowdale's account could have come straight from a text book. The end result, though, is one of the first stories to consider cross-species sex, something that would emerge later in science fiction when exploring relationships between humans and aliens.

Edward Heron-Allen (1861–1943), the man behind the Blayre alias, was a remarkable character with a wide diversity of interests. Although a practising solicitor, his real passions were diverse. He was fascinated with palmistry writing several books on the subject starting with *Cheiromancy, or the Science of Palmistry* in 1883. He studied the violin, not just playing it but making them. His *Violin-Making, As it Was and Is* (1884), was a standard text for decades. He learned Turkish and Persian, undertaking a translation of the *Rubaiyat of Omar Khayyam*, published in 1898. He undertook many scientific studies, worked in military intelligence during the First World War, produced studies on the history and nature of Selsey Bill, where he lived, and was a member of the Society for Psychical Research. And from time to time he turned to fiction, starting with *The Princess Daphne* in 1888, a tale of the transmigration of souls.

On rare occasions copies of that original printing of *The Cheetah Girl* appear for auction, fetching fabulous sums, and in 1998 it was reprinted in an edition of just ninety-nine copies, which also now fetches a king's ransom. It was restored to its rightful place in *The Collected Strange Papers of Christopher Blayre* (1998) in a larger (but not unlimited) print run which is also now scarce. "The Cheetah Girl" thus remains a rare find and a rare read.

The Clockwork Man   E.V. Odle

London: William Heinemann, 1923

This is one of the best scientific romances of the 1920s. Odle not only presents a readable and often amusing narrative but sets a number of conundrums about the future of humanity, not all of which are resolved.

The Clockwork Man—he has no name—appears at the start of the book when he stumbles into a cricket match on a village green. He is first encountered by Arthur Withers, the average man, who finds it difficult to understand the Man's gibberish statements and uncontrolled physical movements. The Clockwork Man makes a few adjustments to become reasonably coherent but no less comprehensible. He asks Arthur what year it is and is both horrified and fascinated to discover it is 1923. In his mumblings he reveals he comes from perhaps eight thousand years in the future.

He is approached by Gregg, the captain of the local cricket team, and one of the players, Dr. Allingham, and because of the team's desperation, the Clockwork Man is co-opted into the team. He proves to be an astonishing batsman—balls vanish from the ground and are found miles away—and an expert bowler, but he has no knowledge of the game. Following another maladjustment he knocks out most of the players with his bat. He then sets off at a remarkable rate, seeming to fly over the hurdles surrounding the ground, leaving those who are still conscious, perplexed.

There follows a series of encounters with the Clockwork Man where, gradually, some explanation of who or what he is, emerges. This also proves confusing. He arrives at a church hall where the vicar is awaiting a conjuror to entertain the children. The Clockwork Man reveals that in the future everyone is a conjuror. His hand and arm momentarily vanish and then produces out of nowhere a parrot in a cage.

At one point he is found having stumbled into a pit and is helped out by a local lad of limited mental capacity. It is discovered the Clockwork Man has lost his hat and wig and reveals a bald head the back of which appears to be glass covering a complex machine.

Gregg convinces himself that the Man has come from the future and is perhaps the next step in human evolution. Allingham refuses to believe this, horrified at what man might become. He convinces himself it is a hoax. Yet it falls to the doctor to help the Clockwork Man when he knocks him down in the road and is intrigued to see that the Man is disturbed by how the doctor treats his car. Evidently the Man has more affinity with machines than humans. The doctor takes him home and provides food and drink and realizes that the Man needs further help. Removing the new hat and wig that the Man had taken (the vicar's!), the doctor discovers the complex mechanism and tries to adjust it, initially with alarming results, but eventually enough to repair the Man and, temporarily, put him to sleep. The doctor summons Gregg and they discuss events, before suddenly finding a label which had fallen from the Man. These are instructions on how he must be operated. The doctor collapses in relief believing that the Man is a toy, a complex one, but still a toy.

Meanwhile, the Man awakes and leaves. He has a final encounter with Arthur Withers and his fiancée where we learn something about the Man and his future. It seems that after the War (and perhaps future similar conflagrations) it became necessary for the lives of men to be adjusted to avoid further conflict. The Makers (we know not who they are) have perfected the Clock, a form of super-computer, which when installed inside men provides them with multiple opportunities. There is no longer one world, but multiform possibilities through the dimensions—in effect a multiverse—and humans no longer need to fight for territory or principles because they can shift through the dimensions to find the world they want. However, in this process, men have lost their sex drive, and women are no longer necessary. Just when you think you're understanding this future, Odle throws another wobbly. The Clockwork Man states that he is not real, but an invention. The Makers are real, and they live in the real world. Women are also real and so the Makers take them to the real world. It suggests that man, because of the trouble he has caused, is allowed to play in a set of multiform realities to satisfy his needs while the real world exists elsewhere. But we learn no more about the Makers or the real world. As the Clockwork Man returns to his future he tells Arthur to "Keep smiling—laughter—such a jolly little world."

The Clockwork Man is a remarkable novel. In a light-hearted way, which makes Odle's ideas more acceptable and meaningful, he proposes not only the adaptation of men into what we call a cyborg, but talks about multiple worlds, subject to a reality run by the Makers, who may be another form of human or alien beings. This was the first novel to feature a cyborg.

Edwin Vincent Odle (1890–1942) was the son of a bank manager and might have been expected to follow in his footsteps. But the family evidently had an artistic gene. The elder son, Alan, became an illustrator and artist of some repute whilst Edwin turned to journalism and writing. He was almost certainly influenced by H.G. Wells—his first novel, *The History of Alfred Judd* (1922), reads like a cross between Wells's *Kipps* and *The History of*

Mr. Polly. Through his brother's wife, Dorothy Richardson, who had known H.G. Wells in more ways than one, Edwin came to know J.D. Beresford, who helped place Odle's first novel.

The Clockwork Man shows elements of both Wells and Beresford—a suspiciously carefree world into which intrudes the unusual that only a few recognize—but it is also richly Odle's own, a book that should be on the shelves of every sf aficionado. It was well received at the time—J. B. Priestley even encouraged Odle to become a writer of scientific romances. But his publisher disagreed, suggesting that sales were poor. Odle had started a thematic sequel, *Juggernaut*, but this remained unpublished, even unfinished at the time, especially once Odle's energies were taken up as editor of the new English pulp magazine, *The Argosy*, a post he held from 1926 to 1936, retiring due to ill-health. He then returned to *Juggernaut* but it remained unpublished. Fortunately bookdealer George W. Locke rescued it from oblivion and it was published in Canada in 2016. The novel follows Samuel Butler's idea that machines would soon evolve into creations superior to humans and these living machines dominate and destroy human civilization. Had Odle followed Priestley's advice he might have become the premier link between H.G. Wells and the more modern science fiction of the 1930s and 1940s. Instead that mantle was bequeathed to S. Fowler Wright, whom we shall encounter shortly.

The Collapse of Homo Sapiens   P. Anderson Graham

London: G.P. Putnam's Sons, 1923

This novel bears comparison with Shanks's *The People of the Ruins*, as it depicts a Britain desolated by a series of wars, two centuries hence (2120AD). And, like Shanks, Graham holds out little hope. It also shares with *Back to Methuselah* the wish for a longer life as the narrator remarks that man's allotted lifespan is too brief to retain a grasp of world events and how we might learn from them.

The book purports to be a manuscript handed over to the "editor" (Graham) by a weary, old, nameless man. This Man had conducted various experiments by way of which he came into psychical contact with an alien being of supreme knowledge and ability, which he calls The Voice. He asks the being if he might be granted a life span of two thousand years but the Voice tells him the human race is not assured that span. He says he will lift a corner of the great curtain and grant the Man a glimpse of the future two hundred years hence. It is only a brief glimpse, but he witnesses a desolate Britain, overrun by nature, buildings returned to ruins, and a brief sighting of humans who seem to have devolved to small vicious apes.

The Man wants to learn more and begs the Voice to grant him a longer visit. This time he encounters a group of normal humans who are trying to restore a semblance of order. They are wearing oddly assorted pieces of armour to protect themselves from the degenerate humans. Their leader is Captain Hart who does not believe the Man's story that he has come from the past and suspects he is deluded. Nevertheless, he takes him in as part of his small group and they return, via a boat, along the Thames to their small settlement, New London. Hart reveals some of the past history, and at this point the book explores a plotline of war between races with sentiments and stereotyping unfortunately not uncommon of the period.

Hart reveals that after the Great War the "coloured races" rebelled against the whites, tired, not just of their domination of the world and their expressed superiority, but because of their indolence and lack of preparedness for the Great War. Britain has become increasingly degenerate, pleasure-seeking with the rise of the labour classes.

Hart still believes the Man, or the Visitor as he is now called, is deluded and sends him to Dr. Turnbull, one of the few medical men who was descended from a line of doctors from the time of the Great War. The Visitor is presented with several old documents which reveal the history of events. The first, written by Dr. Turnbull's ancestor, tells of how he and his wife and child manage to survive when the bombing starts in Scotland and the first of the invasion forces of "coloured" men. British forces were unable to respond and several local rebellions broke out, first in the North and finally in London. A separate manuscript tells of the London revolution and the involvement of a Dr. Binyon, who has invented a new weapon. Its nature is not revealed, though there is a suggestion it was some form of chemical warfare. Binyon uses it indiscriminately in London before escaping. He is not seen again. It is suggested he may have been an agent of foreign powers. A third manuscript reveals the story of a Yorkshire gentry, Sir John Scarlet, who witnessed the final operations of the "coloured" forces, exterminating survivors and destroying all buildings. At one point Scarlet confronts a black soldier who, though armed with a gun, refuses to kill Scarlet but agrees to hand-to-hand combat. The soldier loses but acts honourably having sworn that if he is defeated by a white man he would kill himself, which he does in his plane.

Amongst the survivors is a John Ogilvy who takes on the task of rebuilding Britain. Over a period of half a century he works with others to establish New London. It is a small community at the mercy of weather and pestilence. The Visitor learns there had been a terrible flood, during which time the survivors had become superstitious and drowned an old woman as a witch. After this a young man, called Adam, begins preaching the Christian message and gradually the Christian religion is restored, at least to some. There are still pagan worshippers.

These suspicions return when bad luck descends on the settlement during the time of the Visitor and they tell him to go or face the consequences. Upon leaving he finds himself back in his home in Kent, still holding the documents he had read with Dr. Turnbull. The final implication is that New London will struggle to survive, but its fate is unknown.

Peter Anderson Graham (1856–1925) was a journalist with a long career that included working on the *National Observer* with W.E. Henley, but he was best known as the editor of *Country Life* for twenty-three years from 1900. Hailing from Northumbria, Graham was an authority on northern ballads. He wrote both a book on the highways and byways of Northumbria and a novel set in that county, *The Red Scaur* (1897). His love of the outdoor life is evident in *The Collapse of Homo Sapiens* which may be seen as a condemnation of the stupidity of mankind in forsaking nature and waging war in its desire for progress.

The Last of My Race   J. Lionel Tayler

London: G.P. Putnam's Sons, 1923

John Lionel Tayler (1874–1930) had been a lecturer in biology and sociology at London University, and most of this book reads like one of his lectures. It is subtitled "A Dream of the Future", but it takes the form of a narrative written by a nameless individual, who awakes in the year 501,930AD having been in suspended animation and looked after by myriad generations. He finds himself in a small bungalow with a garden built to replicate the dwellings of his time, but he soon discovers that the flowers and animals that he sees are artificial, and that food is brought to him by automata.

It is not until half-way through the book, that the narrator is visited by a human charged with looking after him. The narrator learns he is the last survivor of what the visitor calls *homo ignoramus*. Though this may be harsh—because the visitor recognizes the geniuses of the day—humans of the twentieth century were incapable of further evolution because the female form could not accommodate the birth of children with larger heads for increased brain capacity. The visitor has a poor view of life in the twentieth century remarking that it "was perhaps the worst century on record for decaying moral and religious purpose."

Unable to evolve, *homo ignoramus* died out to be replaced by *homo sapiens* whose heads were able to grow after birth. The visitor is one of these but admits that his race is also dying out and they remain as servants to the next species in human evolution, *homo sapiens varius*. Humans were adapting to their environment because they could now also live in the sea, the air and underground. The most significant of these was the air species which evolved further into *sapiens minimus*. The side effects of man's evolution, in particular its inventions and scientific products, became dangerous to most animals and birds, many of which died out.

The narrator's visitor concludes his series of talks by saying that already *sapiens minimus* is anticipating the next stage in human-kind's evolution, but he does not speculate further. At that point the narrator wakes up.

A dream ending is always a disappointment, but if we ignore that, Tayler has explored an intriguing argument for the development of the human being. It is clearly inspired by the ideas of H.G. Wells in *The Time Machine* and various essays but also paves the way for future books such as *The Amphibians* by S. Fowler Wright, which is discussed next, and *Last and First Men* (1930) by Olaf Stapledon (see *Star Maker* below).

Tayler was a Unitarian minister (his religious views are evident in this book), a physician, and a lecturer. Amongst his books were *The Nature of Woman* (1912), in which he is supportive of women's arguments for equality, but tempers with his view that "the path of development for the woman should be in harmony with her distinctive attributes..."; and *The Stages of Human Life* (1921) which acts as a precursor to *The Last of My Race* in considering how people should make the most of their allotted life span.

The Amphibians   S. Fowler Wright

London: Merton Press, 1925

In this time-travel adventure you will be projected to an Earth half-a-million years in the future, a world from which all humans have vanished, and encounter an array of bizarre creatures of varying intelligence and threat.

The opening chapter is not very convincing. We learn nothing about the method of time travel, only that the Professor has already sent people into the future who have returned, but we know nothing of their adventures. Of recent explorers, Brett has not returned whilst Templeton, who did return, went back to find Brett, but has not returned. The Professor appeals to a third adventurer, George, though his name is irrelevant as most of the book is his first-person account. George agrees. He takes with him an axe and a knife and wears a fur-lined leather suit. Lest we think he is insufficiently prepared—he has a box of sandwiches.

Once George is in the far future, the magic begins. We witness an utterly alien environment, a world you would not recognize as Earth. Seen through George's eyes, we learn about the world piece-meal, and there's much we don't understand. We do discover that the continents have changed and that this adventure takes place on one of the large land-masses in the northern hemisphere—the stars and constellations still seem the same, although the nights and days are three times longer. There are two major intelligent beings, the Dwellers, who are humanoid, yellow-skinned giants up to thirty-feet tall and live predominantly underground, and the Amphibians, smaller, furry humanoids, with tails, with whom George can communicate telepathically. Although the Amphibians are apparently asexual, their slim appearance made George think of them as feminine and he refers to any individual as 'her', feeling that 'it' was inappropriate.

The Amphibians live on islands off the shore of the continent and have agreed with the Dwellers that they do not enter the land. The Amphibians are non-violent and are horrified how readily George is prepared to kill. They think of him as primitive and though he grows close to one of the Amphibians, who accompanies him on his later adventures, it becomes clear through an unguarded telepathic exchange that she regards touching him as repulsive.

Amongst other creatures, the most dangerous are the Killers who are skilled with weapons, and have an elongated mouth through which they suck the remains of the creatures they cook. There are also bat-winged humanoids who are on the verge of extinction. They were once the pre-dominant creature on the planet, until the Dwellers emerged, and there is a hint that they might be of human evolution.

When George arrives it is dark and it is only as day dawns that he witnesses the strange environment. He is on a radiant pathway in a vast purple-brown plain. Behind him are giant cliffs. Either side of the pathway are plants, like giant cabbages eight-feet high. As George approaches the cliffs where he sees a large cave, a figure rushes out of the cave. Surprised to see George, she slips and treads off the path. Immediately the cabbage-like globes capture her in a mass of tentacles. George frees the victim but receives a telepathic message telling him not to touch the body. He later learns that this being is an Amphibian and the body is dying, but her mind is still active. Although an Amphibian's body may die, their spirit lives on. She gives George a message to take to others of her kind.

So George's quest begins. We follow him through this alien world as he meets creature after creature and peril after peril. He crosses an invis-ible bridge, and ventures down to an underworld, though before reaching the bottom he hides from a giant, whom he later learns is a Dweller, and returns to the surface. Whilst trying to pass through a tunnel he finds that the pressure of his feet on the path causes leech-like grass to shoot up and grab him. He encounters malevolent frog-like apes which seem impossible to kill. He also realizes that there is a barrier around the island in the air over which birds cannot pass.

After surviving many hazards George encounters a party of Amphibians who, defying the Law of the Dwellers, has ventured on to the land to rescue one of their own. This was the individual George had encountered who had been a defiant amphibian who wanted to explore the world. A senior amphibian went in search of her but was captured by the Dwellers who are holding her prior to handing her to the Killers for food. The defiant amphib-ian had discovered this and was trying to return home when George's presence frightened her and her body died. The party of Amphibians is following a route that George can't pursue, but though they think of him as primitive, they believe he has qualities which may help them. He is allotted to one amphibian who seems empathic with him, and it is their adventures to rescue their leader that we follow.

Amongst their later adventures is a battle with the Killers where George must use all his skills to escape, aided by telepathic advice and remarkable agility from the amphibian. George creates a fire, not realizing that this is taboo to the Dwellers. These giants are now disturbed but they encounter the main body of the Amphibians who, perhaps surprisingly, discuss matters in an orderly fashion. The Amphibians are allowed to return with the individual they had come to rescue.

Although that is the end of *The Amphibians*, it is not the end of the story, because George is still in search of his two predecessors. In his travels he had found Templeton's revolver, so knew he was there somewhere. This search and other adventures take place in the sequel *The World Below* which, though not published until 1929, was clearly written as part of the same original book. Later editions were combined and published as *The World Below*.

Wright had self-published *The Amphibians*, using the Merton Press imprint, run by the Empire Poetry League of which Wright was one of the founders (in 1917) and served as editor of their magazine *Poetry*. It was well received critically and sold sufficient for there to be a second edition in March 1926 and a cheap edition the following month. But Merton Press closed down in 1927 and Wright began his own imprint, Fowler Wright, Ltd., under which he issued his next novel, *Deluge* (1927), in which the Earth suffers a cataclysmic flood and most of Britain and Europe are under water. *Deluge* caught the interest of the American Cosmopolitan Book Corporation which issued a US edition of both *Deluge*, and its sequel *Dawn* (1929) and his lost-race novel *The Island of Captain Sparrow* (1928). These last two were also picked up by other UK mainstream publishers.

Although Wright trained as an accountant his heart was in poetry and literary expression. His poetic vision can be seen in many of his descriptions of the future world and is evident from his traveller's revelation at the start of his odyssey:

As the familiar sun rose slowly, a gradual gold spread over the vivid green that sloped toward it, till the whole expanse shone with a dazzling splendour; and as the rising light struck across the path on which I stood, it showed a shining band of opalescence that stretched right and left to the horizon limits, beneath the background of the dark-grey wall. The sky was of a deep unbroken blue, and the whole scene was one of great though alien beauty.

Wright's first book had been a volume of poems, *Scenes from Morte d'Arthur* (1919), and he worked for many years on a translation of Dante's *Divine Comedy*. There is little doubt that both influenced his writing. Wright had intended to complete a third volume about the Amphibians and Dwellers to parallel the three books of the Divine Comedy, but the final volume never appeared.

Sydney Fowler Wright (1874–1965) was Britain's premier writer of the scientific romance during the late 1920s and early 1930s. Later works include *Dream, or the Simian Maid* (1931) and its sequels; *Beyond the Rim* (1932), *Power* (1933), *The Adventure of Wyndham Smith* (1939) and a sequence of future-war novels starting with *Prelude in Prague: The War of 1938* (1935). His stories were collected in *The New Gods Lead* (1932; US as *The Throne of Saturn*, 1949) and *The Witchfinder* (1946).

The Emperor of the If   Guy Dent

London: William Heinemann, 1926

We often speculate about what might happen had events followed a different course, what was commonly called "the 'ifs' of history". What if Harold had defeated William at the Battle of Hastings? What if Napoleon had been victorious at Waterloo? And so on. I shall discuss this in more detail with J. C. Squire's *If It Had Happened Otherwise* (1931). The following was one of the first, certainly in Britain, to explore the idea at full length in novel form.

The plot centres upon Professor Greyne who starts a convoluted discussion with an acquaintance, John Blatherwick, about the nature of the universe which he believes is governed by Thought. This "Thought" is a powerful force which has controlled the course of history. He plans to harness that Thought and use it to study the "ifs" of history. He has acquired the brain of a dead local man and kept it within a skull which he has fed with nutrients not just to keep it alive but to increase its power of thought. He has but to flick a switch and the brain will function.

Greyne intrigues Blatherwick with talk of the digressions of history. Although Blatherwick wants to leave, the professor clamps a helmet on his head, wired up to a machine, and tells Blatherwick he must concentrate and retain a vivid picture of our present reality, because that will provide the link for them to return. Then he flicks the switch.

Unlike most later novels of alternate histories, in which the protagonists venture from our world to another as if through a portal, here that alternate history gradually grows about the two men at an increasingly rapid rate, overlaying the present. The Professor wanted to see how the world would have developed had the Earth not been subjected to the Ice Age. This question was asked of the brain, which tapped into the cosmic Thought, and an alternate world starts to appear. The Professor and Blatherwick leave the laboratory and, taking his car, tour London and the countryside to witness the changes. Before long the roads are disrupted as primeval plants grow through the tarmac. The river Thames assumes its old course and floods along its length. Dinosaurs appear, roaming the city.

Greyne and Blatherwick witness these changes accelerating about them. We learn of other significant changes across the world: Lemuria has risen from the ocean depths, the Sahara has become a shallow sea joined to the Mediterranean, the north of Australia has sunk beneath the ocean. The world has become painfully hot and cities burst into flames. Earthquakes rent the globe, especially in the Americas.

Yet, on their travels, Greyne and Blatherwick encounter an area in England that is stable, and unchanged. Here, in a country house, lives Jane Vandredon and her family. Jane has astonishing willpower. She recognized that the chaos was something evil and through her own power of Thought established a zone of stability.

Jane challenges Greyne's motive for what he's done. She believes he wanted to act like God, creating a superior race of humans who would have evolved further and stronger without the limitation of the Ice Age. Greyne refuses to accept this and he and Blatherwick prepare to leave but his car won't work. They have to walk and Jane's son, Peter, joins them. On their travels they encounter humans who are savages, and Greyne realizes his error.

Blatherwick, who has been held in thrall by Greyne, now rejects him and stumbles away eventually returning to Greyne's laboratory, now buried under piles of rock. As he finds a way in, he realizes Greyne has followed him, but Greyne is prepared to stop the experiment, and switches back the lever. The world returns to their known timeline almost instantly, and only they and the Vandredons have any memory of what had happened.

Under instruction from Jane, Greyne agrees to use his system to project mankind forward and see what it becomes. They find themselves 25 million years in the future. Earth is locked tidally to the sun, with one side in permanent darkness. The moon was knocked out of its orbit and lost millennia ago. Much of the Earth was destroyed at that time. The few surviving humans are ape-like dwarves with huge hands who are there to service the machines. There are two races of machines, called simply Them and They, but they seem to be on a self-destructive course. One of the dwarves who knows English refers to a long sequence of wars that began with the Great Revolt of Machinery, followed by the War to Regain the Mastery and so on through at least six more, each lasting several thousand years. The current state is a stalemate called The War to Decide when the Next War shall Start.

The dwarves have erratic moments of perception and memory. If something moves into their pathway, they have no memory of it being there, and simply walk through it. But if nothing is there now, but had been, the dwarves move round it, believing it is still there. Greyne suspects this is because the cosmic Thought has almost dissipated and this is the end of all time. After a vision of Christ in the sky they return to their laboratory and reinstate the twentieth century.

Greyne has further discussions with Jane Vandredon but Blatherwick has no involvement and so when Greyne vanishes on a third trip, from which he does not return, Blatherwick has no idea where he might be, but suspects he might be seeking to unbind mankind's thoughts from its passion for materialism.

At times *Emperor of the If* is clumsily, perhaps hastily written, as if Dent was desperate to set down his ideas which clearly have a religious basis. The idea that Thought governs the Universe relates directly to the Biblical reference to "the Word" in the Gospel of John: "In the beginning was the Word, and the Word was with God, and the Word was God." This is why Jane thought Greyne was trying to usurp God's role and has the vision of Christ. Dent's message, prompted by the carnage of the Great War, is that mankind is too materialistic and science has advanced too far to be controlled by humans. Dent, through Greyne, wanted to return to basics but it becomes evident that humanity has corrupted the globe.

Guy de Boisragon Dent (1892–1954) came from a military family and his mother's forebears had served in India. Her brother, Guy Boisragon, received the Victoria Cross for his actions in the Hunza-Naga campaign in what is now Pakistan. Dent was born in Aldershot, and raised in the military, serving in the First World War in both the East African Mounted Rifles and the Royal Flying Corps. He turned to writing after the War producing many short stories for the popular magazines, mostly crime and adventure stories and occasional wildlife studies. But he did not write anything else remotely like *Emperor of the If*.

The Man with Six Senses   Muriel Jaeger

London: The Hogarth Press, 1927

This is the story of Michael Bristowe, a young lad with a developing sense of psychic awareness. He is looked after by Hilda, who starts out as something of a mother figure, but becomes much more. The story is narrated by Ralph Standring, who is in love with Hilda and so resents Michael, who takes up much of Hilda's time and attention. As a result we get a negative attitude towards Michael which builds our sympathy towards him. Michael is resentful of his talent, and hostile towards those who do not believe in his abilities. As a consequence, we see Michael as an outcast not only of society but of himself.

Jaeger liked the concept of the outcast. She almost certainly felt one herself, and outcasts feature in all her fiction, especially *The Question Mark* (1926) where a man is projected into the future and though he befriends a family he fails to find a place in this new world and remains forever the outsider looking in. It is the same with Michael Bristowe. He finds it difficult to come to terms with his talent and to convince others it is genuine. Hilda explains this to Ralph at one key point early in the book:

> "...You see, one likes to play sometimes with the idea of one's own exceptional personality, but have you ever considered how appalling it would be to discover that one really was abnormal in some important way?"

Hilda thus handles Michael with kid gloves trying to protect him and at the same time understand his skill. This works only if kept within a small circle of acquaintances, but everything turns sour when the world discovers the scale of his talent. He had been working as a water diviner, the kind of mild skill that the media half-accepted. But one day, while crossing a field, Michael feels something wrong, what Hilda calls his "churchyard feel". Michael has sensed the buried body of a murder victim for which the police had been searching. Press coverage goes ballistic, and Michael is interrogated by the police, suspicious of how he knew the body was there. This has a violent debilitating effect upon Michael and is the start of his decline.

That mood was further aggravated when his services are called upon by various people. He is employed by an elderly mother to find her lost child and by an entrepreneur to find oil deposits. His lack of success in these tasks, neither his own fault, causes him to draw back into himself and increases the demands upon Hilda to help him.

The book is a remarkable study of an individual unprepared for how the world accepts and rejects him. The story builds upon ideas developed by J.D. Beresford in *The Hampdenshire Wonder* and establishes a base for which Olaf Stapledon could create his "superhuman" in *Odd John* (1935). It is the least known of those three books, but to my mind the most accomplished, because Jaeger takes you deep into the psyche of Michael Bristowe and you feel as he does what it is to be the outcast.

Muriel Jaeger (1892–1969) came from a fairly well-to-do middle-class Yorkshire family and clearly had literary ambitions even while at High School in Sheffield, publishing poetry in the school magazine. She obtained a scholarship to Oxford University where she studied at Somerville College. There she began a lasting friendship with Dorothy L. Sayers and was later instrumental in encouraging Sayers to write her first Lord Peter Wimsey novel. During the war she served in the Ministry of Food which focused her mind on the need for controlled agriculture, an idea that forms part of the new world in *The Question Mark*. She turned to writing after the war, obtaining her diploma in journalism in 1920. In addition to being the sub-editor of the weekly paper *Time and Tide*, run by Lady Rhondda, she wrote four novels. Her first was *The Question Mark* which, as with *The Man with Six Senses*, was published by Leonard and Virginia Woolf in their Hogarth Press imprint. After a gap of some years, when she had turned to writing non-fiction and works for the theatre, she completed *Hermes Speaking* (1933), another foray into the world of a gifted and manipulated child, and *Retreat from Armageddon* (1936), a more philosophical book about a group of individuals who retreat from a global war into a country house to discuss the failings of mankind. Her fascination with how lives develop was explored in *Experimental Lives* (1932) where she studied people who lived by their own plans rather than the demands of society. Jaeger continued to write almost up to her death, but she did not return to the world of the scientific romance, even though it is this world that still remembers her and celebrates her work.

Kontrol Edmund Snell

London: Ernest Benn, 1928

Kontrol is one of several competent techno-thrillers, as we would now call them, that had been developing during the 1920s alongside the success of the crime thriller.

During the Great War, in which he was injured, Captain Denis Wildash had met a Russian doctor, Serge Guriev. He had told Wildash of his thoughts about perfecting the human race through brain transplants, making sure that the superior brains were in superior bodies. Wildash called the idea preposterous but Guriev said to check it out in ten years' time.

Chance brings Wildash and Guriev together again ten years later. Wildash is driving his girlfriend, Marjorie, to Sussex where her father, Sir Geoffrey, wants to visit an archaeological site. He is being driven by Jack Adversane, a rival for Marjorie's affections. Sir Geoffrey and Adversane have an accident and are taken to a nursing home run by Guriev and his vicious colleague Leeds-Carlish. Wildash and Guriev renew their acquaintance and Guriev shows Wildash the results of their transplant experiments. Wildash is horrified. At one point, while left alone, he enables one of the victims, a girl with the brain of Sonia Ingerstrom but in the body of another, to escape. Wildash also meets Count Marchetti who is apparently financing Guriev's work as part of a scheme to create a utopia of super-beings on a remote volcanic island in the Pacific.

A few days later Wildash is visited by the missing girl which catapults them both into trouble when Guriev and Leeds-Carlish track her down. Wildash discovers that in their spite over the missing girl, Guriev and Leeds-Carlish have operated on Sir Geoffrey and Adversane, exchanging brains. He discovers you can identify a transplant victim because their eyes are colourless, and he believes that although brains and bodies may still live, their souls have been lost, rather like zombies.

In the ensuing conflict with Guriev and Leeds-Carlish they kidnap both Sonia and Marjorie. Wildash joins forces with a work colleague, Marten, to pursue Guriev, but all of them are ensnared by Count Marchetti. He has a super-plane in which he takes them all to his remote island. On the journey Guriev reconciles himself with Wildash saying that Marchetti was in control and he had exploited Guriev's skills.

Wildash is astonished at the scale of work on the island. There are huge, windowless buildings in which the "zombies" work, and other super-machines are being developed. The island is guarded by a ray that ensures no planes or ships come near, and there are other barriers to stop anyone escaping. There is strict discipline and any who transgress Marchetti are hurled into the volcano.

Wildash realizes if they are to escape, he must bide his time and under-stand the island's routine and defences. Marchetti seems to appreciate him and promotes him to his second-in-command, much to the annoyance of Berkoff who was demoted. Marten, in the meantime, is assigned office work, and has discovered that it is not Marchetti who is funding the whole operation but that he is an agent of the Soviet Union. Marten believes that Russia is preparing for the next war, using an army of super-brains to create super-machines and weapons and an army of super-beings. Between them Wildash and Marten plan their escape.

Marchetti enjoys pitting one man against another but has overplayed his hand with the demotion of Berkoff. While Marchetti is enjoying demoral-izing Wildash by giving Marjorie to Leeds-Carlish, Berkoff kills Marchetti and, in the ensuing chaos, Leeds-Carlish kills Berkoff. In the midst of this, the volcano erupts and as the island is destroyed, Wildash and the others struggle to escape, though not all make it.

Edmund Snell (1889–1972), whose wife was also called Marjorie, was a prolific writer of novels and stories, mostly thrillers, many with an Oriental setting. He travelled extensively, but when at home lived mostly in Sussex, which is how he understood the road system used in the novel. *Kontrol* is probably the best of several sf thrillers he wrote in which scientists develop inventions capable of death and destruction such as the disintegration ray in *Blue Murder* (1927) or the super-x-rays in *The "Z" Ray* (1932). Despite their somewhat formulaic period style, Snell was a capable writer able to infuse both character and humour alongside exotic settings in a driving narrative.

The Ant Heap   Edward Knoblock

London: Chapman and Hall, 1929

This book is a none-too-subtle religious allegory, which it achieves by using one of the key tropes of science fiction—attempts to create life.

The story is told by Tim whom we first meet as an infant and who, when his mother dies, is taken under the wing of his sadistic and egocentric uncle who lives and works on a farm. During his childhood Tim has a fall injuring his leg and spine. Unable to work he spends his time reading and becomes an intelligent youngster. His uncle eventually reveals to him what he has been working on in a barn on the farm. It seems the uncle is something of a Victor Frankenstein or, more appropriately, Dr. Moreau. He has been attempting to create a new form of life by operating upon and fusing life-forms including both animals and plants. Tim is horrified but is so under the spell of his uncle that for a while he becomes his assistant. The uncle believes that society will not progress all the while people remain as individuals. They need to work like a hive mind—his example is the world of the ants each working assiduously under the command of a queen ant—and that there can only be one master. That individual is the uncle who claims, "I'm beyond the reach of *every one!*"

The uncle does not realize that Tim knows a secret about his uncle. Years before, the uncle had fathered a son with the bride on her wedding night while the groom was drunk. This son, Stephen, whom the uncle had little to do with, eventually comes under the uncle's control when one Christmas he nearly dies of pneumonia on the uncle's doorstep. Stephen is a highly sensitive, caring soul and Tim is protective of him. He is horrified when the uncle declares he will reveal to him the secrets of the barn. Before the uncle has a chance, Tim destroys all the monstrosities and creatures held captive. Furious, the uncle sends Tim away to London with £100 and does not expect to see him again.

Tim suffers badly in London, coming into contact with all forms of low-life. He begins to compare his uncle's monsters with those struggling to survive in the city. He is saved from suicide when he comes into contact with two rich sisters, both suffragettes, who work with a group of social-ist activists. Stephen later joins them and it is now that Stephen's abilities to work with people to improve their lives and diffuse difficult situations come to the fore.

With the outbreak of the Great War Stephen is determined to serve but instead works with the hospital service near the Front whilst Tim remains in London, having trained to be a pharmacist. During the War they learn that their uncle has achieved fame by continuing his work with the dead and dying, seeking to use body parts to research his hopes for a new race.

After the War Stephen returns home working with the socialists who have created their own "hospital" to help those struggling to survive in the impoverished 1920s. There is considerable unrest and though Stephen seeks to help the poor and unemployed, at one meeting the mob turn against him because of his association with a rich family, and he is killed. Tim secures the body and returns to the family farm where he buries Stephen in a sacred place.

If it was not already apparent it is now that the religious allegory is made clear. The sisters expect to find Stephen in a local chapel, but he is not there and, like Christ, rumours spread that he has risen again. The uncle confesses that he had seen Stephen as an experiment which had been ruined by Tim's intervention. Stephen was, in the eyes of his megalomaniac uncle, a new messiah.

This is a profound novel and although the science-fiction element of it seems minor, it is crucial in developing the idea of not simply a new physical race of beings but a new spiritual race, because in the uncle's mind, religion robs people of their individuality when they all slavishly follow a god or messiah.

Edward Knoblock (1874–1945) was born in New York of German descent. He was raised and educated in both New York and Germany but in 1896 he came to London and made it his home. He became a British citizen in 1916 when he anglicized his name from Knoblauch. He established himself as a playwright, best known today for *Kismet* (1911) which later became a stage musical and was filmed several times. *The Ant Heap* was his first novel and some reviewers found it difficult to believe he was capable of producing a book which was both engrossing and sordid. Certainly he pulls no punches when depicting the poor in London and the social unrest of the 1920s. The book leaves a vivid image of an inhumane uncle who believes himself superior to everyone and the only one allowed to be an individual but whose experiments are thwarted by others who struggle for their existence by being individuals, striving for the best in everyone. In Knoblock's eyes humanity wins out against science.

Brain   Lionel Britton

New York & London: G.P. Putnam's Sons, 1930

When this play was first performed at the Savoy Theatre in April 1930, despite plaudits from George Bernard Shaw, it was clear from reviews that many believed it held a good idea buried amongst too much talk and difficult futuristic jargon. Some felt Britton should have written it as a story rather than a play, but in fact the script format works well, and once the play was published readers came to understand it better.

The play starts with a discussion between a professor and a librarian at the British Museum. The professor had found an unpublished manuscript, by an author now dead, which discussed the theory of ideas and what constituted consciousness. The professor believed that it might be possible to create an artificial thinking machine. The librarian was horrified believing that such a machine, if allowed to evolve, would become a god.

Alas the professor and librarian are killed in a road accident and the next scene shifts forward 150 years to a group who have rediscovered the manuscript and are considering building the machine, which becomes known as the Brain. The group, which decides it must remain secret, calls itself the Brain Brotherhood and agrees to attract donations from all walks of life. This consists chiefly of white people and, for that matter, the British. It is a highly anglo-centric play.

The Brain Brotherhood keeps its existence and plans secret for two hundred years but the work that is developing in the Sahara attracts attention and the British government meet to consider its response. The Home Secretary reveals he has been contacted by the Brotherhood and is keen to be involved. He is forced to resign, and after he has gone the Cabinet decide they must take over the Brotherhood by whatever means. After the meeting, the Prime Minister talks to a newspaper editor via a televisor about their plans.

Up to this point the play is easy to follow but audiences were perplexed with the following scenes which catapult them forward by thirty, forty or fifty thousand years (the director or the audience could decide) for a series of expressionist and existential episodes, some in the dark. It is evident that the Brain has taken over control of humanity and is dictating events. There is discussion about liberal sex, which must have shocked many audiences, and a scene where ideally one of the men should have been naked, though the playwright accepted this may prove difficult. The surface of the Earth is rebuilt with the Brain synthesizing human ideals about scenery and the environment. The Brain controls all human life, education and child rearing. Children are produced artificially via test-tubes—"lab-pregs" they are called. Some men have fathered thousands of children but have no idea who they are.

The Brain believes that the Earth came into being when a cosmic body collided with the Sun and the planets were created from the material that was ejected. Since this could happen again the Brain becomes concerned that if human life is destroyed, what purpose does It serve, and might It too be destroyed. It believes humanity must leave the Earth and venture to the stars. It is not clear whether this actually happens, though it is implied towards the end.

In the final Act, fifty million years in the future, most human and animal life is extinct. All is dark, and the Brain awaits Its destruction as a distant world approaches the Earth. The Brain, which had regarded itself as "the thought of the world", realizes It is now helpless and the play ends with a blazing flash of light.

The play is provocative and full of ideas, much of which are clumsily handled. The idea of a universal computer had already been presented by E.M. Forster in *The Machine Stops*, but Britton wanted to explore how one such Brain would harmonize the population and improve the race. It was a communist ideal—Britton later visited Russia but returned, disillusioned. Had Britton edited the stream of complicated language, *Brain* might have had more impact.

Britton (1887–1971) did not give up on his pseudo-scientific ideas, as the press regarded them. Another play, *Spacetime Inn* (1932)—apparently the only play to have been performed in the House of Commons—used some of the ideas of J.W. Dunne (of which more later) to establish a location where celebrities from all ages—including Shakespeare, Queen Victoria, Karl Marx, Eve, Napoleon and George Bernard Shaw—discuss and contrast their ideas. Alas Britton's work was too experimental for the audiences of his day. His third play *Animal Ideas* (1935) was overly metaphysical and bombed at the theatre. Britton claimed he was not worried, and continued to write, but no more plays were performed or published. He retired to Hastings and worked as a caretaker. At the time of his death in Ramsgate in 1971 *The Stage* recognized his limited appeal but lauded his "far-ranging mind", noting that he was a "pioneer in bringing time theories into the theatre", something that J.B. Priestley would achieve with much greater effect.

The Seventh Bowl   Miles (Stephen Southwold)

London: Eric Partridge, 1930

In many ways this novel unites the parallel themes of future society and future humans into a cataclysmic finale. Both themes would, of course, continue and prosper within the science-fiction genre, but Southwold's story incorporates so much that we have already seen and presents it as a *fait accompli* in a way that provides some form of closure as the 1920s morph into the 1930s.

We are introduced to Paul Heller, a youth of seventeen in 1924, who is proclaiming to his father that there can be no such thing as God. This reads like a continuation of the argument that concludes Tillyard's *Concrete*, but it rapidly moves on. In 1935 Heller reappears giving an uninvited talk at the British Medical Association which included amongst its guests J.B.S. Haldane, George Bernard Shaw and H.G. Wells. Heller's speech concerns longevity and the need for research on extending human life.

Few take him seriously and, in any case, there are other important scientific advances, including the creation of Phosgon, a gas that can be made plentifully and cheaply. Its inventor, however, is murdered in May 1940 and by September the Great Gas War has erupted resulting in the deaths of 150 million people. (Southwold was one year out for the start of World War II, but got the month and day, 3 September, exactly.)

The aftermath of the War saw the deaths of most national leaders, the League of Nations being replaced by the League of Peoples, a universal language (Abaco) introduced, and a World Council, led by Lord Burfleet, which governed the planet through a Council of Ten in each country. Other scientific advances include landing men on the moon in 1949, a nitrogen-fixer called *floccus* which resulted in increased production of food, and a new drink which replaced alcohol and enhanced mental and artistic perceptions. Building upon Haldane's research, the first ectogenetic child was born in 1957 and by 1960 it was the norm. People were freed from manual labour with the creation of a robot work-force known as *Fermos*.

In 1961 Heller reappears and hi-jacks a celebration dinner of the Post-Victorian Dramatic Society in honour of George Bernard Shaw, who had been killed in the Gas War. Heller reveals he has invented a serum, Plasm Alpha, which utilizes the body's Life Force to cure any disease, to regrow any damaged or lost part of the body and guarantee longevity, perhaps even immortality. Here we are close to the invention in Swayne's *The Blue Germ* and the evolutionary force in Shaw's *Back to Methuselah*. Heller refers to Shaw's play as his inspiration. Heller had demonstrated the effect of his serum to a journalist when he pulled out a fingernail which regrew instantly.

Heller is called before the English governing council who have learned he plans to broadcast the formula for his serum to the world via radio. Burfleet convinces Heller to withhold his announcement for three days, and talks Heller into giving the Council the formula and injecting them all. Heller is now of little use and Burfleet contrives his murder, to look like suicide. Burfleet then announces to the world that the serum was a hoax.

However, the press know otherwise, leading to a confrontation between journalists and Burfleet who announces his plans, the "New Code", issued in November 1961. It sets the total world population at 500 million. The existing population, which is 2,500 million, will be divided into Primaries, selected by rigorous criteria, who will receive the serum, and Secondaries, who will not, but will be allowed to either accept euthanasia or work in Labour Camps with the robots until they die naturally. There will be no more natural births after September 1962. In future all couples must sign a declaration when they marry, agreeing that they will either be sterilized or any children born will be euthanized. Everyone will be allotted work by the new World Council, and any contravention of the Code will be punishable by death, including the Primaries, who will be cremated to destroy the serum.

Initially society accepts the Code. People realize they had much more leisure time, even the Secondaries, most of whom accepted living out their normal life span. There was a crisis at the end of September 1962 with the last legal child-births and the horror of seeing babies born after midnight taken away to be killed. Children became precious but by the 1980s all were adults and it was a child-less world. This affected society, especially women, and by the 1990s adults were acquiring dolls and toys for themselves. There emerged a teller of fairy tales but his stories glorified children and he soon vanished.

The serum had caused a distaste for meat and vegetarianism grew. A new food, Biogen, became the perfect meal producing no waste matter. Eventually all farm animals were destroyed, followed by the wholesale destruction of noxious plants and insects. Butterflies and song-birds were kept. There was a brief resurgence in pets and when this grew out of proportion an Act was passed leading to their destruction.

In the 1980s a virulent plague wiped out some 350 million Secondaries and, by the end of the century, the remaining population of a thousand million was evenly split. Society was segregated with the Primaries living in pleasure domes and the Secondaries ghettoized.

Despite the apparent superiority of the surviving humans a general malaise settles over society because of so much loss. A rebel emerges, Martin Torelli, the last British child born before the closure date in 1962. Martin has invented a new power source, Energen A, which he further develops as the ultimate power, Energen B. Its nature is not described but one may deduce it is atomic. Initially Martin wants to use it to explore other planets in search of life, for he believes that God may have created life in infinite forms. He and his wife defy the Code and have a child, refusing to have it euthanized. Martin challenges Burfleet's rule and states that their utopian dictatorship is at an end and a new world must be born, symbolized by the young child, called Peter. Martin proclaims that if the Council defies him he will use Energen B and cast the moon into deep space. Burfleet is intractable and Martin carries out his threat. Unfortunately, he had not foreseen that this tips the Earth out of its orbit and propels it towards the Sun. All is lost.

Stephen Southwold (1887–1964) was the name adopted by Stephen H. Critten, who worked initially as a primary school teacher until the Great War robbed him of his spirit and he turned to writing. He was not only a victim of the War but of a difficult childhood—he changed his name in order to dissociate himself from his violent father. He used several pen names of which the best known was Neal Bell, under which name *The Seventh Bowl* was reprinted in 1934. In *The Gas War of 1940* (1931) he explored in more detail the War described at the start of *The Seventh Bowl*. That was also reissued under the Neal Bell name in 1934 as *Valiant Clay*. Southwold gave vent to his bleak outlook for the world brought about by the War in several more novels, notably *The Lord of Life* (1933) where twenty people survive the destruction of all life, but only one of them is a woman. *Precious Porcelain* (1931) suggests Southwold's struggles with his own identity by exploring a multiple Jekyll and Hyde type personality, something he returned to in the even more bleak *The Disturbing Affair of Noel Blake* (1932). There is further bleakness in *Death Rocks the Cradle* (1933, as by Paul Martens) which imagines a parallel world divided between healthy but evil vegetarians and unhealthy meat-eating villains. You do not read Southwold's works for any humour or levity but for his sharp realistic depiction of the weaknesses of mankind.

Brave New World   Aldous Huxley
London: Chatto and Windus, 1932

Although this novel is by far the best known of the utopia/dystopias published between the Wars there is little that has not already been explored in many of the other inter-bellum works discussed here. Huxley simply covered it in more detail, added healthy doses of sex—the book was banned in Ireland as immoral—and presented it in such a forceful style that the reader is convinced it is the inevitable future.

Huxley's future society was influenced after a visit to the United States where he had seen the astonishing conveyer belt assembly line that Henry Ford had developed for car production, especially the Model T. Huxley thereby dates his World State as starting from the year that the first Model T was produced, which was 1908. So when we learn we are in the year A.F. ("After Ford") 632 we know that in the old reckoning it is A.D. 2540.

Huxley applies the conveyer belt system to the production of humans, which is how the opening of the novel has such an impact. In a dispassionate way the Director of the Central London Hatchery and Conditioning Centre, along with one of his assistants, Henry Foster, conduct a number of students through the Centre and explain the process. There are no longer any live births. The ideas of mothers giving birth and family units are abhorrent. Instead, the ovaries and removed, fertilized in special receptacles and incubated in bottles. The bottles move along the conveyor belt and the foetus is adapted by a sequence of treatments. There are five castes of humans. The embryos of the lower castes, Gamma, Delta and Epsilon, are subjected to the Bokanovsky Process which shocks the egg into dividing up to ninety-six identical embryos—effectively cloning. These lower castes are little more than human machines, undertaking identical, repetitive tasks but they are conditioned to love their work and in no circumstance would a Gamma want to be an Alpha. The two superior classes, Alpha and Beta, do not undergo the Bokanovsky Process because this can weaken the eggs so they are more individualistic and intelligent.

In a rather distressing episode, the Director shows students how the lower-class babies are conditioned by Neo-Pavlovian electric treatment to abhor certain things—in the example it is books and flowers—so that they won't waste time reading or communing with nature. It had once been believed that it was good to appreciate nature, but it was realized that the natural world was free and thus not profitable for a consumer society. Huxley's World State is built upon consumerism.

SUPER, SUB OR NON-HUMAN?

Elsewhere in the process it is understood that 70% of all females are sterilized (called "freemartins") but males are not. This allows for free sex and one of the features of the World State is the promiscuity of the Alpha and Beta humans. It is male dominated, as there are no Alpha females.

Everyone is educated by hypnopaedia, or sleep-learning, a process which had been invented by Alois Saliger in 1927 but had been predicted by Hugo Gernsback in 1911. This works best at instilling everyone with the same moral code—which is essentially to be happy and not create ill feeling. The slogan of the World State is "Community, Identity, Stability". Anyone with moments of frustration can take a dose of the drug *soma* which restores calm and a satisfaction with life.

To many this is an ideal society, but not everyone is happy. Bernard Marx, a hypnopaedia specialist, who is rather short for an Alpha and, with an inferiority complex, shirks from public gaze. There is talk that he may be exiled as a misfit. He is in love with Lenina, a beautiful girl who works in the Hatchery, but is uncomfortable with her promiscuity and how she openly talks about her relationships. She has recently had a longer-than-usual relationship with Henry Foster, but her friend Fanny, advises her to play the system more.

Lenina decides to go with Bernard and take up his offer to visit the Savage Reservation in New Mexico. This is an area populated by natural-born individuals who are outside the World State. Here they meet Linda, and her son John. Linda had once lived in the World State and had visited the Reservation with others but became lost. She found she was pregnant by one of her colleagues who, we later discover, is the Director of the Hatchery. Ashamed at her condition she did not return home. Bernard decides to bring Linda and John back to London, hoping this will raise his status. When John sees the Director he identifies him as his father, bringing shame and disgrace. Linda takes to her bed, existing solely on *soma*, and soon dies. Having been raised in the Reservation, John has no prior experience of the World State. He had been taught to read but books were few and his main reading had been the works of Shakespeare. It is from *The Tempest* that he quotes the lines from which we find the phrase "Brave New World".

John rebels, refuses to take *soma*, and tries to live by his own ideals, but this fails leading to his own self-destruction. Bernard also fails and is exiled.

Brave New World is a tragedy for any who will not conform to a regimented and superficially ideal society. When first published it shocked many readers and reviewers, perhaps because of the way human life becomes so mechanical. Many aspects of the world he depicted had been portrayed in other works, most notably *Man's World* by Charlotte Haldane and *The Seventh Bowl* by Stephen Southwold. Whilst we cannot be sure how many of these books Huxley might have read it would be surprising if he wasn't aware of *Man's World*, because she was acquainted with Huxley's brother, Julian. Huxley, though, only admitted that the book was, in part, a repost to H.G. Wells's *Men Like Gods*, which he felt painted too ideal an image of a utopian future. Moreover, Huxley was writing at a later period. Europe and America were in the grips of the Depression following the stock market crash of 1929, and the previous year the Soviet Union had launched its Five Year Plan of increased industrialization and collectivization. It seemed that drastic measures were needed. In addition to having seen Henry Ford's conveyor-belt production line, Huxley also saw the rigid organization of the new I.C.I. plant near Middlesbrough. Huxley borrowed the name of the Chairman of I.C.I., Sir Alfred Mond, for his character Mustapha Mond, the World State's Controller of Western Europe. Huxley's "new world" thus emerged out of a need for strict regularization and control, to eliminate the foibles of human emotion and unreliability.

Aldous Huxley (1894–1963) had already had some success with his earlier novels starting with *Crome Yellow* (1921) but the overwhelming reception for *Brave New World* caused him to become a prophet of the next generation, not unlike H.G. Wells. He responded to this with further works of how society might develop. *Ape and Essence* (1948) depicts an appalling post-atomic/bacteriological warfare society in America which has reverted to savagery by the year 2105. *Island* (1962) tries to be more positive, presenting a utopian island-based society controlled by religion and drugs. But Huxley was forever haunted by *Brave New World*. In an introduction he provided to a 1946 reprint he discussed how he avoided revising the text but nevertheless highlighted the two areas he felt needed changing, both of which would clearly spoil the impact of the book. He produced further essays in *Brave New World Revisited* (1958) where he seemed almost apologetic that the world was rapidly taking some of the aspects of his novel, notably drugs and subliminal suggestion. As we shall see with *Nineteen Eighty-Four* one of the dangers with proposing a future totalitarian society is that it can start to influence those who might benefit from it.

" Coming through the bushes by the white sphinx, were the heads and shoulders of men running."— P. 50.

ABOVE: *The Time Machine*, H.G. Wells (New York: Henry Holt, 1895), illustrated by W.B. Russell. Walter Bowman Russell (1871–1963) was an American artist, architect and self-trained scientist who became something of a visionary in later life and worked with Nikola Tesla.

PLATE 1

ABOVE: Scene from *The War of the Worlds* by H.G. Wells from *Pearson's Magazine*, June 1897, illustrated by Warwick Goble (1862–1943). Goble was a leading illustrator for the popular magazines at the turn of the nineteenth century and though he later turned to illustrating children's books, especially fairy tales, his work for *The War of the Worlds* remained memorable, no doubt contributing, according to science-fiction art historian Jane Frank, "to the immense popularity of this historically important work of science fiction."

PLATE 2

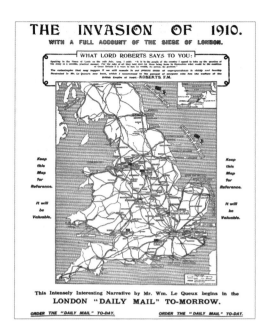

LEFT: "The Invasion of 1910" by William Le Queux, as serialized in the *Daily Mail* from 10 March 1906.

BELOW, LEFT: *The Crack of Doom* by Robert Cromie (London: Digby, Long, 1895).

BELOW, RIGHT: *The Violet Flame* by Fred T. Jane (London: Ward, Lock, 1899).

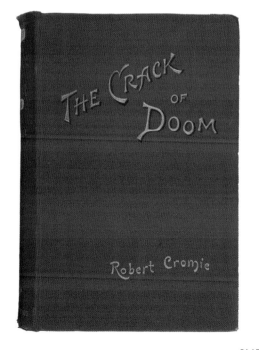

PLATE 3

"A MAN WITH A GHASTLY SCARLET HEAD FOLLOWS, SHOUTING THAT HE MUST GO BACK AND BUILD UP HIS RAY."

"I'VE ASKED HIM TO TEA ON FRIDAY"

LEFT: "With the Night Mail" by Rudyard Kipling (New York: Doubleday, Page, 1909) illustrated by Frank X. Leyendecker. Leyendecker (1876–1924) was a German-born artist resident in the United States from 1882. He became one of the foremost magazine illustrators of his day, especially for *Collier's* and *Saturday Evening Post*, but he fell under the shadow of his better-known elder brother, Joe. He died of a morphine overdose while depressed, aged only 48.

PLATE 4

"SUDDENLY, OUT OF THE DARKNESS, OUT OF THE NIGHT, THERE SWOOPED
SOMETHING WITH A SWISH LIKE AN AEROPLANE."

(See page 616.)

ABOVE: *The Lost World*, Arthur Conan Doyle, from *The Strand Magazine*, June 1912, illustrated by Harry Rountree. Rountree (1878–1950) was a New Zealand artist who settled in England in 1902 and became a prolific magazine illustrator and cartoonist. One of his cartoons depicted a sky so full of aircraft and self-propelled humans that the birds had taken to walking on the ground. Rountree also illustrated the second Professor Challenger serial, *The Poison Belt*.

PLATE 5

ABOVE, LEFT: *Menace from the Moon* by Bohun Lynch, dustjacket possibly by Lynch himself. (London: Jarrolds, 1925)

ABOVE, RIGHT: *The Clockwork Man* by E.V. Odle (London: Heinemann, 1923) illustrated by C. Paine.

RIGHT: *Brave New World* by Aldous Huxley (London: Chatto & Windus, 1932), dustjacket by Leslie Holland (1907–2005). Although this cover is probably Holland's best known work, according to his family, he never read the book. He lived for many years in a religious commune seeking the utopian life.

PLATE 6

PLATE 7

ABOVE: *Star Maker* by Olaf Stapledon (London: Methuen, 1937), dustjacket by Bip Pares. Ethel Pares (1904–77), always known as "Bip", illustrated over six hundred books, many of them crime fiction, but including such science-fiction titles as *The Dumb Gods Speak* (1937) by E. Phillips Oppenheim and, most notably, *Woman Alive* (1935) by Susan Ertz for which she did several striking art-deco interiors.

PLATE 8

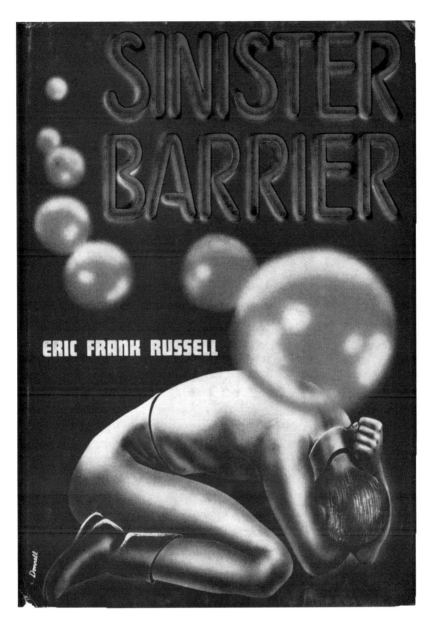

ABOVE: *Sinister Barrier* by Eric Frank Russell (Reading, PA: Fantasy Press, 1948), dustjacket by Andrew J. Donnell. A.J. Donnell (1905–1991)—he never liked his first names—had no interest in science fiction, but he nevertheless became a partner in one of the earliest specialist sf publishers, Fantasy Press, because he worked with the founder, Lloyd Eshbach. Donnell's covers were always simplistic but effective, his cover for *Sinister Barrier* showing an individual menaced by the alien globes.

PLATE 9

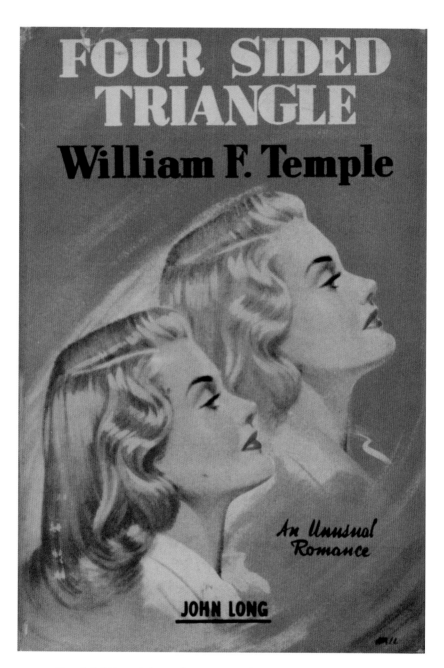

ABOVE: *Four Sided Triangle* by William F. Temple (London: John Long, 1949), dust-jacket by Roger Hall. Henry Hall (1914–2006), always known as Roger, painted many book covers, and is best known for having been the first to depict James Bond on a cover with *Casino Royale* in 1955.

PLATE 10

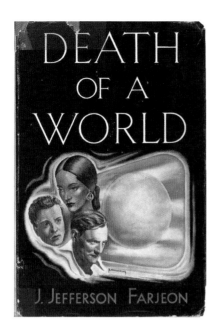

ABOVE, LEFT: *Death of a World* by J. Jefferson Farjeon (London: Collins, 1948), dust-jacket by Norman Manwaring (1912–85) who was better known as a heraldic artist.

ABOVE, RIGHT: *The Day of the Triffids* by John Wyndham (London: Michael Joseph, 1951), dustjacket by Patrick Gierth (1910–94), who did many book covers after the War but was better known as a war artist.

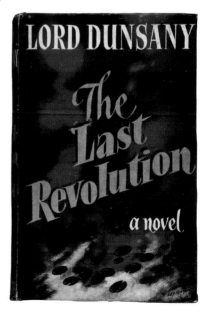

RIGHT: *The Last Revolution* by Lord Dunsany (London: Jarrolds, 1951), dustjacket by Ley Kenyon. Bennett Ley Kenyon (1913–90) painted several book covers, notably the first British edition of Philip K. Dick's *World of Chance* (1956), though he was better known for his underwater scenes—he was an able scuba diver. Besides this, his major claim to fame was his involvement in the Great Escape from Stalag Luft III in 1944 where he forged passports and other papers.

PLATE 11

ABOVE: *The Sound of His Horn* by Sarban (New York: Ballantine Books, 1960), cover by Richard M. Powers. Powers (1921–96) was one of the leading sf artists of the 1950s. Indeed, *The Encyclopaedia of Science Fiction* remarks that with Powers "the packaging of sf could be said to have come of age." His first cover was for Isaac Asimov's *Pebble in the Sky* (1950) but the majority of his covers adorned the paperbacks from Ballantine Books. His work is now highly collectable.

PLATE 12

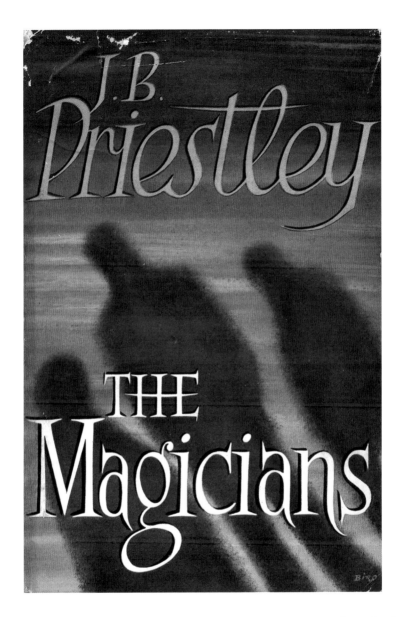

ABOVE: *The Magicians* by J.B. Priestley (London: Heinemann, 1954), dustjacket by Val Biro. The Hungarian-born Balint Biro (1921–2014) settled in Britain in 1939 and became a prolific illustrator of books and magazines. In addition to illustrating many of C.S. Forester's Hornblower books and Nigel Tranter's historical novels he illustrated several sf and fantasy works including Sax Rohmer's *Wulfheim* (1950), Lord Dunsany's *The Little Tales of Smethers* (1952) and Daphne du Maurier's *The Apple Tree* (1952).

PLATE 13

ABOVE: *Childhood's End* by Arthur C. Clarke (London: Sidgwick & Jackson, 1954), dustjacket by Deborah Jones. Jones (1921–2012) was best known for her illustrations for children, especially dolls and teddy bears, but also animals—she ran an animal charity. Her affinity for children, however, made her cover for *Childhood's End* all the more haunting.

PLATE 14

ABOVE: *One in Three Hundred* by J.T. McIntosh (New York: Doubleday, 1954), dust-jacket by Mel Hunter. Hunter (1927–2004) was a popular book and magazine artist of the 1950s and 1960s perhaps best remembered for his series of covers for *The Magazine of Fantasy & Science Fiction* depicting the antics of robots in a world devoid of humans. He also wrote and illustrated several of his own books including a series for younger readers looking at the origin of life on Earth which began with *How Man Began* (1972). In accordance with his wishes Hunter's cremated remains were launched into space in 2012.

PLATE 15

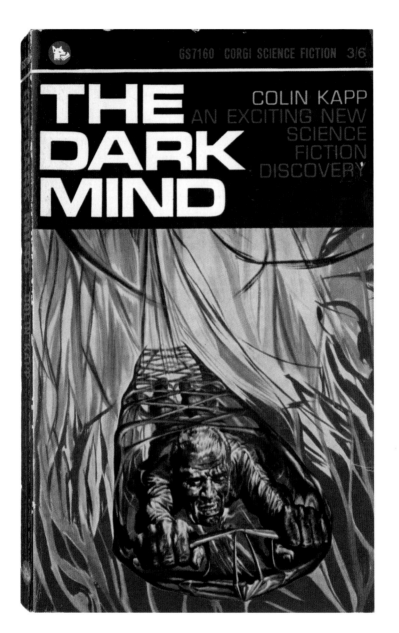

ABOVE: *The Dark Mind* by Colin Kapp (London: Corgi Books, 1965), cover by Josh Kirby. Ronald "Josh" Kirby (1928–2001) was one of Britain's leading book cover artists, mostly paperbacks, for over forty years. His first sf cover was for Dan Morgan's *Cee-Tee Man* (1955) but he is best known for his series of covers for Terry Pratchett's Discworld books. Several collections of his paintings were published, notably *In the Garden of Unearthly Delights* (1991) and *A Cosmic Cornucopia* (1999).

PLATE 16

PHILOSOPHICAL SPECULATIONS

O F THE 100 BOOKS COVERED HERE ONLY TWO ARE NON-fiction and, as both were published around the same time it seems sensible to cover them together. What's more they show a growing interest in exploring the "What Ifs" of life, both in terms of considering the future and reflecting on the past.

Surprisingly we can go back a long way to consider the history of speculation on the future or the possibilities of science. In his *Opus Majus*, written around 1267, Roger Bacon included a chapter, "De Scientia experi-mentalis", on experimental science, which speculated on such possibili-ties as telescopes, microscopes, steam ships and flying machines. Three centuries later his namesake Francis Bacon considered the implications of the invention of printing, gunpowder and the compass in *Novum Organum* (1620). Of special interest are the works of the recently ordained priest, later to become Bishop of Chester, John Wilkins. In *The Discovery of a World in the Moone* (1638) he speculated on the possibility of life on the Moon and, in a revised edition added thoughts on how we might journey there. *Mathematical Magic* (1648) gave further thought to powered flight.

Leaping ahead to the period covered by this book, it is not surprising that H.G. Wells produced a detailed study on what the twentieth century might present in *Anticipations* (1901). He speculated on the rise in motor transport likely to rival the railways, which would also lead to the urbanization of the countryside. He suspected that new technology would revolutionize the class system with financial and business managers at one end of the scale and those with neither property nor employment at the other end—"the abyss". He hoped that a scientifically trained technocrat would become the primary governing influence rather than governors and businessmen who are more likely to provoke wars they cannot manage. He believed that in future wars the advantage would go to those who had command of the air and scientifically improved weapons, though he saw no role for the submarine. Alas Wells also saw the potential of eugenics and the eradication of the weak.

One of the most interesting volumes was *The World in 2030* (1930) by Frederick Smith, the Earl of Birkenhead, a renowned barrister, an active politician and father of the equally rebellious Lady Eleanor Smith. Taking his lead from Haldane's *Daedalus*, Smith considered the future in eight categories plus a general survey. His categories included war, industry, politics, flight, women and everyday life, but he preceded his forecasts by a statement which is every bit as relevant to science fiction:

> ... it is not only in the material world that science is important; ideas and ethics no less than machines develop as the direct outcome of the discoveries of scientific workers.

In other words, science may stimulate the technologies and inventions of the future but they also influence how people utilize those inventions and how this affects society.

Alas, Smith would not have endeared himself to the women readers of the day because although he recognized that there were women of talent and genius, he believed that "even the most gifted woman is less valuable to the state than an exceptional man." Neither did he see equality between the sexes.

So rather than treat Birkenhead's book as one of my select 100, I've chosen two others, which I have singled out because they go further than the Earl and look in two different directions. J.D. Bernal considers scientific evolution far into the future, whilst J.C. Squire looks into the past to consider how the world might be had major history been different.

The World, the Flesh and the Devil   J.D. Bernal

London: Kegan Paul, Trench, Trubner & Co., 1929

The *To-day and To-morrow* series which began in 1924 with J.B.S. Haldane's *Daedalus, or Science and the Future* and Bertrand Russell's *Icarus, or the Future of Science*, continued for over a hundred books to 1931. They included such studies as *Lysistrata, or Woman's Future and Future Woman* (1924) by Anthony M. Ludovici, *Quo Vadimus, Some Glimpses of the Future* (1925) by E.E. Fournier d'Albe, *Automaton, or the Future of the Mechanical Man* (1928) by H. Stafford Hatfield, and such specialist titles as *Hymen, or the Future of Marriage* (1927) by Norman Haire and *Democritus, or the Future of Laughter* (1929) by Gerald Gould. There were titles by authors more closely associated with the scientific romance such as John Gloag with *Artifex, or the Future of Craftsmanship* (1926) and J. Leslie Mitchell with *Hanno, or the Future of Exploration* (1928). We shall encounter both authors shortly.

Clearly some titles were more serious than others and impacted upon the public in different ways, but one that had a lasting impact was *The World, the Flesh and the Devil* by J.D. Bernal. His tripartite title allowed him to divide his discussion between the future of the Earth, the human species and the mind.

After some minor thoughts about synthetic clothing and foods, Bernal moved rapidly on to space travel and how humans might survive in space. He suspected that, with rockets, it would not prove too difficult to escape the Earth's gravity and he recognized the importance of scientific work that could be done beyond the Earth. He suggested the idea of a space habitat in the form of a giant sphere, ten miles in diameter, with an outer shell strong enough to avoid damage from meteors. Inside would need to be facilities for providing breathable atmosphere, recycling waste, and living quarters for perhaps 20,000 people. He also suggested the idea of spaceships powered by solar sails, capturing the solar wind. He was not the first to suggest this—the Russian Konstantin Tsiolkovsky had proposed it a few years earlier—but Bernal popularized the concept. He presented it as an obvious technology to develop.

When he turned to the human body he considered the inevitable changes arising from evolution but maintained that humans were now in a position to control those changes, which no previous species could. He foresaw that any shortcomings could be overcome by humans merging with machines, in effect cyborgs, though he doesn't use that term. He considered how these machines might be linked, most likely by wireless but controlled by the human mind, so that the machines could think collectively, in effect a hive mind, but again he doesn't use that term.

He continued this thinking in the section on the human mind where he felt that humans had a small ability to think ahead, but augmented by machine (really a computer, another word he doesn't use) that ability to forecast, or predict, might be extended from moments to days, or even longer.

He proposed many other ideas—the book is a fountain of possibilities—but he added that for any of this to develop, governments needed to have a significant input from scientists and that, ultimately, scientists should be in control.

This last idea was the basis for Aldous Huxley's *Brave New World*, as we have seen, and it's very likely that Huxley read Bernal's booklet. It has been recognized as influential. Arthur C. Clarke called it "perhaps the most remarkable attempt to predict the future of scientific possibility ever made," adding that he was "astonished to see how many of my own concepts and ideas I really owe to Bernal!" Clarke certainly used the idea of the solar sail in his story "The Wind from the Sun" (1964). Olaf Stapledon acknowledged his debt to it in his preface to *Star Maker*, and its impact passes down through the works of such recent authors as Stephen Baxter and Alastair Reynolds.

John Desmond Bernal (1901–1971) was born in Ireland, but his mother was American. He pioneered the work of X-ray crystallography to help understand in more detail the structure of matter. Although he joined the communist party in 1924 this did not stop him becoming a chief scientific adviser to the government during the Second World War, helping plan and map the D-Day landings on the Normandy beaches. He went with the troops and was one of the first to land. His enthusiasm for his interests was infectious and he has been called "one of the most influential scientists of his generation."

If It Had Happened Otherwise J.C. Squire
London: Longmans, Green, 1931

The exploration of the "what ifs" of history is a game enjoyed as much by academics and historians as it is by writers of science fiction. Such works have been called alternate histories or counterfactual or uchronia or imaginary histories but no matter the name, one of the most influential books in the early development of imaginary history was *If It Had Happened Otherwise.* John Collings Squire (1884–1958), the poet, parodist and often inflammatory editor of the *London Mercury*, commissioned various historians to explore how history might have changed had some key event happened differently or not happened at all.

The book contains eleven essays some closer to fiction than others. Some are pure wish fulfilment, such as Hilaire Belloc's "If Drouet's Cart Had Stuck". Drouet was a French postmaster who recognized Louis XVI when he fled from Paris in disguise in 1791, during the Revolution. Drouet blocked the bridge at Varennes with his cart. Belloc muses on what might have happened had he not managed to move the cart and the king escaped. In reality not much would have changed. Drouet had already alerted the authorities and there's little doubt that the king would have been captured. But Belloc launches himself on a flight of fancy where Louis marshals his forces, and with the help of the British, defeats the powers of the revolution, as well as Napoleon, and restores the monarchy, leading to a different outcome of the Great War.

Belloc's partner in crime, G.K. Chesterton, explored "If Don John of Austria had married Mary Queen of Scots" and proposed that they would have made a formidable pair capable of ruling a united Catholic Britain.

In "If the Emperor Frederick had not had Cancer", Emil Ludwig considers a better fate for the German Emperor Frederick III. He became Emperor upon his father's death in March 1888 at the age of 90. Frederick was still only 56 but he had been diagnosed with cancer and died just three months later. He was succeeded by his son, Wilhelm II, who was Kaiser at the outbreak of the First World War. Had Frederick survived, his liberal outlook would almost certainly not have promulgated the events that led to the War and Emil Ludwig suggests that had he died in 1914 when his son was fifty-five, the Great War may not have started.

In "If Napoleon had escaped to America", H.A.L. Fisher suggests that Napoleon might first have established a federal republic in South America but would then have mysteriously disappeared in 1818 in order to establish himself in India. Ronald Knox sees Britain becoming communist in "If the General Strike had succeeded". Milton Waldman believes that had Abraham Lincoln survived he would have soon been discredited as a warmonger and would have been impeached had he not died prematurely in "If Booth Had Missed Lincoln."

The most creative essay is by Winston Churchill, "If Lee Had Not Won the Battle of Gettysburg", because he writes it from the viewpoint of an historian living in an alternate history where the Confederate Army had won at Gettysburg in 1863. It allows Churchill to suggest an alternative to the after effects of the battle in our own history where Britain, the Confederacy and the Union develop stronger ties and consequently help reduce the likelihood of the Great War.

Squire himself, who enjoyed parodies and had already scored points off various orators with his volume *Imaginary Speeches* (1912), contributed an essay to show what would happen if it was proved that Francis Bacon had written the plays of Shakespeare—it's an amusing journey along the trail of commercialism, tourism and rebranding.

The book was a success partly because not all contributors took themselves seriously, and even those who did posed some fascinating ideas about how significantly one small event can affect the world stage. We have already seen how Guy Dent explored this is *Emperor of the If*, and the idea would soon become a staple feature of science fiction.

INTO THE COSMIC

A S WE ENTER THE 1930S THREE FACTORS BEGAN TO INFLU-
ence the development of science fiction—although that phrase had
yet to enter general British parlance. The looming threat of a Second World
War, which everyone tried to ignore, is sufficient to discuss separately, and
I shall cover this in section XI. The other factors are a greater awareness
of the far future prospect of humanity—assuming it had one—and the
emergence of "science fiction" itself.

We have already seen how, inspired primarily by H.G. Wells's depiction
of humanity 800 millennia hence in *The Time Machine*, John Lionel Tayler
and S. Fowler Wright depicted mankind's fate in *The Last of My Race* and
The Amphibians. These were followed by such books as *Tomorrow's Yesterday*
by John Gloag (see below), and the books of Olaf Stapledon, starting with
Last and First Men in 1930. This is discussed below with Stapledon's *opus
gigantus*, *Star Maker*, published in 1937, which takes us on a trip through the
future of the universe over 100 thousand million years.

Star Maker is as much a religious experience as one of science and any
book which takes us on a journey of such magnitude has to take into

account how we as humans fit within the cosmos and this became a new factor in taking science fiction forward. It could be a religious allegory, as in C. S. Lewis's *Out of the Silent Planet*, or an awareness that we are not alone in the universe, and not masters of our own domain, as in Eric Frank Russell's *Sinister Barrier*.

There was also the growing awareness of the connection between space and time and that time might play tricks with our perceptions of the world. Time travel or a distortion of time featured in an increasing number of books, whether the time viewer in Gloag's *Tomorrow's Yesterday*, or a genuine shift in time as in J. Leslie Mitchell's *Gay Hunter*. Mitchell used some of the principles laid down in J.W. Dunne's *An Experiment with Time* (1927) and this book influenced many writers, especially J.B. Priestley, whom I discuss later.

At the same time humans were becoming increasingly aware of our tiny place in a vast universe. The American magazine market allowed writers and experimentalists to give free rein to their imagination in the newly dubbed field of "science fiction".

Tales of scientific adventure had been a part of the American pulp magazines since their emergence in the 1890s and even more so following the success of the novels by Edgar Rice Burroughs, including his Barsoom series set on Mars. Other writers who developed a reputation for their tales of weird science in the years during and just after the Great War were Homer Eon Flint, Abraham Merritt and Ray Cummings. In 1923 the magazine *Weird Tales* was launched and although it concentrated on tales of horror and the supernatural, it ran a fair quota of scientific adventures and began the career of Edmond Hamilton.

The inventor and publisher Hugo Gernsback had settled in the United States from Luxembourg in 1904. He had long seen how stories of scientific adventure could inspire readers, especially the young, to experiment and invent. He included one or two stories in his technical magazines *Modern Electrics* and *The Electrical Experimenter* (renamed *Science and Invention* in 1923). These tales usually involved a young inventor producing something of world-shattering importance. Gernsback wanted his readers to become the next Thomas Edison, Nikola Tesla or Lee de Forrest. In April 1926, Gernsback published the first all-sf English-language magazine, *Amazing Stories*. He relied initially on reprints, including works by H.G. Wells, but he soon developed a stable of regulars including David H. Keller, Jack Williamson, E.E. "Doc" Smith and Edmond Hamilton.

In 1929, due to his financial mismanagement, Gernsback lost control of *Amazing Stories* but he fought back with several new magazines including two that soon merged as *Wonder Stories*. Until now Gernsback had called the material he published "scientifiction", a rather clumsy contraction of "scientific fiction". That word had become a trademark on the cover of *Amazing Stories*. When he lost control of that magazine, he was advised not to use that word elsewhere, so he came up with "science fiction" which he promoted relentlessly. It was an easier phrase to remember, so soon caught on—at least in the United States.

The success of these magazines caught the attention of other publishers and at the end of 1929 *Astounding Stories* appeared from William Clayton. It was a purely commercial venture, with no interest in inspiring young inventors, and it published unadulterated adventure fiction, with little regard for scientific accuracy. The reputation of science fiction suffered. Gernsback and his editor David Lasser did what they could to restore its reputation in *Wonder Stories* but because of the Depression and Gernsback's poor payment system, authors switched to *Astounding Stories* which, since 1933, had a new publisher and editor. It was here, first under F. Orlin Tremaine and then, from 1938, under John W. Campbell, Jr., that science fiction recovered some of its reputation but, more significantly, moved away from the raw adventure story, to stories which expanded our understanding of science and placed it in the hands of human beings. Campbell told his writers that he wanted stories you could read as contemporary to someone in the future. Under Tremaine and Campbell writers who would transform science fiction emerged (or, in the cases of Jack Williamson and Clifford D. Simak, re-emerged)—including Robert A. Heinlein, Isaac Asimov, Theodore Sturgeon, A.E. van Vogt and, representing Britain, Eric Frank Russell.

In Britain, although publishers would issue the occasional work of imaginative or philosophical science, the magazine market was shrinking, and the scientific romance found itself being shunted out of the adult market into magazines for juvenile readers.

A case in point is George C. Wallis. He had started his career in 1895 selling regularly to the leading adult markets. One such story, "The Last Days of Earth" (1901) is set thirteen million years in the future on a frozen Earth from which the last few survivors attempt to escape with tragic consequences. As these adult markets faded Wallis found himself contributing more to the boys' magazines where his reputation lingered. His cousin, Bruce, who lived in Canada, was aware of the growing American market, notably *Weird Tales* and *Amazing Stories*. He encouraged George to contribute to the pulps, and they collaborated on several stories, including the serials "The Star Shell" (*Weird Tales*, November 1926–February 1927), set on Jupiter, and "The World at Bay" (*Amazing Stories*, November–December 1928) where the Earth is in peril from a race of underground beings with super-weapons.

Wallis was the first British writer to find a regular market in the American specialist magazines. Others followed. John Beynon Harris, who twenty years later would become world renowned as John Wyndham, first sold to *Wonder Stories* in 1931. Benson Herbert also debuted that year. His 1935 serial in *Wonder Stories*, "The Perfect World" was one of the few to receive a hardcover publication in Britain where it appeared as *Crisis!—1992* in 1936 (see below). The wonderfully named Festus Pragnell, in real life a Southampton policeman, began his sales in 1932 and, like Herbert, had a serial in *Wonder Stories* in 1935 which saw British publication in 1936 as *The Green Man of Kilsona*. John Russell Fearn, the most prolific British contributor to American pulps, debuted in *Amazing Stories* in 1933 with "The Intelligence Gigantic", whilst perhaps the most popular contributor of the late 1930s and 1940s was Eric Frank Russell, whose *Sinister Barrier* is also discussed below.

Both John Gloag and Olaf Stapledon were aware of this growth in science-fiction magazines in the USA and in Britain, where *Scoops* appeared in 1934 and, more importantly, *Tales of Wonder* in 1937. Stapledon remarked to Gloag that this growing interest in tales of space and time was "symptomatic of our period" whilst Gloag remarked that the writers have created "a golden age of their own". Indeed, the late 1930s in America is often seen as the birth of the Golden Age of science fiction, and it had its effects in Britain.

To-morrow's Yesterday   John Gloag

London: George Allen and Unwin, 1932

It takes some perseverance to read *Tomorrow's Yesterday*, because it is presented in two guises, as a play and as a novel, and at the same time tries to be a social satire and a futuristic drama. Gloag (1896–1981) had conceived it as a film script and when that did not sell he converted it into a novel by retaining the script and bookending it with an introductory chapter about how the play was to be staged, and a final chapter on the aftermath. But it's the play that is the real story, and it works as a script because it's a series of images seen through an interactive time viewer by two individuals from the far future.

The first few episodes viewed from the future are set in the 1930s and demonstrate the commercialism of the day, from the viewpoint of the world of advertising, and the superficiality of society, with an emphasis on changing fashion and glamour. Some of the sexual images described probably contributed to the film script being rejected. The images then leap to 1963, showing how disrespectful society has become. One of the characters reckons that within the decade marriage will be out of fashion.

There is a brief flashback to the end of ancient Rome suggesting that the social decline that resulted in the fall of the Roman Empire would also lead to the end of the British Empire. Sure enough, a world war breaks out in the 1990s and we see scenes of devastation and destruction. Mankind reverts to savagery and we witness activities to show that mankind never learns as humans fight for supremacy amongst the tribes across Britain.

We discover that mankind never did recover. The race which has evolved to take over the world and to create a time viewer not only to witness the past but bring people from the past into the future are not related to the apes at all, but are cats!

Gloag's view of mankind is cynical, not surprising since he had been gassed in the First World War and regarded most governments as incompetent. He had a passion for arts and crafts having already built a reputation as an expert in architectural design and furniture before he turned to fiction—references to furniture abound in his novels. His thoughts on the superficiality of society re-emerge in *The New Pleasure* (1933) where a drug enhances the sense of smell which becomes the primary sense in how people choose their partner and influences life. *Winter's Youth* (1934) again appeals to vanity when a process for rejuvenation leads the government to consider how society might be rebuilt. Later novels include *Manna* (1940), about a fungus that appeases all hunger but which also creates a sense of lethargy, not unlike the serum in Martin Swayne's *The Blue Germ*, and *99%* (1944) where a drug allows takers to tap into their ancestral memory.

Gloag's works on furniture and design kept his reputation alive for many years but his science fiction was forgotten, yet his cynical view of fashion and society is every bit as relevant today as it was in the 1930s.

Gay Hunter   J. Leslie Mitchell

London: William Heinemann, 1934

For clarity's sake, the title of this book is a person's name, Gay Hunter, a young American archaeologist who has spent some time in Wiltshire, England. She recognizes the irony of the name when she finds herself forced to hunt for survival. At one point the name almost becomes a title.

Nearing the end of her stay in England she meets Major Ledyard Houghton who is abrupt and insolent. She takes an instant dislike to him. Houghton is friends with Lady Jane Easterling who runs the local branch of Fascists. Just before this book appeared the British Union of Fascists had been formed, in 1932, by Oswald Moseley.

Forced to dine with Houghton at her hotel, Gay talks about her work and discusses the subject of time. She tells Houghton the theories of J.W. Dunne who, by recording his dreams, was intrigued with how many seemed to come true. He developed his theory of serial time in *An Experiment With Time* (1927), and later books, where he suggested that whilst the brain perceives normal time, there is a higher dimension, in which our higher consciousness (a form of transcendental ego) can monitor normal time but is aware of the future. Although Houghton thinks this is all rot both agree to experiment when going to sleep that night, during which there is a powerful thunderstorm.

Gay wakes the next day in the open, naked, and soon discovers Major Houghton, also naked. Before long Lady Jane appears. It is not until Gay observes the night sky that she realizes they have somehow been projected thousands of years into the future long after civilization has collapsed and mankind reverted to barbarism.

The three set out to find other humans, but Gay tires of her companions and travels on her own, accompanied by a wolf, which has clearly been domesticated. The wolf helps catch food and within a few days Gay meets the wolf's owner, Rem, a Singer from a local tribe. After a few days together Gay meets the rest of the tribe and discovers they have captured Houghton and Lady Jane. Whereas Gay enjoys life with the tribe, Houghton and Lady Jane rebel. From the elder Singer of the tribe Gay learns about the fall of civilization following the release of many atomic bombs and the spread of radiation. It seems the Wars had been started by the Fascists who here are called the Hierarchs.

Some ancient buildings survive, including a giant dam, but most have reverted to Nature. However, they learn that London does survive, better than elsewhere, now called the Shining Place. Houghton and Jane leave the tribe with some of the folk heading to London and it becomes clear when they reached there because the tribe hears explosions and sees fires.

Houghton discovers that some of the ancient machinery and weapons can be restored, which he plans to do to rebuild civilization.

Gay realizes she must venture to London to confront the Major, and though she travels most of the way with some of the tribe, she goes the final distance alone, so as not to antagonize the Major. Even then she is attacked by Jane who tries to kill her using one of the existing Fire-Beams. Gay also encounters rats that have evolved into kangaroo-like creatures. The final encounter is as much a battle to save the world of the tribes rather than rebuild civilization.

James Leslie Mitchell (1901–1935) was a bold and original writer, who created an alter ego, Lewis Grassic Gibbon for his novels and writings set in Scotland. As Mitchell he produced four sf novels of which *Gay Hunter* was his last before he died tragically young of peritonitis. *Gay Hunter* is a companion piece to *Three Go Back* (1932). In that novel three people are projected via a timeslip to the Stone Age in Atlantis. Mitchell depicts the honourable savage as heroic and the ancient world as an Eden, just as he does in the post-civilization future of *Gay Hunter*. Mitchell takes time to explore this future world and its people so that the reader feels a genuine affinity. *Gay Hunter* is certainly one of the best post-catastrophe novels of the period.

Adrift in the Stratosphere   A.M. Low

Scoops, 17 February–21 April 1924, as "Space"; Glasgow: Blackie & Son, 1937

This is what is commonly called a "boys'" book, written for a juvenile readership, recounting the adventures of three lads, aged 23, 20 and 18. I fear not a single woman appears in the entire story.

I include the book because at this time in Britain science-fiction adventures were regarded as boys' books and not to be taken seriously. None of the books we have discussed so far, and none for the next decade, would be called "science fiction" or given any genre title. They were described as being in the tradition of H.G. Wells, or pseudo-scientific, or future war, or imaginary future—there was no single adjective, and that's because the genre had yet to be born in Britain. It had emerged in the United States in the pages of *Amazing Stories, Wonder Stories* and *Astounding Stories*—magazine titles that hardly endeared themselves to an adult market, with covers of monsters and machines that fascinated younger readers. The thrills-a-minute adventure aspect of science fiction rapidly acquired a juvenile image and that also happened in Britain.

Britain had a long history of boys' magazines of which the best known was the *Boy's Own Paper* which ran from 1879 to 1967. It had a certain acceptability amongst parents because it was published by the Religious Tract Society. It serialized some of the first English translations of Jules Verne, including "The Clipper of the Clouds" (1886–7) and "An Antarctic Mystery" (1898–9). Arthur Conan Doyle sold some of his early stories to the *Boy's Own Paper*. Edgar Rice Burroughs's *At the Earth's Core*, which had appeared in the American pulp *All-Story Weekly* in 1914 was serialized in Britain in *Pluck* in 1923. Edgar Wallace's sf adventure "Planetoid 127" first appeared in *The Mechanical Boy* in 1924. Cassell's magazine *Chums*, regularly published science fiction, and even reprinted stories from Gernsback's magazines such as Jack Williamson's "The Second Shell" in the May 1931 issue. A highly popular series by Murray Roberts featuring Captain Justice ran in *The Modern Boy* from 1930 to 1935. Justice, a favourite of the young Brian Aldiss, operated from Titanic Tower in the mid-Atlantic saving the world from every imaginable disaster.

Although science fiction was a regular, highly imaginative part of these magazines, there was no single boys' magazine devoted to the field until 1934 when C. Arthur Pearson published *Scoops*, which called itself "The Story Paper of To-morrow". A two-penny, small tabloid magazine on cheap paper it had lurid covers and small print cramming in as much wordage as it could in its 32 pages. It was edited by Bernard Buley who provided the first serial, "Master of the Moon", though almost all stories were published anonymously. But its real scoop was a serial called "Space" where the author was named: Professor A.M. Low (1888–1956) a renowned populariser of science and a pioneer in the fields of television and rocketry. The serial was issued in book form as *Adrift in the Stratosphere* in 1937.

It is a totally unpretentious adventure story with, despite Low's standing, little reliable science. The three young men discover a combined rocket-ship/balloon, the *Aeronauticus*, in a hangar when they seek help after one of their motor-bikes breaks down. The rocket had been built by Professor Slater to explore the stratosphere and he was going to test fly it after lunch, so it was unattended. The boys check it out and accidentally launch it. Trying to control it they inadvertently fire the rockets and the *Aeronauticus* speeds off into space. The boys are overcome by the acceleration, and experience turning transparent when they pass through a belt of X-rays beyond the Earth's atmosphere. Thankfully they soon master the rocket and discover there is food on board in the form of super-vitamin tablets.

Peril follows peril. They are menaced by a mile-long monster which they evade by firing rockets at it. Unfortunately this propels the rocket into an unknown direction. The boys had already been working the rocket's radio, tuning in to a football match that had been broadcast two weeks before, and now pick up a signal in a language unknown to them. Fortunately, the professor had written a book on the Martian language and they discover he has created a machine that will translate any alien language. They find the message is indeed from Mars. The Martians regard the rocket as a threat and are determined to destroy it, bombarding it with yellow radium rays. Once again the professor's notes come to their aid when they read "Death Rays—How to Deal with Them."

The Martians try to drive them insane by broadcasting weird sounds which the lads overcome by destroying the radio. The Martians send a Death Ship to destroy them which almost succeeds until the rocket passes through some new ray in space which saves them. They encounter a series of islands in the upper stratosphere of Earth which are home to a superior, utopian race. These have been seen from Earth but mistaken for comets. The boys tour the islands where they have further life-threatening

adventures before, thanks to the king of these worlds, they are given dia-
grams on how to return to Earth, safe and sound.

I first read this book when I was about ten, and thoroughly enjoyed it.
It was with much trepidation that I re-read it recently, and understandably
so. The book is dreadful. I cannot imagine any child finding it enjoyable
today, as it was to me in the 1950s and probably others in the thirties. I have
included it because it is representative of the boys' adventure fiction of
the day and, unfortunately, of how appalling much of that was. Despite
Professor Low putting his name to it, it is so full of scientific inaccuracies
that I find it hard to believe he wrote it, and suspect he may have provided
an outline that was expanded by one of the regular boys' writers. Yet I don't
doubt it thrilled a generation of young readers who may have been inspired
to study science for themselves and that alone would make it worthwhile.

Planet Plane   John Beynon

The Passing Show, 2 May–20 June 1936 as "Stowaway to Mars"; expanded, London: George
Newnes, 1936

Scoops ran for only twenty issues and its failure suggested that an all-sf
magazine for youngsters wouldn't work. That didn't stop publishers experimenting, especially amongst a more general readership. In 1932 Odhams
rejuvenated their weekly humour title *The Passing Show* as a brash, full
colour magazine, running more fiction including both speculative articles
and science fiction. The first few issues had Ethel Mannin proclaiming
that marriage would soon be outmoded and Julian Huxley writing about
eugenics and life expectancy.

The first science fiction it ran was a short piece by Hugh Pilcher whereby
radiation can be beamed down the telephone to disintegrate matter. By the
end of 1933 it was serializing the novels of Edgar Rice Burroughs, beautifully illustrated by Fortunino Matania. Other sf serials included "When
Worlds Collide" and "After Worlds Collide" by Edwin Balmer and Philip

Wylie and, in the summer of 1935, "The Secret People" by John Beynon. This was the first novel by the author who would become world famous as John Wyndham fifteen years later and tells of a secret world discovered beneath the Sahara.

John Beynon was the preferred alias of John Beynon Harris (1903–1969) who had been selling science fiction stories to Hugo Gernsback's *Wonder Stories* since 1931, starting with the time-travel conundrum "Worlds to Barter". The absence of a regular British market meant he continued selling to America, but the expansion of *The Passing Show* at last allowed him to appear in Britain. "The Secret People" was not the best debut, but the next novel, "Stowaway to Mars", serialized during 1936 was another matter.

It shows the difference when an author knows his subject. The novel reveals Beynon's wide reading of science fiction and understanding of science—unlike Professor Low's weak *Adrift in the Stratosphere*. Curiously both novels start in almost the same way—the revelation of a spaceship being built in a secret hangar—but there the similarity ends. Dale Curtance has followed in his father's footsteps as a pioneer in rocketry, especially the development of rocket planes and in setting world records. Now, in 1985, he is creating his own rocket-ship, the *Gloria Mundi*, hoping to win the American Keuntz Prize of five million dollars to be the first to travel to and return from another planet. There had already been attempts to land on the Moon, all of which had ended in disaster. There are attempts to sabotage his plans as others are also hoping to win the prize.

Dale is accompanied by four others—a young pilot (Dugan), an engineer (Burns), a reporter (Froud) and a doctor (Grayson). All goes well but soon after launch they realize a variance in the amount of fuel used suggests extra weight and they discover a stowaway, a woman called Joan. It is a while before they discover why she's there, which is to exonerate the reputation of her father. Some years before he had discovered a weird machine which he is convinced came from Mars. He kept it secret while he and his daughter examined it. They believed it was some kind of robotic rover, which the Martians had sent to explore Earth. When his secret is exposed, the father holds a press conference but the alien machine destroys itself leaving everyone to suspect a hoax. In stowing away, Joan wants to prove him right.

There is some sexual tension on board the ship in the twelve-week trip to Mars, but Joan is strong-willed and highly capable. She spends time teaching the others what she learned from the alien machine, including the rudiments of a pictographic Martian language. Dale remains aloof and sceptical.

The travellers find the journey to Mars tedious. Apart from scientific observations much time is taken up in discussion and debate with such subjects as the nature and potential of machines and why women in general seem less interested in machines than men.

Once they reach Mars, landing in a desert, they discover the air is breathable if tenuous (requiring oxygen masks). They soon find one of the enormous canals which has poor vegetation along it banks. The sexual tension on the flight suddenly bursts when Burns decides to take Joan for himself and threatens the others. Returning with her to the rocket, Burns is killed by the Martian machines and Joan is captured. The others believe Joan has also been killed. They manage to get back to the *Gloria Mundi* just as another rocket arrives. Beynon had predicted the space race. The Russians arrive safely, but the Americans which soon follow, crash and are killed.

Joan is taken to the city of Hanno, one of seven such cities, once the home of millions, but now only several thousand Martians survive. She meets Vaygan, an elderly Martian, who is humanoid but with an enlarged head and chest. They try to communicate by writing but this takes too long. Vaygan hypnotizes Joan and manipulates her brain so that they can converse. She learns that the machines are intelligent and self-replicating and will be the successors to the Martians when the race dies out. A health check on Joan reveals she has germs which could infect the Martians (and vice versa) and the surviving Martians insist that she and the others must return to Earth.

The novel has a shock ending, which I will not reveal. Beynon also shows that many of the population believed it was a hoax just as happened with the first Moon landing in 1969. The Russians are hostile claiming the British abandoned their comrades, whilst the Americans do not believe their rocket crashed. It is surprising that Beynon, who considers much technological advances, did not consider radio contact between them and Earth during the expedition.

Yet Beynon does have some original ideas. Apart from the conspiracy theories, he foresaw that Joan's extra weight at the start of the journey could have jeopardized the expedition and there is a debate about whether she should be ejected into space, a dilemma which is usually heralded as originating in "The Cold Equations" by Tom Godwin published in 1954. He also explored what benefits might arise from space exploration, though the discussion centres primarily on the advance in knowledge. Finally, taking a lead from Olaf Stapledon, Beynon considered that humans are simply the current dominant being in the evolution of life on Earth and that at some future age, the race will almost certainly be superseded.

There are elements of the novel which seem barely above the juvenile, particularly in the relationship between the men, and compared to our understanding now of space flight it seems remarkably poor. Yet Beynon was nevertheless aware of the knowledge of the day, at a time when all too few believed space flight was possible, and this novel was one of the first to attempt a serious study of how it might happen.

Odhams reprinted the serial in abridged form as "The Space Machine" in their glossy new magazine for boys *Modern Wonder* in 1937 but one of the editors changed Joan to John, a ridiculous piece of meddling which caused problems and required Beynon to provide further changes. Beynon wrote a short sequel, "Sleepers of Mars", for the second issue of the new sf magazine *Tales of Wonder* in 1938, tracing the fate of the Russian cosmonauts on Mars.

I shall return to Beynon when he donned his Wyndham persona.

Crisis! — 1992   Benson Herbert

Wonder Stories, October 1935–January/February 1936 as "The Perfect World"; London: Richards Press, 1936

This quirky novel, which was serialized in the American *Wonder Stories* in 1935 as "The Perfect World", has some highly original ideas sadly tarnished by absurd characters.

Earth is threatened by a rogue planet which is likely to collide in a few weeks. There is the inevitable panic and suicides, and plans hoping to save mankind come to nought. Then an astronomer notices that the planet has suddenly shifted its course and will miss the Earth.

By the year 1992 rocket planes, called soarers, are commonplace, but there has been no advance in interplanetary travel because there is no fuel sufficiently powerful. This has been the goal of German chemical engineer, Otto Lieben, and his efforts have at last been achieved. The financier and rocket expert Henry Guidance plans to launch a new kind of Soaring Rocket, and learning of Lieben's breakthrough decides to test the Rocket by flying to this new planet, which has been called Arion, a journey of 600,000 miles.

After rapid preparations the Rocket is ready to launch complete with an overly eccentric crew and passengers. Besides Guidance and Lieben, are the two astronomers who had detected Arion and plotted its course, a geologist, who is drunk at the time of the launch, a journalist and former rocket pilot, and various others. Just before launch there are two incidents. The final consignment of fuel bursts into flames before delivery and police try to board the rocket believing a burglar has taken refuge. Once launched discrepancies are found in the amount of fuel and they discover two stowaways, Lieben's daughter Ilse, and a Welsh criminal who refuses to give his name.

The presence of the stowaways is a problem because of the fuel consumption and food supplies, though there seems to be plenty of unnecessary commodities on board including wine and port. Although Benson Herbert was a qualified teacher of physics and mathematics, he gives scant thought to the problems of an interplanetary flight and has his passengers wandering about the rocket as if they were on an ocean liner.

The adventurers reach Arion but encounter a mist and though this clears, the rocket crashes. The atmosphere is breathable, and there is drinkable water, so they begin exploring. It is a world of dense vegetation and not without its perils. At one point they are surrounded by a giant lizard with two heads, two tails and ten legs. Although harmless, its size and uncontrollability cause problems. There are also odd moments of weightlessness and disorientation when the terrain shifts so that a plain becomes a steep slope and a mountain is flattened. The transformation of the landscape causes some of the crew to become lost.

Suddenly they encounter an intelligent creature—in fact several, whom they had already seen but mistaken for trees. The tree-being has no way to hear or speak but can communicate by writing which Ilse rapidly learns. The explorers learn that Arion is not a natural planet but a spaceship, created artificially around the shell of an old planet. It had come from the direction of Betelgeuse in search of other life and wanted to observe Earth, which they found of little interest. The shifts in terrain are caused by reorienting the spaceship.

The tree-man provides some of the travellers with a quick tour of Arion in superior flying machines, but we learn little of the planet's true nature because the tree people's limited communication. Meanwhile mayhem continues with the other explorers, caused partly by the chaotic appearances of the giant lizard, and by pits created by the tree-people to hinder the lizard. Some of the travellers fall into the pits and are killed. Others attempt to repair and escape in the soarer, but it crashes. The Arionians, whose super-science abilities have only been glimpsed, help the remaining survivors build a new rocket for their return to Earth.

This uneven novel has some moments of brilliance and others of absurdity. So far as I know, Herbert was the first to suggest the idea of a small planet being converted into a spaceship, hollowed out and used as a home. The idea was used by Arthur C. Clarke in *A Rendezvous with Rama* (1973). Much that is original, though, is spoiled by the ridiculous characters all of whom have ulterior motives for being on the expedition. The most bizarre relates to the Welsh stowaway who wants to murder Guidance for having once killed his pet parrot. To this end he has smuggled a giant bird onto the rocket to peck out Guidance's eyes.

Evidently, Herbert (1912–1991) did not take much of this seriously, and one can only wonder what he hoped to achieve. He wrote a few other minor short stories and, during the Second World War, secured such paper as he could to publish a series of science-fiction booklets. He became better known in the 1970s when he was involved with the British branch of the International Fortean Organization, which explored unusual phenomena of the type once researched by the American Charles Fort.

Star Maker   Olaf Stapledon
London: Methuen, 1937

Star Maker is not really a novel but an extended, cosmic thought experiment. It was a natural extension, or expansion, of his first book of imaginative fiction, *Last and First Men*, published in 1930. That book had been inspired to some degree by the writings of J.B.S. Haldane, especially the essays in *Possible Worlds* (1927). It follows the evolution of mankind from First Man (us) to Eighteenth Man, two thousand million years in the future. It tracks the rise and fall of their civilizations and the growing transcendence of each stage until the final humans are near immortal and almost all thought. Alas they are destroyed in a nova.

Star Maker sees the span of *Last and First Men* as just a phase in the hundred thousand million years of the cosmos. The story is narrated by an individual reflecting upon his own existence and regarding our insignificance in the universe. Sitting on a hillside the narrator has a vision, or rather experiences a mental voyage, as he moves away from Earth into the solar system and beyond—way beyond. He is travelling in both space and time, able to witness the evolution of many life-forms on a wide variety of planets. These life-forms also progress from system to system as if he is witnessing a cosmic evolution.

As he ventures further from Earth, and further from humanoid creatures, he discovers much stranger forms, such as six-limbed beings that evolve into centaurs, or humanoid echinoderms which evolved from starfish and developed a communal culture. There are nautiloids, or intelligent tentacled ships, and there are two symbiotic races, the fish-like ichthyoids and the crab-like arachnoids.

Star Maker is impossible to summarize because of the scale and wealth of Stapledon's creative imagination. His narrator witnesses events on a vast scale leading to conscious worlds and living galaxies until he arrives at the ultimate consciousness and creator, the Star Maker itself. There we witness a being that for eons has experimented with one new cosmos after another constantly looking for change and improvement. But there is no empathy, no compassion. The creation of life is simply an experiment, almost a game and it is only when it has created the ultimate in life that there is any emotion in fulfilment.

Frustrated and indignant the narrator's scorn at this discovery drives his mental self back to the hillside where he finds welcome relief in the "littleness" of Earth.

Stapledon had embarked on the future history as an exercise in mythmaking, but it became more than that. His religious beliefs had been suffocated by the horrors of the Great War, and he had been torn between his father's atheism and his mother's religious moralism. Stapledon wanted to explore what the Creator was trying to achieve and whether that process was leading to an ultimate "ecstasy"—a word he uses repeatedly. Yet neither *Last and First Men* nor *Star Maker* are religious books, not in the theocratic sense. They are philosophical exercises that nevertheless require a transcendence because the human mind is limited in what it can visualize.

William Olaf Stapledon (1886–1950) was by training a philosopher but by vocation a writer. He worked as a lecturer, but did not enjoy it, and his writings earned little, so he was fortunate that a family inheritance gave him the financial support he needed. His first book was a study of the moral attitude towards ethics, *A Modern Theory of Ethics* (1929). His other novels include *Odd John* (1935), the story of a superman which reworks some of the ideas from *Last and First Men*. Stapledon explored the theme again in *Sirius* (1944), this time about a dog with enhanced intelligence and its inevitable limitations. All these works consider how humans are restrained by their inherent and limited abilities and it requires a metaphysical transcendence to progress further, something which may only be achieved by an external influence.

Stapledon had no knowledge or awareness of science fiction, even though he was friends with S. Fowler Wright, and was surprised when he discovered how he and his books were held in such high regard by sf fans. At the time it was published L.P. Hartley believed it was the most "ambitious" novel he had ever read, calling it at times "lofty and impassioned … almost forbidding." Brian W. Aldiss later called it "the most wonderful novel I have ever read" whilst Arthur C. Clarke called it "probably the most powerful work of imagination ever written".

Out of the Silent Planet   C.S. Lewis
London: The Bodley Head, 1938

This highly regarded novel is the first in what became called the Space Trilogy, along with *Perelandra* (1943) and *That Hideous Strength* (1945), but it stands better on its own. It is an allegorical religious fantasy with science fiction concepts and was inspired to some degree by David Lindsay's *A Voyage to Arcturus*, though Lewis's allegorical images are clearer.

Elwin Ransom, a philologist, is on a walking holiday in northern England when he is drugged and abducted by Dick Devine, whom Ransome

had known long before at school, and his accomplice Dr. Weston, a boor-
ish physicist, full of self-importance. When he recovers Ransom discovers
he is in a spaceship bound for Malacandra, which he later learns is the
native name for Mars. In their parlance Earth is Thulcandra and Venus is
Perelandra.

The spaceship is powered by "solar radiation" and although Lewis later
said this was "pure mumbo-jumbo" he was, in fact, ahead of his time in
imagining the solar wind as a power source.

Ransom overhears that he is to be a sacrifice for the Malacandrans. The
name Ransom takes on its allegorical meaning, since Jesus was the ransom
sacrifice to restore humanity to God's grace. Although Ransom does not
know this at the time, it is evident that Ransom is a payment for Devine
and Weston's plans. Devine is keen to mine the gold which is plentiful on
the planet, whilst Weston wants to develop Malacandra for human habita-
tion if and when Earth becomes uninhabitable.

When they arrive on the planet, Ransom encounters two of the *séroni*,
a tall, humanoid species which he describes as "spooks on stilts". They
are the intellectuals of the planet, but he believes it is to them he is to be
sacrificed. Ransom escapes. He travels across the landscape marvelling at
the beauty of the planet and such oddities as the lakes and rivers being
warm, before encountering other life-forms. He discovers there are two
other sentient species, the *hrossa*, who are the most primitive but whom
Ransom likes and from whom he learns the language, and the *pfifltriggi*,
who are the workers and artists. Above all of these are the *eldila*, an angelic,
spirit-form, who are masters of the planet, ruled by the arch-*eldil*, Oyarsa.
Ransom learns that each of the inner planets have their *eldil*, but Earth's
archangel has fallen whereas Malacandra and Perelandra have remained
Edenic. That is why Earth is the "silent planet".

Ransom's journey across the planet helps him understand the spiritual
significance of Malacandra. He discovers that Oyarsa had summoned him
to learn more about Thulcandra, and about the evil in human hearts.
Weston and Devine are captured and banished from Malacandra. Ransom

is given the choice to stay or go and he decides to return to Earth rather than pollute Malacandra. Oyarsa provides their spaceship with sufficient supplies to last ninety days and they only just make it. It is then that Ransom dictates his story to Lewis himself, who appears in the book's final chapter.

Although Lewis's Mars is nothing like the real place, it feels very real within the story and Lewis does a remarkable job at creating individual races in their environment. Its religious element is not out of keeping within a science-fiction setting. It is a true landmark of the genre.

It also sets the scene for the next two books, *Perelandra*, set on Venus, which is in the form of a Garden of Eden and must be protected, and *That Hideous Strength*, set on Earth after the Second World War, which highlights the evils arising from scientific research.

Clive Staples Lewis (1898–1963) is best known for his children's series about Narnia which began with *The Lion, the Witch and the Wardrobe* in 1950, but his Space Trilogy, and especially *Out of the Silent Planet*, is arguably a Narnia for adults. Lewis was always experimenting with fantasy right from his first book *Dymer* (1926) under the alias Clive Hamilton, through to almost his last *Till We Have Faces* (1956). He had started another work in the Ransom series, which is hinted at at the end of *Out of the Silent Planet*, involving time travel, but it remained unfinished and was published posthumously in the collection *The Dark Tower* (1977). Lewis was a member of the Inklings group at Oxford along with J.R.R. Tolkien and Charles Williams.

Sinister Barrier Eric Frank Russell

Unknown, March 1939; Kingswood, Surrey: The Worlds Work, 1943

If you walk down Marchmont Street in London towards Russell Square and look to your right you will see on the wall a blue plaque to Charles Fort (1874–1932) the founder of Forteanism, defined as "the study of anomalous phenomena". Fort was an American journalist who travelled extensively, and spent many hours in libraries reading newspapers and magazines, building folders full of reports of strange events. This took form as *The Book of the Damned*, published in 1919, followed by *New Lands* (1923), *Lo!* (1931) and *Wild Talents* (1932). All four books collect unexplained phenomena, grouped by category and with occasional commentary. Fort did much of his research at the British Museum in London, where he lived from 1921 to 1928, hence the plaque.

Fort let readers make up their own minds about the weird facts he presented, but amongst the few deductions he made was that "we are property". He suggested that perhaps we are owned by another race of beings which may occupy the upper atmosphere or the ocean depths. His work reached a broader and rather specific readership after his death when *Lo!* Was serialized in *Astounding Stories* in 1934. There had already been interest in his work amongst science-fiction writers, notably Edmond Hamilton, but his leading advocate came with the British writer Eric Frank Russell (1905–1978).

Russell had sold several stories to *Astounding*, starting in 1937, most of which were imitative of Stanley G. Weinbaum, featuring humorous and bizarre aliens in exotic locales. But then he gathered together his thoughts about Fort's theories and submitted a manuscript to the new editor of *Astounding*, John W. Campbell, Jr. It was called "Forbidden Acres" but after Campbell suggested some revisions, Russell rewrote it as *Sinister Barrier*. Although accepted for *Astounding*, Campbell was planning a new magazine of fantasy and horror, *Unknown*, and decided that the novel should lead off the first issue. Russell's core idea was that Earth is co-occupied by a race of beings visible only in the far infrared and which feed upon human emotions, especially fear and rage. These aliens are large blue spheres, not unlike ball lightning.

The story is set in the year 2015 in a rather futuristic world with video-phones and gyrocars. It follows a police investigation, led by Special Officer Bill Graham. Russell had read enough American pulp magazines to develop a passable American style which endeared him to US readers. At the outset there are a number of mysterious deaths amongst scientists, put down to heart failure, but when Graham encounters the suicide of a scientist he knew, he becomes suspicious. He discovers there have been some eighteen such deaths worldwide, and all in strange circumstances. As he seeks to contact other scientists who were part of a network researching into optics he is thwarted by yet more deaths before he can reach them, but at last he tracks down Professor Beach, who had invented a new photographic emulsion that can capture the beings on film, and he tells the full story.

It seems that these creatures, which have been called Vitons, treat humans like cattle. They feed upon their fears and anxieties. Indeed, the Vitons aggravate situations, through their mental control, so that conflicts arise upon which they can feast. But the Vitons don't want humans to know this, so they have been killing the scientists before the full facts can be revealed. Both Beach and Graham are now in great danger, as the Vitons can read their thoughts. Graham has to keep imagining pleasant images so as not to attract the Vitons. His investigation has been elevated to national importance and he reports to his senior in the Intelligence Service. It is agreed that the whole world must know about the Vitons even though it is clear the Vitons will try to stop this. However, there are far more humans than Vitons, so it is hoped the Vitons cannot react against everyone at once.

The Vitons, though, stir up anxieties across the world in danger spots and before long a new world war has eruption with Asian forces in China and India, against Europe and the Americas. Graham and the Intelligence Service now battles against time to find how to defeat the Vitons.

The novel proved very popular in *Unknown* and contributed to the success of the magazine which, until stopped by wartime paper rationing, was the leading fantasy magazine in the United States. It was also circulated in Britain so it would have been possible to read the story at that time, but it did not appear in book form in Britain until 1943 in a hardback edition with all the wartime restrictions. It established Russell's reputation as Britain's leading writer of genre science fiction and as an advocate of Forteanism. He contributed several articles about Fortean phenomena to *Unknown* and later compiled *Great World Mysteries* (1957). He returned to the Fortean theme in *Dreadful Sanctuary* (serial 1948) alongside a wealth of other science fiction. He was the first British writer to win the American Hugo Award for his short story "Allamagoosa" (1955), a typically British yarn about bureaucratic chaos.

PREPARING FOR WAR

I T SEEMS WE ARE NEVER FAR FROM H.G. WELLS. THE PHRASE "the war to end all wars", relating to the Great War, came from Wells, though he originally said "the war that will end war", which became the title of a book published at the end of 1914. The phrase caught on and mutated to "the war to end all wars" by 1918 and perhaps at the time many believed it.

As we have seen, though, there were many who did not believe it. *The People of the Ruins* and *Theodore Savage* showed how writers feared a future war with powerful and devastating new weapons, especially atomic bombs. This fear which grew in the 1920s was even more tangible in the 1930s, especially with the emergence of the Nazi Party in Germany and the appointment of Adolf Hitler as Chancellor in 1933. In *Prelude in Prague* (1935), S. Fowler Wright predicted a War in 1938— in fact his original draft had proposed 1939. Wright had been commissioned by the *Daily Mail*, the same newspaper that had worked with William Le Queux on *The Invasion of 1910* in 1906, and it was seeking to emulate the same sensation. Wright went to Germany in January 1935 to study their armaments preparation and began work on his serial as soon as he returned in early February. The *Daily Mail* ran it under the title "1938". Wright predicted one of the trigger moments of the next war being Germany's annexation of the Sudatenland and the occupation of Czechoslovakia. Wright depicts a series of atrocities and the use of new weapons, including chemical warfare. The book ends with a German ultimatum to Britain, and Wright continued the story, with its visions of chemical and biological warfare in *Four Days War* (1936) and *Megiddo's Ridge* (1937).

It is well known that the British government believed they could reach a deal with Hitler and continued their policy of appeasement opposed stolidly by Winston Churchill, who was denigrated as a warmonger. But plenty of writers also saw the potential horrors of a war with Germany, not least Katharine Burdekin, writing as Murray Constantine, with *Swastika Night* (see below). She took the vision forward seven hundred years to a Nazi-controlled totalitarian Europe where Hitler is worshipped as a god. Likewise, in *The Strange Invaders* we find a future Russia returned to a feudal society after a war but where Karl Marx, Lenin and Stalin are worshipped as a holy trinity.

In *Lost Horizon*, James Hilton accepted the inevitability of war and looked to a hidden society that would guard the treasures of the world awaiting the end of conflict and the re-emergence of civilization.

A breath of fresh air came with Susan Ertz's *Woman Alive* where the sole surviving woman of a chemical war finds that her existence gives her the power to stop war. As a counterpoint is Herbert Best's bleak *The Twenty-Fifth Hour* where a war wipes out almost everyone and the survivors try to establish a new world.

Evidently in the minds of many, there would still be plenty of wars to end all wars.

Lost Horizon   James Hilton

London: Macmillan & Co., 1933

Lost Horizon is one of my favourite novels and favourite films—the 1937 version, that is, directed by Frank Capra; we'll draw a veil over the 1973 remake. The chances are that everybody knows one fact about this book even if they've never read it or seen the film, and that is the name of the lamasery buried deep in the mountains between Tibet and China, the magical Shangri-La.

The story begins with a group of men reminiscing at their Club and by chance the name of "Glory" Conway comes up. Everyone remembered him from either university, or as a hero in the Great War, or his achievements in the consular service, but no one had seen him recently. Travelling to his hotel, Rutherford admits to the narrator that he had encountered Conway in the Far East. Conway seemed to have lost his memory but it returned following an incident when Conway was playing a Chopin piano piece and a colleague claimed he knew everything by Chopin and that wasn't amongst them. Conway revealed that he'd learned it from a pupil of Chopin's—even though Chopin had died over eighty years before. Conway revealed the tale of his experiences to Rutherford who now unburdens himself to the narrator. His record of Conway's account forms the bulk of *Lost Horizon*.

Conway and three others are the last white occupants of Baskul in Northern India to be evacuated during a revolution. The others are Mallinson, a civil servant, Henry Barnard, an American, and a missionary Roberta Brinklow. Mallinson does not recognize the pilot and the plane is heading over unexplored mountains on the China-Tibet border. The plane is forced to land in poor weather, and the pilot dies, but soon the four travellers are met by a party of porters with their master, Chang. He leads them through difficult terrain and a narrow pass to the Valley of the Blue Moon and the lamasery of Shangri-La.

Despite the hostility and cold of the surrounding mountains the valley, which is almost a mile deep, has its own microclimate and is warm enough to grow a diversity of crops. The lamasery is well equipped not only with beautiful baths, bedrooms and dining facilities but a well stocked library all of which puzzle the visitors. They are astonished that there is even a piano which had to be brought in through the narrow pass. The piano is played by a seemingly young girl, Lo-Tsen.

Mallinson is anxious to return home, but the others are content to stay until the next delivery of goods by porters which may not be for two months. It is discovered that Barnard is travelling under false pretences and that he is really a crook called Bryant, which is why he is happy to stay, whilst Miss Brinklow wants to work as a missionary with the locals. Chang is happy to show them around the lamasery and valley, but is cautious how much he reveals about Shangri-La. Conway has realized, though, that their arrival there was no accident.

After they have been there for almost two weeks Conway is summoned by the High Lama from whom he learns the history of Shangri-La. In 1734 a Capuchin monk called Perrault, then aged 53, and the last survivor of a group of four who had set off fifteen years earlier seeking any outlying remnants of the Nestorian faith in Asia, had stumbled into the valley near to death. He survived and grew in health. Perrault became venerated by the locals because of his advancing age and he set about building the lamasery on the site of a decaying monastery. Over time he even developed telepathic skills. An Austrian, Henschell, arrived and helped with the lamasery, taking advantage of a deposit of gold in the valley to establish a trade route to the outer world. Conway sees a painting of Henschell made just before his death when he was an old man, yet the painting shows him in the prime of youth. Apparently the atmosphere of the Valley is conducive to longevity. Conway suddenly realizes that the High Lama is Father Perrault, now approaching 250 years of age.

Perrault had brought Conway to Shangri-La to continue his work as he was sure he would soon die. He saw Shangri-La as a haven against the wars and revolutions of the outside world, and that at some future time, if mankind has survived the Dark Age almost certain to descend upon civilization, the learning and heritage kept safe in Shangri-La, would help restore the World. It takes a while for Conway to take all this in but Chang, now prepared to tell him more, introduces him to other leading individuals in Shangri-La, including the erstwhile pupil of Chopin.

But Mallinson is still determined to leave and has convinced Lo-Tsen to accompany him. Following a second meeting with Perrault, Conway starts to believe he would take on his new role, but he also feels a duty of care to Mallinson and the girl. Despite misgivings, he accompanies them as they leave. He has been warned that once they leave the atmosphere of the Valley their body will age. Mallinson does not believe that Lo-Tsen is very old.

Conway's story ends at the point that he leaves and when the narrator meets up again with Rutherford in India he enquires what more he has learned. It seems the fate of Mallinson was unknown but Conway had been brought to a mission hospital by a very old woman. Conway was determined to return to Shangri-La but whether he found it remains a mystery.

Lost Horizon was a bestseller for many years, helped by being reprinted as the first mass-market paperback in the United States by Pocket Books in June 1939. Since this was just before the outbreak of the Second World War, Perrault's vision of a future catastrophe and Dark Age was all the more real.

James Hilton (1900–1954) was born in Lancashire but settled in the United States in 1938 and became involved in the film industry. Aside from *Lost Horizon* he is best known for *Goodbye, Mr. Chips* (1934) about the eponymous and much venerated school-teacher who, like Perrault, lives to a great age and becomes something of an anachronism. Alas Hilton was not able to emulate either Mr. Chips or Perrault. He died of liver cancer when only fifty-four.

The Peacemaker   C.S. Forester

London: William Heinemann, 1934

If there was ever an understated weapon of mass destruction it is the one suggested in *The Peacemaker*. It may seem strange to imagine that the famous author of the bestselling Hornblower series or *The African Queen* could write a science-fiction novel, let alone such a mild, almost inoffensive one. *The Peacemaker* is a sleeper. For the first half of the novel little happens and then it steadily builds but it is not until the final two chapters that it explodes.

The book is about shy, hen-pecked Dr. Edward Pethwick, a teacher of mathematics and physics at a public school, not unlike Dulwich College which Forester had attended. Through an understanding of a complicated mathematical puzzle, Pethwick has come up with a device that cancels anything magnetic that falls within its beam. He realizes the machine works when a class at school is unable to do any experiments with a bar magnet and compass.

Pethwick hopes he can use his device for world peace, because many machines operate using electro-magnets and he believes, used properly, his device would stop bombing raids and military machinery. Though married, Pethwick has fallen in love with Dorothy, the headmaster's daughter, and she loves him until he discusses his device with her when she is horrified at its potential.

So Pethwick goes it alone. He uses what little money he has to rent an office in central London where he installs his device and tests it on the local roads. All vehicles that come within the beam cease to operate, causing traffic chaos. The vehicles need towing away, even after the beam is switched off. Pethwick had informed *The Times* that he would conduct this experiment, but they ignored his letter. He wrote to them again and now *The Times* posts his communications, all signed "The Peacemaker", where he sets out his hopes for world peace.

He discovers, though, that his experiments, which he repeats daily on different roads, turn the public against him. It becomes worse when we reach the climax and Pethwick uses his machine on a power station and the railways. In one accident several children and a woman are killed. Pethwick is distraught and the public become a mob. One man who had helped Pethwick buy a car had guessed he must be the Peacemaker and a mob descends upon his house. Although Dorothy returns to save him, she is too late.

The Peacemaker is what we would now call a techno-thriller with only a minor science-fiction element, but it's barely a thriller, until the last few chapters. It's a character study of a man hoping he could bring peace to the world only to realize he had caused death and destruction. A modern-day writer would use this device in the hands of terrorists to wreck the world, but Forester is more subtle than that. He demonstrates very calmly and simply that any invention that might be used for good, can also be used for ill, and mankind always suffers.

C.S. Forester was the pseudonym of Cecil Lewis Troughton Smith (1899–1966). He had yet to have the success that came with *The African Queen* (1935) and the Hornblower series which began in 1937, and though most reviews regarded *The Peacemaker* as rather slight compared to earlier novels they recognized a mood of hopelessness that individuals have against authority. Forester did write further science-fiction stories including a future Utopian high-tech Britain in "Maturity and Modernity" (1944) and the alternate history novella "If Hitler Had Invaded England" (1960). Science-fiction writers also enjoyed the Hornblower series and it has been seen as an influence on several later space-faring series such as the Rim World books by A. Bertram Chandler and a model for Captain Picard in *Star Trek: The Next Generation*.

The Strange Invaders   Alun Llewellyn

London: George Bell & Sons, 1934

This is another post-catastrophe novel, but with a difference. It takes place in a future Russia struggling to cling to its old beliefs, even though most of the surviving feudal society no longer understands them.

We do not know when this takes place but it's far enough for most surviving books to be rotting, for everywhere to be in a state of ruin, for a new Ice Age to be returning, and for giant lizards to have evolved in the hotter south and to be heading north.

The society, which exists in a city some way south of Moscow (which is now buried under ice) but north of the Caucasus, is ruled by a Council of Fathers who ensure citizens adhere to the Faith. The details of the Faith are not clear except that it has a holy trinity—Marx, who introduced the doctrine, Lenin who first made the doctrine work, and Stalin who used it for power. These three have become something like saints, but little is known about them by the general populace. The Fathers keep much of their knowledge, drawn from any records that survive, secret and preach that one must worship the unknown in order to ensure faith. The Council is supported by the Swords, an army led by Karasoin, but he has a mind of his own, seeking total power, and shows little support for the Faith.

One of the sub-plots that drives the narrative is the rivalry between Karasoin and Adun Bayatan, a herdsman, both of whom love Erya, the daughter of a blacksmith. Karasoin is powerful and could take Erya by force, but she also has a mind of her own and does not want to be owned by any one man. Adun's brother, Ivan, is a trainee in the Council of Fathers and provides Adun with what would otherwise be confidential information.

Adun serves as a watchman looking for the arrival of the next caravan with supplies, but it is long overdue. A troop of Tartars arrive with a sole survivor from the caravan but he has lost his wits from whatever happened.

The Chief of Fathers believes the Tartars destroyed the caravan to steal the supplies and Karasoin prepares for an invasion from the main army of Tartars, even destroying a bridge to a nearby river island, despite the Chief of Father's wish that the bridge be saved.

When the Tartar army arrives it is obviously fleeing from something rather than invading. Some Tartars are brought into the city but when it is realized the lizards are also approaching, the gates are shut. Most of the Tartars flee but many are killed by the Swords and the lizards.

The Chief of Fathers refuses to believe the lizards are real stating that they are a vision sent by the gods as a warning to those not adhering to the Faith. He argues that people have been corrupted by the Tartars and he decrees that all those within the city walls should be slaughtered, a needless genocide that Ivan can no longer reconcile with his beliefs.

Even when the lizards storm the city walls the Chief of Fathers refuses to believe leading to a confrontation with Karasoin in which the Chief is killed. Karasoin orders everyone to leave the city and make for the river island, as they believe the lizards cannot cross water. In the evacuation Karasoin attacks Adun and leaves him for dead.

Adun recovers and manages to elude the lizards, reach the island and kill Karasoin, and though he and Erya escape, it is a constant battle to elude the lizards and stay alive, especially as winter descends. With the cold the lizards become torpid and the survivors realize they might just survive another winter back in the city. Thereafter the future is unknown.

At the end of the novel Adun's brother Ivan reflects upon the nature of mankind which has the power to create and destroy, to love and to hate, and wonders whether the race of Man will survive or be supplanted by another. Although set in Russia, which can allow us readers to distance ourselves, Llewellyn makes it clear his message is as relevant to Britain where the rise of fascism was bringing a similar threat.

Alun Llewellyn (1903–1987) was a barrister known for his political satires, including a collection of sharp tales set in different imaginary countries, *Confound their Politics* (1934), and *Jubilee John* (1939), an amusing exploration of how London night-life is experienced by an elderly Welshman. Llewellyn visited the Soviet Union to observe communism first-hand but was not impressed. He was attached to the League of Nations prior to the Second World War and worked for British Intelligence during the War. He was a strong advocate of the Commonwealth and the development of African nations.

Brian Aldiss discovered this book in his early teens and claimed it was the one book that converted him to science fiction. In 1977 he resurrected it in New English Library's SF Master Series.

Land Under England   James O'Neill

London: Victor Gollancz, 1935

Subterranean worlds have been a key part of science fiction for centuries, certainly as far back as *Mundus subterraneus* (1665) by Athanasius Kircher, and the Danish writer, Ludvig Holberg's *Nicoli Klimii iter subterraneum* (1741). The idea of a Hollow Earth, proposed by the American John Cleves Symmes in 1818 was lampooned by the pseudonymous Adam Seaborn in *Symzonia* (1820). The best known subterranean adventure is Jules Verne's *Voyage au centre de la terre* (1863), with its dinosaurs and vast central sea, whilst Lord Bulwer Lytton's *The Coming Race* (1871) reveals a race of superior humans with telepathic powers living in a utopian world underground.

O'Neill may have borrowed from both Verne and Lytton, along with a dose of the ancient Roman story of Aeneas. In Book 6 of Virgil's *Aeniad*, Aeneas searches for his father in the underworld where his soul survives.

O'Neill's novel is also about a son's search for his father. Our hero is Anthony Julian—the Roman names are evident from the start. His father is obsessed with ancient Rome, and believes a family legend that somewhere near their home, close by Hadrian's Wall, is an entrance to an underworld where Romans escaped and survived. After the War, the father becomes even more obsessed, neglecting his family and living by an ancient pond which in summers of extreme drought runs dry. When the father disappears young Anthony becomes obsessed to find him.

He eventually finds the entrance by accident, which propels him down a shaft and starts him on a long journey. Anthony has to survive a fungus forest, giant spiders, slugs, toads and serpents plus a perilous river journey until he finds himself by a vast central sea where a Roman galley is moored.

This world is not what Anthony expected. He had hoped for a sympathetic society, but he finds a highly regimented one, run by an elite who control all minions by telepathy. Minds are rewired by thought control to produce automata who carry out set tasks. The Master of Knowledge, who seeks to control Anthony, states the rigid belief that the populace is happy having been "absorbed" into a society where everyone knows their place. Anthony is told that his Father has been "absorbed" because he was happy to become one amongst the Romans.

Although the Master advises Anthony not to look for his father he still wishes to do so and is sufficiently strong-willed that the Master finds it hard to control him. Allowed to explore, Anthony is horrified by his first encounter at a school, where he discovers that children are reprogrammed to eradicate their childhood wonder and delight and become mindless automata.

Anthony is twice left to wander, always hoping he will find his father, and twice he returns. Eventually the Master agrees to let him see the man who was once his father, provided he would return home and not come back. Anthony is still of the belief that he would return to rescue his father, but the final anguish in his search for the man, and his endeavour to return home, his mind increasingly delirious, provides the book with a potent climax.

A contemporary reviewer called it "One of the most powerful novels of recent years." The celebrated Irish writer George Russell ("Æ"), who provided an introduction to the book, stated that O'Neill had "elevated the 'thriller' into literature."

One can read into O'Neill's description of the ruthless totalitarian Roman state an interpretation of both Stalinist Russia and Hitler's Nazism, as well as a potential Fascist Britain. O'Neill (1884–1953) had lived through the Easter Rising, at which time he was a schools' inspector. With the creation of the Irish Free State he became Secretary of the Department of Education. He followed *Land Under England* with *Day of Wrath* (1936), a future-war novel set in 1952 when civilization is wrecked with the introduction of an advanced aircraft.

Curiously, when *Land Under England* was reprinted in 1987 in Penguin Books' Classic Science Fiction series one reviewer—a lecturer in English literature—commented that the book is "hardly a classic and is certainly not a work of science fiction in any generally accepted sense of the term." Such is how the literary establishment choose to delete from the realms of science fiction anything that is good.

Woman Alive   Susan Ertz
London: Hodder & Stoughton, 1935

The narrator, Dr. Selwyn, meets a medium, who uses the time theory of J.W. Dunne to project an individual's consciousness into the future, to inhabit their own body at that time. Selwyn agrees to an experiment and asks for his consciousness to be projected fifty years to April 1985, thereby inhabiting his eighty-eight year-old body.

The transition happens immediately and there is instant awareness, because the body in which the thirty-eight year-old consciousness resides is aware of its own world and so the future world does not need explaining. Naturally the reader still needs to understand, so the future Dr. Selwyn reflects on the horrific circumstances of 1985.

The future world has advanced scientifically mostly for the benefit of civilization—wonderful new buildings (mostly of glass), great transport systems, universal access to a new power derived from the atmosphere, ample food. There were some aspects similar to *Brave New World*—people could select the sex of their children, and usually had a boy first, and there is a drink called Euthanol which works like *soma* and makes you calm and happy.

However, human greed and intolerance has not changed. There had been a War in 1950 which reshaped Europe and America. There was a United States of Europe (USE), of which Great Britain was not a part, as Britain and its Empire had joined the United States to form the League of English-Speaking Peoples.

A division within the USE led to war between the factions (the sides are not identified). The aggressors had developed a gas, celadon, which poisoned as well as burned. Too late it was discovered that celadon was lethal to all females and the female population was soon declining by the million. Death cars patrol the streets collecting bodies for burial at sea.

When Dr. Selwyn's consciousness awakens in 1985 his first vision is of a young child that collapses in the street and dies. Selwyn has lost his wife and daughter, but he goes to meet his daughter's fiancé, Alan, a pilot (cheap air travel is available to all) who has been searching for any female survivors. Alas, all women have succumbed to the gas.

Even the Queen of England (Henrietta) has died and the monarchy is abolished. Mankind struggles to adjust to the bleak future. Some throw themselves into work, trying to rebuild a world even though it will last but a generation. The fears are for the children, knowing they will be growing up in a world with no future.

Selwyn is contacted by a boy who tells him that his Aunt Stella won't wake up, but he asserts she is not dead. When Selwyn visits her, he discovers she is still alive but under the influence of Euthanol. A few hours later she awakes. She is very healthy. She reveals that she acted as a guinea-pig in an experiment with a young scientist who claimed he had created a process which gave immunity to all known diseases and so it proved. Alas, he was killed in the recent war so the secret of his process was lost. Before Stella wakes, Selwyn discovers a note she wrote where she declaimed all men.

"Men! Without them how happy we could have been," and her note ends by cursing all men.

Selwyn fears for the girl's safety and visits the Prime Minister, Mr. Hardy, who immediately visits her. He discovers that Stella is strong willed with firm convictions. She despises all men for having created this problem because of their passion to fight, and Hardy does not help matters by reminding her that men will soon be fighting over her. It had been her desire to stay at home but she is convinced by Alan, that she should heed Hardy and be protected by guards in the royal palace. She refuses to be treated as a Queen but realizes that, as the only woman in the world, her life is no longer hers to lead.

Nevertheless, her willpower, her steadfast logic and her hatred of warfare, dictates progress. One nation (unnamed) claims it has chosen a mate for her and if he is not selected they will declare war on Britain. Hardy had planned to retaliate but Stella admonishes him, summons that country's ambassador, and by blistering logic and diplomacy wins his support. There is later an attempt to kidnap her but thanks to the heroism of Hardy, she survives. She eventually marries and we are left with the hope that the world will slowly be repopulated, this time a world of peace.

Ertz poses the conundrum that because Selwyn has experienced this future, his younger self could do something about it, and we are left to ponder that paradox.

Susan Ertz (1887–1985) was born in England of American parents (her father was of German descent). Though she occasionally visited America, much of her childhood and adult life was spent in England. She married a Royal Air Force officer, Major Ronald McCrindle in 1932. He had been a flying ace during the War and could well be the original for Alan. She lived her final years in Kent. She wrote over twenty novels, starting with *Madam Claire* in 1922, but her fame came with *Nina* (1924), about a woman in the grip of a faithless husband. All her books feature strong women in difficult circumstances, none more so than *Woman Alive*, a profound and provocative work. The original printing of this book included several

art-deco illustrations by Bip Pares of which the most striking is the memorial to mankind.

Swastika Night   Murray Constantine (Katharine Burdekin)
London: Victor Gollancz, 1937

With remarkable prescience Burdekin followed the development of the
power of Adolf Hitler's Nazi regime to predict what might happen if
Germany was victorious in a future war.

This novel takes us 720 years into a future world locked in stalemate
between two powers, Germany and Japan. Japan rules Asia, the Americas
and Australia, and Germany rules the rest. In this German empire, history has been rewritten. Hitler is worshipped as a god. Jews have been
exterminated. Christians are filthy outcasts and all women are treated as
sub-human, kept in concentration camps, their heads shaved, serving only
for breeding.

The Hitler myth was created a century or so after his death. To sustain
it, all pre-Hitler books and records were destroyed. By the time of the
twenty-seventh century all Germans believe this revisionist history and
worship a creed of violence. Sympathy is a weakness.

In the first chapter we witness this violence when a Knight of the
Empire, Hermann, encounters a German boy attempting to rape an
underage Christian girl. He attacks the German for although he has no
sympathy for the girl, any contact by a German with an underage female
is perverted. His savagery is stopped by his English friend, Alfred.

That Hermann and Alfred are friends is surprising because they hardly
agree on anything. Alfred is suspicious about the cult of Hitler. Britain
was the last country to be conquered by Germany and although all
records have been destroyed, Alfred was close to memories passed on
from recent generations that Britain had once been a great country, with
its own Empire.

When Alfred insists Hermann take the injured boy to hospital they are met by the high-born Knight, Friedrich von Hess who takes an interest in Alfred, especially when he learns he can fly an aeroplane. Flying is restricted to senior officials, but von Hess orders Alfred to fly him to Munich and back. The Germans have a grudging respect for the English and von Hess asks Alfred to visit him the next day.

Von Hess reveals the shocking truth about the Hitler cult. He is a descendent of Hitler's Deputy, Rudolph von Hess and, unknown to others, has kept a photograph and compiled a book about the pre-Hitler world. Von Hess is the last surviving member of his family and with no heir, wishes to pass the documents to Alfred, to keep alive the true history.

The central part of the book involves long, philosophical discussions between von Hess and Alfred about how the Hitler cult grew, the nature of religion, especially Christian and Jewish faiths, and the role of women. Under the Nazi regime any contact with women other than for breeding is anathema. It is believed that women have no souls or virtue, and that the strength of men is passed on solely by the male seed. Alfred had also been indoctrinated with these views but has always had doubts. He has been on a Holy Tour of Germany and is returning to England. He takes the book and photograph with him, hiding them in an ancient British burial mound on Salisbury Plain—the Nazis have a fear of Stonehenge.

Once in Britain Alfred realizes the enormity of his task. He confides in his sons, but all realize that change can only happen slowly and by example, not by violence. Alfred's woman, Ethel, has given birth to a baby girl and she is mortified for having let Alfred down, but Alfred wants to hold the baby and dream about how that child might grow. He also visits a shunned Christian community to learn their history and knowledge.

It is but a small start and by the end of the book you are left wondering what, if anything, can be achieved, but you are also reminded of how Jesus's followers changed the world, and maybe that could happen again.

It was unusual at that time for a novel to speculate on the future of another country and name individuals alive at the time of publication. I do not know what the German reaction was to the book, but at least one English review commented that it was uncomfortable and nightmarish because it was so "infernally probable."

Katherine Cade (1896–1963) hoped to study at Oxford but her parents denied this and instead at eighteen she married Olympic rower Beaufort Burdekin who had recently been invalided home from France. They had two children and in 1920 they moved to Australia. The marriage was unhappy and she turned to writing. They divorced that same year and she returned to England. She began to use sf concepts in *The Burning Ring* (1927) where an individual acquires magical powers that allow him to move in time. *The Rebel Passion* (1929), which she regarded as her first major novel, has a twelfth-century monk witness the twenty-first century with a eugenically controlled population and where women are equal.

Her views became increasingly political and she created the Murray Constantine persona in 1934 to hide her identity. In *Proud Man* (1934) she has an androgynous mental time traveller interrogate an individual in the past to explore gender roles. The nature of this book, exploring the transformation of *homo sapiens*, caused some to speculate that Murray Constantine might be Olaf Stapledon! Certainly the author was considered to be male. Burdekin kept this identity secret for the rest of her life and it wasn't uncovered until the 1980s. A companion volume to *Swastika Night*, which had not been published, at last saw print in 1990 as *The End of This Day's Business*.

The Hopkins Manuscript   R.C. Sherriff

Good Housekeeping (UK), August 1938–April 1939; London: Victor Gollancz, 1939. Reprinted as *The Cataclysm*, London: Pan Books, 1958

This disaster novel is, at different times, absurd, naïve, comical—perhaps the cosiest of all "cosy catastrophes"—but also powerful, frightening and despairing. Sherriff brings this off by the sheer simplicity of his narration, though therein lies the first absurdity.

A foreword by the Imperial Research Press of Addis Ababa, written in the thirtieth century, tells us that this manuscript, written by Edgar Hopkins, is all that survives to describe in detail the destruction of western civilization when the moon fell out of its orbit and struck the Earth in March 1946. The manuscript had been discovered in a "small vacuum flask" buried under the ruins of a house. Britain had been so desolate that the civilization rebuilt by the Arabs had not bothered to visit the islands, so it is only now that the facts are being discovered. Alas, according to this foreword, the manuscript is so full of personal detail that it provides little historical data on British or European history.

Hopkins tells us he is writing by the light of a piece of string soaked in bacon fat. When he has finished his account he will seal it in his thermos flask, but how he acquired sufficient paper or ink we do not know and, more significantly, how he managed to fit over 300 pages of manuscript into a vacuum flask stretches credulity.

Considering the conditions under which Hopkins is writing, it is surprising that he spends so long talking about the minutiae of life—we learn more about poultry contests than the impending disaster in the first half of the novel. Hopkins is an amateur astronomer and he learns from his local society that the moon has shifted from its orbit and is slowly spiralling towards Earth. It will strike in seven months. The society members are sworn to secrecy as, presumably, are all astronomers and politicians worldwide because the public know nothing about this for four months. It is hard to imagine how anyone could keep this secret, especially once the moon is twice its apparent size in the sky. What's more, the terrifying tidal effects and earthquakes that a closing moon would have on the Earth are ignored until the last few weeks before the moon strikes. Evidently Sherriff was not concerned about scientific accuracy but about how humans behave in such cataclysmic circumstances.

And it is here that the book succeeds. In that first half Sherriff contrasts the attitudes of people in the countryside, where Hopkins lives in a small village, and those in London. Initially few people understand what is happening, and many don't believe it, suspecting a hoax. Even when it becomes obvious, the locals are determined to play a final cricket match. In London (and presumably elsewhere—Hopkins doesn't bother much with a radio) there is greater panic and looting, but again only when the disaster is imminent. The government has been building underground shelters across the country, though most people believe these are for an impending war.

At the given hour most of the villagers retreat into their dugout, but Hopkins stays at home. Despite a night of storms, floods and changes in atmospheric pressure, he survives—even though he learns that the moon passed five hundred miles overhead. Unaccountably the moon does not break up until it lands in the Atlantic, just off the coast of Cornwall. It was this that caused the floods. You learn little about devastation elsewhere and although many houses were destroyed, and those in the dugout suffered a disaster, much of the village survived. Hopkins soon found two others and together they start to rebuild their lives.

That is not the end of the story, though. The moon had created a land bridge between Europe and America. It blocked British navigation to her Empire and Britain wanted to create a channel into the Atlantic. Once it was discovered that the debris of the moon was rich in minerals, the nations of Europe and North America wanted their share. Britain still wanted its share and its channel. As ever greed rules over common sense and before long a war breaks out between the Confederated States of Europe and Britain, a war that causes more destruction than the Moon. As Europe battles itself into oblivion a new power arises in the Middle East and it is they who become masters of the world.

All of this is told by Hopkins in his scribbled manuscript tucked into a vacuum flask. It is one man's account of life coping with two disasters. Sherriff had originally called the novel "An Ordinary Man", and, rather like Wells's narrator in *The War of the Worlds*, we witness disaster through an everyday individual. It is this that makes the story both exasperating and fascinating, even if scientifically absurd. As a science-fiction novel *The*

Hopkins Manuscript leaves much to be desired, but as a story of human resilience against adversity, it is most worthy.

Robert Cedric Sherriff (1896–1975) established his name with the powerful play *Journey's End* (1928), where we witness the horrors of the First World War through the eyes of officers in the trenches. Sherriff wrote sixteen other plays and several film scripts including *The Invisible Man* in 1933 and *The Dam Busters* in 1955.

OUR DARKEST HOURS

PAPER RATIONING WAS INTRODUCED IN BRITAIN IN FEBRUARY 1940 with strict controls over how much paper could be used for existing publications, let alone new projects. Amongst the casualties were the fledgling science-fiction magazines. *Fantasy*, published by Newnes, ceased after three issues even before the war began, its paper being saved for its companion magazine *Air Stories*, which ceased in April 1940. *Tales of Wonder*, from World's Work, survived until early 1942, ending after sixteen issues. These magazines had run a fair quota of reprints from the American pulps, but did provide a market for a few British writers amongst them John Russell Fearn, John Beynon Harris, William F. Temple and Arthur C. Clarke. Clarke's first professional sales appeared in *Tales of Wonder*, both speculative articles, "Man's Empire of Tomorrow" (Winter 1938) and "We Can Rocket to the Moon—*Now!*" (Summer 1939). Several potential careers went into hiatus until after the war, and such science fiction as was published in wartime Britain continued in much the same vein as before the War.

You might think that authors would be encouraged to write positive fiction to raise public morale but at the start of the war some novels were extremely bleak. Some were started before the war began, but the fact that publishers still issued them shows a degree of despair. The belief, resurrected from the First World War, that it would all be over by Christmas, was not so readily accepted.

An especially bleak novel was *Man Alone* by Horace Horsnell, published in February 1940. The protagonist, Johnson, suddenly discovers that he is the last person alive, at least in Britain. He knows not how or why. Animals and plants have survived. He is surprisingly accepting to begin with but before long this turns to despair and then madness. The poet Alfred Noyes also contributed to this theme with *The Last Man* in June 1940. Combatants have invented an "ethereal" ray which stops human hearts and petrifies the bodies. One man believes he is the last survivor, having been in a submarine, but our hero discovers others, including a religious community in Assisi. Initially very bleak was *The Twenty-Fifth Hour* by Herbert Best, issued in Britain in August 1940, which is discussed below.

In *Manna*, released in March 1940, John Gloag considered the effects of a new wonder food that should solve world starvation. Unfortunately it also produces a lethargy and the government is concerned that as war looms, the British might be too enervated to fight.

Other works explored the horrors of a Nazi victory. We have already seen Katharine Burdekin's vision of a future Nazi society in *Swastika Night*. *Loss of Eden* by Douglas Brown and Christopher Serpell, published in August 1940 (discussed below), sees an increasing subjugation of British society by Nazi rule. *Then We Shall Hear Singing* (1942) by Storm Jameson is an especially powerful novel of a European country, called the Protectorate, where Nazis seek to eradicate all past memories through an operation on the brain, believing this will lead to total control. But they overlook the significance of how deep in our memories is a resonance for the songs of the past. In *When Adolf Came* (1943), Martin Hawkin invoked the title of Saki's *When William Came* to show how the Nazis tried to appease the British through a more humane domination. Warwick Deeping looked back to a previous invasion of Britain in *The Man Who Went Back*, published in September 1940. His hero, an engineer, finds himself catapulted back in time to Roman Britain when it was under threat from the Saxons. He uses his engineering knowledge to help the Romans which boosts morale, a lesson which comes in handy when he returns to his equally war-torn time.

H.G. Wells, who was still producing literary visions fifty years on, took a rather sanguine view of the war in *All Aboard for Ararat*, published in October 1940. God tires of mankind and decides to have another global flood, selecting a new Noah who is rather less dedicated than the original. Wells's friend, J.D. Beresford, took the same idea literally in *A Common Enemy* (1942) where an earthquake and extreme weather sinks Germany beneath the waves enabling the survivors to build a new world. Closer to the real thing was Bernard Newman's *Secret Weapon* (1942), discussed below, with Germany defeated by deviousness.

Olaf Stapledon, whose far future visions in *Last and First Men* and *Star Maker* showed the transitory nature of humanity, holds out little hope in *Darkness and the Light* (1942). Although he follows two threads of civilization, one leading to a dystopian desolation and the other to a harmonious enlightenment, he still believes that the road to utopia is long, difficult and dangerous. Stapledon's most uplifting novel of the war years was *Sirius* (1944) about a sheepdog with enhanced intelligence. It allows Stapledon to study human society and beliefs through the eyes of a being which, whilst loyal to humans, also has its own attributes, notably the desire for hunting, which gives Stapledon the chance to comment upon human frailties.

Instead of a super-dog, John Russell Fearn created a superwoman, Violet Ray, known as the Golden Amazon, who can avenge the human race. The character proved so popular that Fearn wrote another twenty books. The first volume is discussed below.

The other two novels in C.S. Lewis's cosmic trilogy, *Perelandra* and *That Hideous Strength*, were also written during the War. *Perelandra*, which envisages Venus as a garden of Eden being fought over by good and evil, had its obvious wartime connotations. It appeared in April 1943 and was written at a time when some features of the war were at last turning in the allies' favour. *That*

Hideous Strength appeared in August 1945, after VE Day and just at the time that the atomic bombs were dropped on Hiroshima and Nagasaki. The title thus resonated with readers over the awful power of the atom and empha-sized Lewis's argument about the potential evil of scientific experimentation.

At the same time Lewis's book was issued, George Orwell's *Animal Farm* appeared, to my mind the best of all allegorical fantasies showing how easily a totalitarian regime can develop despite the will of the people. Its publication served as a frightening bridge between the Nazi threat of the previous decade and the fragility of Europe against Stalinism.

The Twenty-Fifth Hour   Herbert Best

London: Jonathan Cape, 1940

This slow and at times ponderous novel is bleak, tinged with some, but not much, hope. Best was writing at the start of the Second World War and saw the conflagration spiralling out of control. At the start of the novel, set in the late 1940s, though no date is given, we learn that Europe has been destroyed by internecine wars and all that now survive are bands of soldiers set upon by savages or the few survivors still holding property. We see one leading British soldier, Hugh Fitzharding, who has been serving in Europe, take command of a small castle and kill all its occupants except for a few servants and the mistress of the house.

Alongside this we see the United States, initially in a better state, but soon to be overcome by germ warfare developed by other American coun-tries, which is steadily wiping out the population. Two individuals, Ann, and her ailing brother Geoff, take to their boat. They sail between the islands of the Caribbean securing provisions. They witness the island population declining until eventually they settle on an island now uninhabited. Geoff takes the boat to search for other survivors without success and by the time he returns, months later, he is very weak. They believe there is no hope left in America and so sail to Europe.

Meanwhile Fitzharding is now alone and wandering through Europe in scenes reminiscent of M.P. Shiel's *The Purple Cloud*. He decides not to return to England and heads for Gibraltar. There, where the Atlantic enters the Mediterranean, he spies a boat coming ashore. Armed with his bow, in an impulsive response he kills the man who comes ashore. This turns out to be Geoff, leaving Ann alone. Fitzharding respects her and she comes to accept him and together they sail into the Mediterranean wondering if civilization survives anywhere. They finally discover that Egypt, the original cradle of civilization six thousand years before, still clings to life, and Fitzharding even meets an old friend there. It seems that once again Africa, and specifically Egypt, will see the world's rebirth.

The novel is probably longer than it needed to be, but there is a mood of desolation and hopelessness created by the long passages showing the homeless survivors struggling to find food and avoid death. Reviewers found the novel "tough" but a pertinent warning to all nations to limit hostilities and plan for the aftermath.

Oswald Herbert Best (1894–1980) was born and educated in England and served in the First World War. For the next thirteen years he was a colonial administrator in Nigeria before moving to the United States in the early 1930s where he married and settled down. It was in New York that he wrote *The Twenty-Fifth Hour* and where it was first published, though an English edition followed within weeks. Most of his books were for children. He eventually returned to England after his wife's death, dying peacefully in Devon, in a Britain that had survived the War he depicted so bleakly.

Loss of Eden   Douglas Brown & Christopher Serpell

London: Faber and Faber, 1940; retitled *If Hitler Comes*, London: British Publishers Guild, 1941

Published in August 1940, a year into the Second World War, this book was labelled "A Cautionary Tale". It was a warning against seeking a peace with Nazi Germany and a commentary upon the policy of appeasement which the British government had followed before the War, seemingly oblivious to the duplicitous nature of Hitler and his officials. The image of Neville Chamberlain returning from Munich in September 1938 waving the worthless "piece of paper" in his hand and claiming that he had negotiated peace with Hitler is seared into the memories of many and to whom this book would have meant so much.

Like many works at this time, the book is meant to be a manuscript discovered by an archaeological team in the ruins of Wellington, New Zealand. It was purportedly written by a New Zealand reporter who had been operating in Britain at the start of the Second World War. Although the start of the manuscript is missing, what remains is substantial and follows the fate of Britain after reaching a peace treaty with Nazi Germany. The authors are cautious about dates. They state that the Peace of Nuremberg which brought an "end" to hostilities between the British Empire and Germany was signed in September. Soon after they refer to the fateful day on Friday, 10 March following the treaty, and the only year during the War when 10 March was a Friday was 1944, implying the treaty was in September 1943. Since the authors had no knowledge of the progress of the war between when they wrote the book, presumably in early 1940, and September 1943, they could only refer to the constant loss of life, the suffering of home life, and the impact on the economy. The book was already in press when the Battle of Britain was at its height and before the Luftwaffe's systematic bombing of London and the south-east. Yet this escalation of the war at home would have made the plot of the novel even more significant.

The authors follow the inevitable progress of Hitler's policy towards Britain after the peace treaty, notably the rapid insinuation of British parliament by Nazi officials and advisers. Propaganda claims that all of Nazi Germany's actions are in order to protect and benefit Britain, even though this includes exiling the royal family, and ensuring there is a Nazi presence in all governing bodies. The British army had already been dispersed. There is immediate unrest and resistance in Britain which is initially dealt with by the British Fascist movement, here nicknamed the Greyshirts but effectively the same as Oswald Mosley's Blackshirts. Propaganda soon promotes the belief that the unrest had been caused by the Jewish communities. The Greyshirts progressively round up all the Jewish population along with others who have shown any resistance to Germany, and before long there are concentration camps established at various locations. This process is accelerated when one Jewish activist attempts to assassinate Hitler when he visits England.

Hitler's presence had been part of a purported protection of Britain against the United States where the President had shown concern over the obvious German occupation of Britain. It is only a matter of months from the signing of the peace treaty before the Nazi regime is installed in Britain with a puppet government.

Without having to fight the British army, Hitler's forces are greatly enhanced and he soon overruns Europe and Russia and, before the end of the book, is planning campaigns in Africa and the Far East. Warning messages are sent to the United States. At that point the reporter who is recording this finds an opportunity to escape with his wife to New Zealand where he is able to complete the document for future generations.

The reviewer in *The Sphere* claimed that the book "demands attention from every intelligent person in this country." The book's dedication must have encouraged British resolve: "To Those who will Not Let This Happen". A paperback edition was issued the following May retitled *If Hitler Comes* to further supportive reviews. Today the book is long forgotten, but it still reads very effectively as an alternate history of how Britain could so easily have capitulated to Hitler.

Both Douglas Brown (1907–1976) and Christopher Serpell (1910–1991) were journalists on major British newspapers. Brown continued to work as a foreign correspondent during the War, finding himself at one point stranded in Portugal when his ship had been bombed. Serpell worked for Naval Intelligence under Ian Fleming and, after the war, became the BBC's correspondent in Rome and Washington DC.

Secret Weapon   Bernard Newman

London: Victor Gollancz, 1941

Censorship in both the United Kingdom and the United States forbade any reference that might suggest either country developing new forms of weapon, especially the atomic bomb. There was a major incident in America when John W. Campbell, Jr. printed Cleve Cartmill's story "Deadline" in the March 1944 issue of *Astounding SF*. The Intelligence services descended on the publisher and at Cartmill's home even though Campbell, in his usual challenging way, informed the officials that the story only used references readily available elsewhere.

In *Secret Weapon*, Newman plays this game—in fact he *uses* the game. A new form of bomb has been invented by the beguiling scientist David Drummond. He is determined to keep control of his invention and not let it be misused by bungling British officials. Although he describes his super-bomb in vague detail—it certainly isn't an atomic bomb—the story focuses on how the secret of the bomb may be maintained and how propaganda and false news can mask the real events whilst promoting others, including operations that seem to have gone wrong. Newman is a past master at this. He writes himself into the novel, both as narrator and activist—he undertakes a secret mission into Germany. He also refers to incidents in his own life—his experiences as a lecturer and reporter, for example—and to his previous books. His novel *The Cavalry Went Through* (1930) had been an alternate history where the First World War had been won as a consequence of different military tactics being used before and during the Battle of Verdun. Since that book is referenced here, Newman is living in his own alternate history through both World Wars. Various contemporary figures appear, a few renamed. In both books Winston Churchill becomes Worton Spender.

The story follows Drummond's strategy. He is rapidly made a Member of Parliament and Secretary of State in order to have the authority to direct the actions relating to the use of the bomb. Part of the story deals with ensuring Drummond is protected and here Newman brings back a character from an earlier book, the French police detective Papa Pontivy. Drummond's plan is highly effective and within weeks the Germans surrender. The climactic scenes first between Drummond and an insane Hitler and then between Drummond and Mussolini must have been read with tears of joy. Japan is mentioned only at the end of the book, because their direct involvement had happened only a month before the book was published. By adding a reference, perhaps at the final proofs stage of the book, Newman recognized the growing potential of Japan.

If ever there is an exercise in wish fulfilment, this is it—though Newman denies this in the book's final paragraphs. He was convinced a super-weapon would be created and he was, of course, correct.

It is interesting to compare this book to *Loss of Eden*. There, British naivete and bigotry led to Britain being overrun by the Nazis. Here the tables are turned and British ingenuity, determination and wit (humour plays a big part) show how the Germans could be duped. Newman's ability to manipulate facts to make them even more convincing had already been demonstrated in his book *Spy* (1935) which many believed to be a true account of how a British agent infiltrated the staff of the German general Erich Ludendorff during the First World War and helped accelerate his mental collapse. Newman's explanation of military tactics in *The Cavalry Went Through* were so original and detailed that the military strategist Sir Basil Liddell Hart used the book in his training with students.

Bernard Newman (1897–1968), a grand-nephew of the writer George Eliot, lectured unceasingly during the War on behalf of the British Expeditionary Force and the Ministry of Information. He gave a radio talk on how German spies work in July 1940 and his lecture tour on Europe under Hitler during early 1942, which also helped promote his book, drew audiences of thousands. Newman toured Europe extensively during the 1930s living with gipsies in the Balkans and working in a circus in Poland. In 1938 he stumbled across installations at Peenemunde in Germany where he learned that the Germans were experimenting with a new type of rocket. This became the V1 and V2 developed by Wernher von Braun. When Newman reported this to the British Secret Service he was ignored.

The Golden Amazon   John Russell Fearn
London: World's Work, 1944

At the time his books started to appear in Britain, John Russell Fearn was already Britain's most prolific writer of science fiction. Few in Britain knew this beyond the dedicated reader of the American sf pulps, and even they couldn't have known the full picture because Fearn appeared under a host of pen names. It was under one of those pseudonyms, Thornton Ayre, that Fearn wrote a series of four stories for *Fantastic Adventures*, from 1939 to 1943, featuring the super-woman Violet Ray, known as the Golden Amazon. Violet was orphaned on Venus when the spaceship carrying her parents crashed. The child was raised on Venus where "that environment did things to me". She matures as a strong, intelligent golden-skinned avenger determined to seek retribution on the villains who had caused the crash.

Fearn had plans to continue the series but changed his mind. With the wartime restrictions and fluctuating American market, Fearn sought to develop his outlets in Britain, and began writing for the British publisher The World's Work. The first of these books was *The Intelligence Gigantic* in 1943. This had been his first published work in America, serialized in *Amazing Stories* in 1933. According to Fearn's biographer, Philip Harbottle, when it appeared in Britain, the publisher proclaimed the book "A Master Thriller Science-Fiction Novel", the first time a British book was labelled as science fiction on the cover.

Fearn reworked his idea about Violet Ray and started the novel in the midst of the Second World War. James Axton, a scientist and surgeon, is convinced that by operating on humans' glands, whilst they are still infants, they would grow far stronger and more intelligent. Axton believes that all of the world's problems have been created by men, and that if he could create a super-woman, she would take control and bring peace to the world. The Medical Research Institute, however, will not grant Axton permission to further his research.

Axton is visited by his friend and fellow surgeon, Alfred Prout, who is dubious about the ethics of Axton's plans, but is prepared to support him. But before he can proceed the area near Axton's laboratory suffers bombing during the Blitz of 1940. Searching through the ruins of adjacent houses Axton and Prout discover a baby whose parents are killed. Axton believes this is providence and, taking the baby, immediately operates on her. He achieves this by using a special ray, not unlike modern laser surgery, and the whole procedure is completed in an hour. The baby is drugged to enable her recovery. Then the bombs strike again and a direct hit on Axton's house destroys the laboratory and kills Axton. Prout, himself injured, is able to escape with the child and staggers through the night to in a nearby village. With his last action, he hands the child over to Vernon Brant, telling him that her name is Violet Ray. Brant and his wife try and discover the child's identity, without success, and eventually they adopt her.

The action moves on twenty years to 1960. Brant has become a prosperous industrialist. He has his own daughter, Beatrice, who is kind, generous and doting. Then there is Violet: rebellious, undisciplined and seemingly uncaring. Although Brant tries to control the girl it has the opposite effect and she leaves. Unknown to Brant and his family, Violet's superior strength and intelligence had allowed her to create her own laboratory and build an aircraft-cum-helicopter, the *Ultra*. She is now on a mission to destroy the government of men and establish herself as the dictator of Britain.

The old adage that absolute power corrupts absolutely is proven here. Violet has no compunction in following her course of action and seeking revenge even when it means destroying an airliner full of passengers. She deals out death and destruction until she at last meets her match in a character who, it transpires, is her own mother. At the end Violet is outwitted just enough to allow her to be killed—or so we believe.

Fearn may have planned a sequel but even he could not have imagined the success that would arise from that book. The Canadian Toronto *Daily Star* published a Saturday supplement, the *Star Weekly*, featuring a full length novel. It reprinted *The Golden Amazon* in the issue for 3 March 1945. It proved so popular that the *Daily Star* asked for a sequel and "The Golden Amazon Returns" appeared on 3 November. More followed and the *Star Weekly* eventually published twenty-four novels. The series only stopped with Fearn's death in 1960, aged fifty-two. At that time, the Golden Amazon was the longest regular science-fiction series, but British readers did not benefit, as only the first six were published in Britain, spread over ten years, until 1954.

Unfortunately, Fearn's reputation had suffered in Britain. Fearn (1908–1960) could deliver a sense of wonder in spades, but he wrote more than his talent allowed. Much appeared under pseudonyms, the most notorious being Vargo Statten. When other publishers jumped on the bandwagon to extort what they could from the growing popularity of science fiction, much of what they published also appeared under pen names. Little had any merit, but Fearn became tarred with the same brush and his popularity sank to an all-time low. It never really recovered but his best work is worth exploring for its abundance of ideas.

Four-Sided Triangle   William F. Temple

London: John Long, 1949

Despite its 1949 publication date, this book belongs here because it's an example of what British writers had to endure during the War whilst trying to work. This novel began as a short story, published in the American *Amazing Stories* for November 1939, which went on sale of 10 August, three weeks before the outbreak of war. So, the growth of the novel spans the war years.

Although the basic plot was essentially the same between story and novel, Temple's expansion developed the characters significantly, making the chain of events and the outcome a more convincing and dramatic human dilemma.

The events are narrated by the village G.P., Dr. Harvey. He has two close friends, Bill Leggett and Rob Heath, who have been working on a significant invention which we eventually learn is a matter duplicator. They plan to duplicate works of art on commission.

Harvey introduces them to one of his patients, Lena Maitland, a strange girl who has attempted suicide. Bill, despite his wariness of women, finds her fascinating and learns about her difficult background. She had been orphaned and struggled to survive. She is artistic but is never satisfied with her work and constantly moves on, whether it's painting, sculpture, music or fashion. It was her failure to achieve artistic success in any of these spheres that caused her to try and end it all.

Bill suggests that she come and work for them, despite their lack of money. Inevitably, both Bill and Rob fall in love with her, but it's clear she wants to marry Rob. Bill is distraught but comes up with a scheme. Using their matter duplicator, they decide to duplicate Lena. This is long before the concept of cloning, though the end result is much the same. With Lena and Rob's consent, a perfect duplicate of Lena is created, whom they call Dorothy or Dot. In due course she marries Bill.

But all is not happy. Dot is so perfect a duplicate of Lena, including her emotions, that she too is in love with Rob. Hence the four-sided triangle which plays itself out through not one but two tragedies the last of which leaves us guessing which girl is which.

The book proved popular. In Britain, Eileen Bigland proclaimed it "An outstanding first novel," whilst John Keir Cross, reviewing it for BBC Radio, felt it may well be "a better book even than the author altogether intended...". The two leading American sf critics were full of praise when the book appeared there in 1951. Groff Conklin remarked that it was as perfect "as any science fiction I have ever read," whilst P. Schuyler Miller called it "a strong contender for the best science fiction novel of 1951." The book was filmed in 1952 by Hammer Films, starring Stephen Murray and Barbara Payton.

To achieve this success, however, Temple had to write the novel not once, but three times. With the outbreak of War, he was conscripted and assigned as a field artillery signaller. In December 1942 he set off on a troopship for Egypt via South Africa, a 10,000-mile trip that allowed plenty of time to work on the novel. He continued it as the Army marched through North Africa to Tunisia, engaging Rommel's troops. He had completed about half the novel when his satchel, holding the manuscript, fell from his truck during the battle of Takrouna in April 1943, and vanished into the desert.

From Africa, Temple was involved in the invasion of Sicily in July and while there, spurred on by the news of the birth of a son in September 1943, he started the novel again. His battalion fought through Italy and was involved in the fierce battle of Anzio which raged from January to May 1944. Temple had again reached the half-way point in the novel when the manuscript vanished after his jeep got bogged down in the mud. Temple was out of communication with home, so it was months before he learned that his son had died when only seven months old. Devastated, it was not until he was on leave in Rome that he returned to the novel and saw it almost to its conclusion. He finished it in snowbound barracks in the Alps. Once home in October 1945 he typed the final copy. Rejected by four publishers, the novel was eventually published in July 1949, nearly seven years after he had started.

Temple (1914–1989) was born in Woolwich in South London. He entered the London Stock Exchange as a clerk in 1930, but his interests were of a different speculative nature. He was one of the early band of British science-fiction fans and was active in both the newly formed Science Fiction Association and the British Interplanetary Society. He became firm friends with Arthur C. Clarke and for a while they shared a flat which became the centre of various fan activities. He sold several stories before the War but it was only after the success of *Four-Sided Triangle* that he risked becoming a full-time writer. It was a bumpy ride but Temple persevered, and although he never had the same success as he had with *Triangle* he was one of Britain's most popular writers. His books include *The Three Suns of Amara* (1962), *Shoot at the Moon* (1966) and *The Fleshpots of Sansato* (1968).

POST-ATOMIC DOOM

YOU MIGHT IMAGINE THAT WITH THE END OF THE SECOND World War in September 1945 there would be a flood of books looking to a bright and hopeful future. But the detonation of the atom bombs over Hiroshima and Nagasaki cast a mushroom cloud of gloom and desolation over that. Virtually none of the British books classifiable as science fiction in the five years after the War was optimistic and most were frighteningly pessimistic.

Besides the seven I cover in this section there were many other visions. In *Future Imperfect* (1946), a comedy-of-manners which reads more like a play than a novel, Bridget Chetwynd depicted a totally feminist society in 1965 where men are denied the vote and confined to domestic duties whilst women run the country. She speculates that this had its roots in the War when women could have resolved the problems more efficiently than men.

An almost Chestertonian novel was *Domesday Village* (1948) by Ian Colvin, set in 1986. A reorganization of counties and local government had somehow missed a village which carried on as usual without any of the apparent social or scientific progress in the rest of Britain. People soon realized that this agrarian enclave is a far more pleasant land. The book seems to presage the real-life Findhorn Village which began in the 1960s.

These are the more optimistic of the immediate post-war novels contrasting with the harsh dystopian visions in Aldous Huxley's *Ape and Essence* (1949) and George Orwell's *Nineteen Eighty Four* (1949; discussed below).

With the advent of the Atomic Age many writers looked ahead to what was an all-too-likely outcome. *The Maniac's Dream* (1946) by South African writer, F. Horace Rose, is set in South Africa, though Rose lived for many years in Britain and the book was first published there. Its bold dustjacket shows an atomic mushroom cloud declaring it "A Novel of the Atomic Bomb". A growing number of atheistic and somewhat deranged scientists, disgusted with the state of the Earth, consider how to remedy it. One of them sets off an atomic explosion which knocks the Earth out of its orbit. Equally apocalyptic was *Spurious Sun* (1948) by the pseudonymous George Borodin, where the release of an atomic bomb destroys the nitrogen in the atmosphere and ignites the Oxygen, turning the Earth into a ball of flame.

Slightly less melodramatic but no less intense was *The Story of My Village* (1947) by H. DeVere Stacpoole. Set in a small Essex village the narrator considers the "progress" of mankind and the horror of Hiroshima which leads to a plague of blindness. Civilization stumbles and reverts to village societies where people can help each other.

In fact, the imaginative fiction of post-war Britain was not unlike that of pre-war Britain with the country facing any number of catastrophes, with the threat of the atomic bomb now only too real. World War III, or some similar holocaust, seemed inevitable and writers considered how any survivors might cope. J. Jefferson Farjeon, better known for his mystery novels, felt compelled to explore this fate in *Death of a World* (1948; see below). In *Life Begins Tomorrow* (1948) Sydney Parkman envisages a plague that wipes out most of Britain. *The Moment of Truth* (1949) by Storm Jameson depicts a Britain overwhelmed by a third world war with the Russians as victors. In *The Terrible Awakening* (1949) by Kathleen Lindsay (writing as Hugh Desmond) Earth is threatened by a planetary fragment and a select few humans must escape to another world. In *Address Unknown* (1949) Eden Phillpotts has an alien race debate whether humankind is worth saving, and *Not in Our Stars* (1949) by Edward Hyams, explores an ecological disaster arising from a fungus that could be developed as a biological weapon. It is fair to ask whether the books by Hyams and Stacpoole had any influence on John Wyndham and *The Day of the Triffids* (1951; see below).

Hyams's novel points a finger at scientists and the chaos they have caused and in *The Last Revolution* (1951, see below) Lord Dunsany went so far as to consider what might happen if the latest machines became so superior that they would take over mankind.

Not all writers had finished with World War II and the consequences had Hitler won. The diplomat John Wall, writing as Sarban, considered this in *The Sound of His Horn* (1952).

There were a few glimmers of hope. Perhaps the most original post-World War II story was *The Flames* (1947) by Olaf Stapledon, a short but a highly original novel, where a man discovers he is in contact with intelligent beings from the Sun trapped inside Earth's rocks. The flame-beings offer to help mankind cope with their problems but the man suspects they are planning to take over the Earth and tries to destroy all flames.

Robert Graves shifted from his usual genre of historical or pseudo-mythical novels to a future satire, *Seven Days in New Crete* (1949), where a twentieth-century poet has been transported into the far future to an apparently utopian society established along the lines of ancient Crete. This future society has become so ideal that life has become tedious, and the magicians who summoned the poet hope he will inject some disorder into their lives.

It seems that humankind cannot exist without chaos and disaster!

Death of a World   J. Jefferson Farjeon

London: William Collins, 1948

Joseph Jefferson Farjeon (1883–1955) was best known for his crime and mystery novels and *Death of a World*, his only work classifiable as science fiction, was promoted as a mystery novel. Indeed, were it not for the prologue, its first few chapters would seem like any other of his books.

But that prologue sets us on a very different path. It is written by a being from another world. Farjeon does not tell us which though we may assume Mars or Venus, since the writer tells us of a long interest in the Earth, and of several attempts to reach it. Eventually, an atomic rocket-ship makes it to Earth and discovers it is devastated, with everything turned to dust and ash. By remarkable luck, one of the explorers stumbles over a metal box in which is encased what turns out to be the diary of John Smith. Farjeon has thus used an identical device to that used by Sherriff in *The Hopkins Manuscript*, except that the diary is discovered by aliens rather than Arabs.

The aliens manage to translate the diary, helped by the box containing a dictionary and the works of Shakespeare, but they do not understand most of it, and the transcription has many footnotes, many an amusing commentary on human foibles.

The diary starts with John Smith on a walking holiday in a remote part of Wales. The year is not given, only the date Monday, 1 September. As later internal references suggest we are at least twelve years after the end of the Second World War, and more likely twenty or thirty, then the year is possibly 1969, 1975 or 1980. Smith learns of a murderer on the run and is alarmed when he stumbles across the man as a mist comes down. The murderer, Carver, is also surprised and in trying to escape from Smith falls over a cliff, landing on a ledge. Wrestling with his conscience, Smith tries to rescue him only to captured by a third man who forces Smith (and, later, Carver) through a hidden doorway in the cliff and deep underground.

A day or two later, Smith learns that this well-stocked, well-built refuge, is one of thirty around the world, each housing some two hundred people, who will become survivors of a Third World War. The scheme was devised by Benjamin Harsh who had disappeared, believed dead, twelve years before. He was convinced there would be another War and his agents kept track of growing weapon arsenals and political situations around the world. These weapons included not just more powerful atomic bombs (Farjeon was writing before the nuclear hydrogen bomb was created), but biological weapons, weather control and something akin to laser beams. They also discover there is a disintegration beam or gas which turns solids to dust. The refuges have been designed to support life for at least ten years and once the warning reaches them that the War has begun, the entrance / exits are sealed.

Inside it becomes a study of a society in miniature exploring how everyone is to be entertained, kept fit and healthy, kept working and kept sane. There is always the worry that individuals or groups might rebel, and it is not long before there is growing unrest and incipient madness. It is exacerbated by the sounds of bombing which reverberate through the rocks to the refuge, and added concerns with a pervasive, acrid smell, a continuous droning sound and polluted water. There is the also the fear of the murderer, Carver, whose eventual fate seals the fate for everyone.

Because the prologue has already prepared us, the story becomes one long decline into inevitable doom, and yet there is always hope, and it is a message of hope by the aliens which concludes the novel. Written so soon after the War it is a good example of the fears that everyone was experiencing as to the potential annihilation that a Third World War would bring, a fear that has never entirely gone away.

Nineteen Eighty-Four George Orwell
London: Secker & Warburg, 1949

Even if people haven't read Orwell's *Nineteen Eighty-Four*, it's one of those books that surely everyone has heard of, or knows a phrase from it, such as "Big Brother" or "Room 101", both possibly because of television series, or "Newspeak", the adapted language of the totalitarian society that exists in Orwell's future, or the "Thought Police".

The year 1984 is almost forty years in the past, so Orwell's setting is no longer our future, but we can see it as an alternate past, one that might have been. The perceptive writer Rupert Croft-Cooke, reviewing the book in *The Sketch*, noted that if this book was sufficiently widely read "it may never happen", adding: "The more successful as a publication, the less true as a prophecy." Maybe he was right. Maybe Orwell's novel made such an impact that society in Britain would never allow a totalitarian regime to emerge—or so we might hope.

The book's plot is deceptively simple. In Orwell's future, Britain, known as Airstrip One, is part of the continent of Oceania, which includes the British Commonwealth and the Americas. According to the news being constantly broadcast, Oceania is allied to Eastasia in a war against Eurasia. Our main protagonist, Winston Smith, a minor member of the English Socialist Party or IngSoc, has a vague memory that this was not entirely true. He dislikes the Party because it seeks to abolish individuality and free speech. Smith is intrigued by a Party member called O'Brien, whom he thinks might be a member of a secret organization, the Brotherhood, which seeks to overthrow the Party.

All activity is monitored, mostly through the ubiquitous two-way telescreens that are in every home. Smith starts a private diary in which to note his thoughts even though this would be regarded as criminal if discovered. He spends his evenings in the poorer parts of London which are less rigorously monitored, where he might find fellow believers. But he must be careful. Everywhere are posters declaring "Big Brother is Watching You."

Smith works for the Ministry of Truth where he changes historical records to meet the Party's revisionist view of the past. Another of the Party's slogans is "Who controls the past controls the future. Who controls the present controls the past." There are many Party slogans such as

"War is Peace", "Ignorance is Strength" and the double bluff "Freedom is Slavery" and "Slavery is Freedom".

Also working at the Ministry is an attractive girl, Julia, and one day Smith receives a note from her saying "I love you." The two begin an affair and to avoid this being monitored Smith acquires a room with no telescreen from a man called Charrington who runs a second-hand store in the poorer part of London.

Smith is contacted by O'Brien and he and Julia visit him in a luxurious apartment. O'Brien convinces Smith that he is a member of the Brotherhood working against the Party. But Smith is being deceived. Neither the Brotherhood nor its apparent leader, Emmanuel Goldstein, regarded as the most dangerous man in Oceania, may exist and may be a propagandistic trap.

One day when he and Julia are in Charrington's room, soldiers burst in and arrest them. Charrington was one of the Thought Police and O'Brien is a spy for the Party. Smith is subjected to weeks of torture and brainwashing to make him conform. He resists until O'Brien sends him to Room 101 in which are our greatest fears—in Smith's case, rats. At the prospect of having his face eaten by rats Smith submits and betrays Julia. The Party has won, Smith now loves Big Brother, and we are left with that final sentence pounding in our mind.

Nineteen Eighty-Four is as chilling today as it was in 1949. In addition to the threat of the Nazi regime, which had only recently been overcome, Orwell had witnessed totalitarianism first-hand in the Soviet Union and Spain. He wanted to write a warning of what might happen if governments exert too much power. One measure of his success might be that the book is one of the bestselling of all time and one of the best known.

George Orwell was the pseudonym of Eric Blair (1903–1950) a journalist and essayist who became renowned for his social and political criticism. Amongst his other books is the remarkable *Animal Farm* (1945), a clever allegory where farm animals, seeking to build a utopia, create a world even more harsh than before. It includes the famous phrase "All animals are equal but some animals are more equal than others", which still resonates today.

Time Marches Sideways   Ralph L. Finn

London: Hutchinson, 1950

To most readers of the day, Finn was known as a sports columnist, especially football, about which he wrote several books. But he had another
passion, and that was Time, in particular the theories of J.W. Dunne, which
inspired three novels. *The Lunatic, the Lover, and the Poet* (1948) considered
the consequences of past, present and future existing simultaneously.
Twenty-Seven Stairs (1949) explored precognition through dreams, which
was at the heart of Dunne's original theory of the serial universe. With
Time Marches Sideways, he brings both ideas together in a time-romance.

The book is divided into two halves. The first half, "The Discovery",
takes rather too long to cover its territory. The first-person narrator, Ray
Jessimer, has worked his way up through an advertising agency until he
is second-in-command. When his new secretary, Jill Marond arrives there
is a sudden spark between them as if they both recall meeting before.
Jessimer overwhelms Jill with his theories about time when he tries to
explain that they must have met before and fallen in love but in some
other existence. Jill spoils Jessimer's dreams by revealing she is married,
to an American airman, after a whirlwind romance. He has returned to
the States and only keeps in touch by letter. Jessimer tries to win her
over but its an uphill struggle. During this Jessimer meets another girl,
Pat, who is more sympathetic and understanding and seems a better
prospect for him than Jill, but he is so fixated on Jill that Pat can only
listen and advise.

We learn much about the advertising business and copywriting, almost
too much, but the core thread is that one of their clients turns out to be
a rogue and his inability to pay leaves the agency in financial straits, with
the threat of a scandal. Jessimer had feared this and had told his boss, but
when he raised it again his boss fires him in a rage. His mind in a whirl,
Jessimer staggers aimlessly about London. When he comes to his senses,

he discovers to his horror that he has slipped back in time to 1945, just before the end of the War.

The second half of the book is called "The Search". Jessimer realizes he is back at the time just before Jill met her American airman and he hopes that if he can find her he can win her over and change everything. At this point the book comes alive as we follow Jessimer on a chaotic search for Jill which leads him into all manner of trouble. Even when he finds her his troubles are not over. Through Jessimer, Finn explores all the conundrums of time, whether the past can be changed, just what future or futures exist, and what influence one individual can have. Jessimer considers at one point whether he could make a fortune gambling on events before he realizes his recollection of the previous five years is vague, and he cannot recall which horses won the major races, or what teams won the FA Cup, and so on. There are some things he can recall and when he puts plan into action regarding the rogue builder it is interesting to see what effects it might have.

After several traumatic experiences, and mixed success with the 1945 Jill, Jessimer finds himself back in 1950. He now wonders whether he dreamed it, which is what both the 1950 Jill and Pat suspect, but he notices at least one small change that makes him suspect he really had managed to influence the future from 1945.

In a surprising climax which provides more than a maze of twists, turns, bluffs and double bluffs, we finally discover what happens between Jessimer, Jill and Pat. The book is really a convoluted romance, but the timeslip element and Finn's thoughts on time, are a key part and raise more issues than can be answered.

Ralph Leslie Finn (1912–1999) was born and raised in the London East End, which he wrote about in his engaging autobiography *No Tears in Aldgate* (1963), later reissued as *Time Remembered* (1985), a title with more affinity to his novels. He wrote two other works of science fiction, which he churned out in a couple of weeks, both of which are best forgotten, *Freaks Against Supermen* (1951) and *Captive on the Flying Saucers* (1951). They were notorious in their day for their erotic content.

The Day of the Triffids   John Wyndham

Collier's, 6 January–3 February 1951 (abridged); London: Michael Joseph, 1951

We previously encountered John Wyndham with *Planet Plane*, under his John Beynon alias, a contraction of his real name John Beynon Harris. Only fifteen years separate that novel from this, his best known work, but it could have been a lifetime. Harris had sold some twenty stories before the outbreak of War, but the main British markets vanished with paper rationing. Harris initially worked as a censor but in November 1943 he was called up and became a cipher operator in the Royal Signal Corps. He was involved in the push into Europe through Holland. His experiences left him depressed after the War, a mood aggravated when he barely sold any fiction. Much of that bleakness pervades *The Day of the Triffids*.

As the novel developed, he had trouble deciding the ending and set it aside for a year. When he returned to it, he was still not satisfied but sent the typescript to his friend Walter Gillings, who saw its potential. He sent it to Frederik Pohl in New York, who was then running a literary agency. Pohl sold the novel to publisher Doubleday and secured serialization in the prestigious *Collier's*. Harris also sold the novel to British publisher Michael Joseph. The income from these sales was more than Harris had earned in over a decade from his writing. As a deliberate split from his earlier work he chose to run it under his new alias, John Wyndham.

There are three versions of the novel with the British edition being the preferred text. Doubleday not only Americanized the text but reduced it by over ten thousand words, whilst *Collier's*, which serialized it under the title "The Revolt of the Triffids", cut the text in half, and used an earlier version. Wyndham had originally suggested that the triffids came from Venus, which is how it appears in *Collier's*. But Pohl queried how appropriate this was in the post-war environment and Wyndham revised it to imply the triffids were the result of Russian biological experiments and seeds had been spread round the world in an aircraft disaster.

Wyndham avoids dating the events but it is at least a generation after World War Two. It is far enough ahead for there to be artificial satellites in orbit.

The story is narrated by Bill Masen who is recovering in hospital following emergency work on his eyes after they were squirted with a poisonous sting from a triffid. The triffids are genetically engineered plants from which can be extracted a highly refined oil. They were also carnivorous and can walk in a stumbling way. One of Masen's colleagues suspects they have a form of intelligence and can communicate by clacking stems together.

While Masen is in hospital there is a strange green meteor shower which renders blind all those who watched. There is later speculation that this was radiation from satellites. Masen was saved because of his bandaged eyes. In the turmoil that follows, Masen discharges himself and discovers he is one of only a few people who can see. He stumbles through London witnessing the growing alarm and disorder, and rescues a sighted woman, Josella, from a man who had ensnared her and was using her as his eyes.

They learn that most public services have ceased, looting has started, and the blind are desperate to find anyone who can see. Bill and Josella stay together and return to her home where she discovers her father is dead. They realize that some triffids in Regents Park have escaped their stakes and are free to wander. Their whip-like branch can render a toxic poison which kills quickly. The blind are especially vulnerable.

Overnight they see a signal from a university tower. Making their way there next day, they discover several sighted people, under a man called Beadley, have come together to plan an escape into the country. There is a dispute as to whether the sighted people should save themselves or help those who cannot see. One man, Coker, believes the latter and captures several sighted people, including Bill and Josella, and manacles them to the blind. It is soon realized this is a hopeless idea and is abandoned, but Bill and Josella have become separated.

Coker admits the error of his ways, and joins forces with Bill to find Beadley and Josella. Much of the remaining half of the novel is their quest across southern Britain, witnessing the death and destruction caused by the blindness and the growing menace of the triffids. Coker tries to help a colony establish itself in Wiltshire while Bill continues his search for Josella. They are eventually reunited but find themselves trapped on a farm by the triffids. They fortify their surroundings and dig in for the long term.

Meanwhile Beadley has succeeded in establishing a colony and others are emerging on islands, which were natural defences against the triffids, such as the Isle of Wight and the Channel Islands.

The Day of the Triffids wasn't the first of the post-war disaster novels. Both H. DeVere Stacpoole's *The Story of My Village* (1947), with its plague of blindness, and Sydney Parkman's *Life Begins Tomorrow* (1948), where another plague wipes out the human population, might have influenced Wyndham indirectly. Yet it was Wyndham's that captured the public imagination. It has been filmed and adapted for radio and television. The word "triffid" has passed into the English language to cover any invasive or menacing plant.

The success of the novel encouraged others and the 1950s saw such books as *White August* (1955) by John Boland, *The Death of Grass* (1956) by John Christopher and *A Scent of New-Mown Hay* (1958) by John Blackburn. Wyndham left the novel's ending sufficiently open for the chance of a sequel, but he chose not to write one. However, to celebrate the novel's fiftieth anniversary, with the estate's permission, Simon Clark wrote *The Night of the Triffids* (2001).

The Last Revolution   Lord Dunsany

London: Jarrolds, 1951

It was his passion for the wild outdoors that made Edward Plunkett (1878–1957), 18th Baron Dunsany, one of the fathers of modern fantasy with such volumes as *The Gods of Pegāna* (1905), *The Book of Wonder* (1912) and *The King of Elfland's Daughter* (1921). It was that same yearning for the days of yore, and concern over an increasingly industrialized Britain that caused him to write *The Last Revolution*. The book is full of references to man creating things that he can no longer control. "We are no more suited to towns," says Pender the inventor, "than birds are to cages." Whilst the narrator, ruminating on events, says to himself, "...my forbodings told me that machines were our slaves, and not likely to think well of us, if they were able to think."

And so it is. Pender is a clever gadget man and has made a living inventing small things that help society overcome the niggles of life. His patents bring in enough money to allow him to experiment further and he creates an intelligent brain. Dunsany would have been aware of the first general purpose computer, ENIAC, created in 1946, which weighed twenty-six tons and filled a room. Pender believes that small is beautiful. His brain is housed in a machine about the size of a dog but looks like a crab, with a hundred pincers and four legs.

This brain has already acquired significant intelligence, starting with everything that Pender knows. Dunsany does not explain how this has happened but his message is that often we do not know how one thing develops and improves. He was doubtless remembering what Samuel Butler wrote in *Erewhon* (1872):

Is it not plain that the machines are gaining ground upon us, when we reflect on the increasing number of those who are bound down to them as slaves, and of those who devote their whole souls to the advancement of the mechanical kingdom?

Pender's machine—he does not use the word robot but that's what it is—is self-replicating and it builds hundreds of replicas. Pender has housed most of them in the North Kent marshes where one of his old retainers, Eerith, looks after them when they need oiling. Pender sees no harm in the machines but the narrator becomes more fearful. When the primary machine defeats him at chess he realizes its superior intelligence, and when he also witnesses how jealous the machine is of Pender's fiancée, Alicia, he becomes concerned for her safety and that of all humans.

The narrator gathers evidence to convince Pender of the danger. He discovers that the master machine can influence other machines—trains start to run late, cars and motor-bikes can be controlled, telephones cease to work. It is only when the machines attempt to capture Alicia on her motor-bike that Pender realizes what he has done. But what chance does he have against his creations once they ignore his orders?

The last half of the novel finds the protagonists under siege on the marshes defending themselves against the relentless machines and it is Eerith, with his knowledge of the machines through tending them, who knows their weakness and wins the day.

Yet, as Dunsany notes, even if that battle was won, the war is only just beginning. Despite being written over seventy years ago, Dunsany's message about the growing power of artificial intelligence is even more relevant today.

Most of Dunsany's works were fantasy, though occasional science-fiction ideas creep into his short fiction. His only other novel classifiable as science fiction, *The Pleasures of a Futuroscope*, though written in 1955 was not published until 2003. Through a time-viewer the narrator looks ahead six centuries to see a Britain struggling after a nuclear holocaust.

The Sound of His Horn   Sarban (John W. Wall)
London: Peter Davies, 1952

We have already encountered several novels in which Hitler was victorious in the Second World War, notably *Swastika Night* by Katharine Burdekin and *Loss of Eden* by Douglas Brown and Christopher Serpell, but *The Sound of His Horn* is very different. It does not show us a Nazi-dominated Britain. It does not really depict a Nazi-dominated Europe. All of that is taken for granted. Instead we are trapped in a forest ruled by a hunter.

The story is told by Alan Querdilion who has been repatriated after spending several years in a prisoner-of-war camp. His friends and family notice he has changed, not physically but something has affected his psyche. Querdilion opens the story, blurting "It's the terror that's unspeakable", when he is listening to a discussion about fox hunting. He later confesses to a friend what happened to him during the War.

He and another had escaped from a prisoner-of-war camp and went their separate ways. Querdilion soon encountered problems with lack of food and water and a loss of direction. He stumbles through a forest and suddenly experiences intense pain and a flash of light before he loses consciousness. He awakes in what seems to be a hospital bed, except that the place doesn't feel like a hospital. As he recovers he learns from the doctor that he had passed through part of the forest protected by Bohlen Rays which are normally fatal but in his case they have projected him over a hundred years into the future, after Hitler's victory.

He is on the estate of Count Johann von Hackelnberg, the Reich's Master Forester. It is his domain with his own laws and the Count, the modern equivalent of the Wild Hunstman of folklore, loves to hunt. Not just animals—deer is an especial favourite—but humans, especially the "under races". He even has women genetically altered to resemble and run like cats.

The doctor keeps Querdilion hidden but while showing him the revolting celebrations of the Count and his guests, Querdilion is spotted. He is let loose in the forest, his only haven being an old hut, and he has to survive against the hunters. He is helped by a young girl who has herself been adapted to be a specialist quarry.

Wall's description of the Count and his lifestyle is an image in miniature of how he could see a Nazi regime grow and fester in the years after their victory in Europe. However, because the book appeared seven years after the War, and had minimal political relevance, it did not capture the wider public taste at the time, although critics were complimentary on the quality of the writing and the moments of horror. Yet the book's reputation spread and over the years it was reprinted and became one of the best known of the "Hitler Wins" sub-genre, certainly until Philip K. Dick's *The Man in the High Castle* in 1962.

Some have suggested that *The Sound of His Horn* might have been inspired by the story "The Most Dangerous Game" (1924) by Richard Connell, filmed as *The Hounds of Zaroff* (1932) where an obsessed Russian general lures victims to his island so he can hunt them. But any similarity is coincidental as Wall had neither read the story nor seen the film.

John William Wall (1910–1989) was a British diplomat who served at a number of consulates through the Middle East and Egypt. It was while he was in Cairo in 1950 that he wrote *The Sound of His Horn*. He became better known for his stories of the strange and supernatural collected as *Ringstones* (1951) and *The Doll Maker* (1953). He adopted the alias Sarban for its romantic connotations. It was the Persian name for a storyteller who travelled with the caravanserai along the trade routes.

The Magicians   J.B. Priestley

London: William Heinemann, 1954

We have already seen how the theories of J. W. Dunne proved a significant influence upon many writers. He is referred to in the works of Lionel Britton, J. Leslie Mitchell, Susan Ertz and Ralph L. Finn, and you can also trace his influence in some of the later works of H.G. Wells, Algernon Blackwood, E.F. Benson and John Buchan. But the author who explored his ideas in the greatest depth and with a perceptive insight was John Boynton Priestley (1894–1984). Dunne's theory, first expressed in *An Experiment with Time* in 1927, was that time was a constant, and that all past, present and future were accessible, perhaps visibly, and possibly experienced, provided one had the right mental aptitude. Time did not pass, rather we passed through time.

Priestley had explored this concept in several short stories starting with "Mr. Strenberry's Tale" (1930 as "Doomsday"), the best of which are

collected in *The Other Place* (1953). It also became the mood behind several
of his plays, starting with *Time and the Conways* (1937), but he explored it
at greatest depth in this novel, *The Magicians*.

He also incorporated some of the ideas proposed by the Russian mystic
Pyotr Ouspensky whose *The New Model of the Universe* (1931) fascinated
Priestley. Ouspensky suggested that time exists as a circle meaning we
might continually relive our lives, but he developed this, proposing that
higher intelligences could improve their lives so that the circle becomes
a spiral moving upwards into a higher dimension, another theme hinted
at in *The Magicians*.

Following a boardroom coup, Sir Charles Ravenstreet is ousted as
Managing Director of an electrical engineering company. Rather than stay,
he retires, with a rewarding payout, but he's at a loss over what to do next.
Years earlier he had married the daughter of the company Chairman, as
much to help his career than out of any romantic attachment, but she had
died after a short marriage. He is not ready for another attachment. Instead
he meets three entrepreneurs, Karney, Prisk and Lord Mervil, who have
a business proposition. They have been working with research chemist,
Sepman, who has developed a tablet which enhances the taker's mood,
reducing anxiety and increasing a feeling of wellbeing.

Ravenstreet shows interest in the project and a further meeting is
arranged with Sepman in Cheshire. Ravenstreet has his own house in
the Cotswolds and on the way there he witnesses the crash of an RAF
plane which destroys a public house. Staying at that pub were three men,
Wayland, Perperek and Marot and because his house is nearby Ravenstreet
offers them his hospitality to stay for a few days. These three are the
Magicians of the title, but it's a phrase of convenience as they do not practice magic in any accepted sense. Ravenstreet never fully understands who
they are or what they do, but it's clear they somehow exist both across and
beyond time. Marot provides Ravenstreet with the facility to experience
what Priestley calls "time alive", whereby he re-visits an event in his life.
This is no simple reliving a memory but genuinely experiencing it again,

being present in his own past body, with the knowledge of his future self. It was one of those crucial moments when life could take one of two key turnings. He was with a former girlfriend, Philippa, with whom he could have stayed and taken a new job offer, but he opted to return to his Company and marry the boss's daughter.

Later, Ravenstreet has another "time alive" experience during which he had a greater sense of omnipotence and briefly felt he could stand back and see his whole life as one tableau. He does not know how to achieve this on his own, but any one of the Magicians could facilitate the process.

They also become involved with Ravenstreet's meeting with Sepman when it is arranged that he and his wife will meet at Ravenstreet's house along with Karney, Prisk and Mervil. At this meeting everything goes from bad to worse, somehow engineered by the Magicians, and yet they seem to do nothing but bring each individual's alternate or inner lives to the fore.

Priestley follows events to two separate climaxes, one of which relates to a passing comment made by Perperek that Ravenstreet may have children and grandchildren of whom he is unaware. As the novel progresses Priestley succeeds in making you believe that we have a limited understanding of our presence in time, and that we could be more aware of a greater life. The Magicians have this greater awareness and because they understand or can see each individual's past, present and future, they know how to manipulate events for the better.

Early in the novel Wayland tells Ravenstreet that their purpose is "to save Man", and by extension "save the human race", which seems so pertinent in this complicated, post-atomic world. The comment meant nothing to Ravenstreet at the time but, as events unravel, he realizes that there are those who operate beyond the Realities of life for the benefit of mankind. At this moment their role was to influence Mervil's plan to manufacture Sepman's drug which evidently would not have benefitted mankind. There is a hint that Mervil also has this power but that his strength is "from the other side". Priestley thereby explores that constant battle between Good and Evil, and The Magicians lifts the veil on one small battle.

SCIENCE FICTION BOOM

STRANGE THOUGH IT MAY SEEM BUT THOUGH WE HAVE already covered seventy-seven books in the fifty years since H.G. Wells's *The Time Machine*, the phrase "science fiction" had yet to enter common parlance in Britain. It was hardly ever used in the marketing of books and critics rarely used the phrase, preferring to call such novels "futuristic", "Wellsian", "pseudo-scientific" or simply "thrillers". The phrase had been slowly leaking out, usually in local papers when reporting upon gatherings of fans. For instance, the *Yorkshire Evening Post* for 28 August 1936 reported upon the founding of a "Scientific Fiction" club in Leeds, and then defines "science fiction" as "Wellsian stuff". But this term would have meant little to most people and even when the first two adult science-fiction magazines, *Tales of Wonder* and *Fantasy* appeared in Britain just before the War, the phrase was rarely used on the cover.

After the War, the atomic bomb alerted everybody to the awesome power that science had released. The potential for further scientific advance became an everyday discussion allowing the literature of science fiction to grow and be better appreciated. But that did not happen overnight.

None of the books discussed in the previous section were referred to as science fiction either in their marketing or review. It would not be until 1953 when there was a change, not just in awareness but an acceptance of the genre.

In the summer of 1946 a new science-fiction magazine had been launched, *New Worlds*, edited by John Carnell (usually called "Ted"). This magazine would become the backbone of science fiction in Britain, but it was touch and go. It ceased publication after three issues, but was relaunched in 1949 with a company financed by sf fans and professionals, including John Wyndham. It acquired a companion magazine, *Science Fantasy*, and provided a reasonably steady market to British writers some of whom—John Wyndham, Arthur C. Clarke, William F. Temple, A. Bertram Chandler and Peter Phillips—had hitherto sold primarily to the American magazines.

The apparent success of *New Worlds* attracted competitors, the best of which became *Authentic Science Fiction*. It appeared in January 1951 and was the first regular British publication to use the phrase "science fiction" in its title. Although it had various magazine features, including reviews, a science column and readers' letters, *Authentic* ran one full-length novel per issue, which proved popular. Amongst the authors *Authentic* published in its early years were E.C. ["Ted"] Tubb, who later edited the magazine, and Bryan Berry.

Scotland produced its own magazine in 1952, *Nebula Science Fiction*, edited and published by Peter Hamilton. This always operated on a financial knife-edge, but helped broaden the market for quality. Unfortunately, the development of the market meant that other publishers jumped onto the science-fiction bandwagon, even though they had no idea about the field, and felt they could publish anything provided it included spaceships, monsters and atom bombs. Unfortunately this rash of titles rapidly gave science fiction a poor image, associated with cheap, formulaic fiction. It would be years before the genre was able to prove itself in the wider literary world and *New Worlds* played a pivotal role.

Thankfully, most of the dreadful magazines had ceased publication by 1954, leaving four superior titles—*New Worlds, Science Fantasy, Authentic* and *Nebula*—which between them established a solid British market for science fiction and developed a new generation of writers, including Brian W. Aldiss, J.G. Ballard, Kenneth Bulmer, John Brunner, James White, J.T. McIntosh and Bob Shaw.

To add to this mix, and of vital importance in encouraging younger readers, was the debut of the *Eagle* comic in April 1950, its front page depicting the adventures of Dan Dare, Pilot of the Future, created and meticulously drawn by Frank Hampson.

The pivotal period in this development was during 1953 and 1954. The get-rich-quick titles were fading away. *New Worlds* had a new publisher with reliable financial backing and despite a few more hiccups, became a regular monthly magazine from April 1954. *Authentic* had become a standard magazine, with more short stories and serials rather than long novels. To compensate the publisher, Hamilton & Co., began a companion series under the imprint Panther Books. Other publishers started their own imprints which regularly published science fiction: Transworld launched Corgi Books, initially reprinting science fiction from America, but soon running home-grown novels, starting with Arthur C. Clarke's *The Sands of Mars* in 1954. Brown-Watson started its Digit imprint, and New English Library Four Square Books, both of which regularly published work by British writers. From 1954, even Penguin Books included science fiction as part of its schedule, including Wyndham's *The Day of the Triffids*.

By the mid-1950s science fiction was a regular part of the British publishing scene, to which we can add radio and television, which have a significant impact and generate a vast audience for this apparently new genre. The summer of 1953 saw two of the most influential science-fiction programmes. Television brought us *The Quatermass Experiment* whilst radio ran *Journey Into Space*. Both series have gone down in history, their very names conjuring memories amongst old-time devotees.

The Quatermass Experiment   Nigel Kneale

BBC Television, 18 July–22 August 1953; Harmondsworth: Penguin Books, 1959

The first of six episodes of *The Quatermass Experiment* began on BBC television on Saturday, 18 July 1953 at the surprisingly early time of 8.15 in the evening. These days we are used to the watershed at 9.00p.m., but although the first episode contained little that would frighten children, the BBC were nevertheless cautious and prefaced the episode with what would become a familiar warning, announcing that the programme was "unsuitable for children or persons of a nervous disposition."

We are introduced to Professor Bernard Quatermass, head of the British Experimental Rocket Group. Britain has launched the first rocket into space from a base at Tarooma in Australia—the actual British base was at Woomera. The plan was for the rocket to orbit the Earth and return to Tarooma, but all contact was lost with the three astronauts for over fifty hours. When a signal is received from the rocket there is no message from the crew. Quatermass takes control separating the capsule containing the men from the rocket. Having overshot any landing in Australia it crashes into a residential area in south London. Locals believe it to be a bomb, and Quatermass hurries to the site before they or the emergency services can do any damage. The capsule has been super-heated during its descent through the atmosphere and although desperate to learn if the crew have survived, everyone must wait until the capsule has cooled.

When they can open the hatch only one astronaut steps out—Victor Carroon. There is no sign of the others, Charles Greene or the German Ludwig Reichenheim. Carroon is psychologically disturbed and finds it difficult to communicate, which makes it all the more surprising when at one point he starts talking in German and betrays a deeper knowledge of the rocket's operating system than they would expect.

Research in the capsule reveals that there is a large amount of a jelly-like substance which had found its way into the recesses of the equipment.

Analysis does not immediately reveal its origins, but along with clues arising from Carroon's rantings plus the wire-recording within the capsule,
Quatermass suspects that some kind of energy being must have entered
the capsule. It reduced the bodies of two of the astronauts to jelly but their
consciousness entered the mind of Carroon who is a gestalt of all three. The
energy being continues to function within Carroon. When he is taken to one
of the ruined houses near the capsule he grasps a cactus which somehow he
absorbs. He escapes and in a dramatic television moment that ends episode
four, viewers see Carroon's enlarged hand now grey and covered in spikes.

The remaining two episodes, which were broadcast after 9.00pm, and
which captured the nation, continue the search for Carroon and the battle
to overcome the energy being, which has been absorbing other plants
and has turned Carroon into an amorphous plant-like entity. The climax
happens inside Westminster Abbey where it is important that the monster
is contained. If spores escape they could affect all plant-life and take over
the world.

Tension for viewers was aggravated on the original broadcast when,
half-way through the final episode, a faulty microphone led to a loss of
sound and all vision was faded. It was six-and-a-half minutes before everything was restored.

The Quatermass Experiment was a huge success, the final episode being
watched by five million viewers. The BBC immediately commissioned a
sequel, *Quatermass II*, broadcast in October–November 1955 and a third,
Quatermass and the Pit, perhaps the best known, over Christmas and New
Year 1958–59. In November 1959 the original script of *The Quatermass
Experiment* was published by Penguin Books. There was no attempt to
novelize it. The BBC had only kept recordings of the first two episodes
and the remaining four were lost, so the complete script was the only
record of the full serial. The book included photographs of moments
throughout the serial.

Nigel Kneale (1922–2006) became something of a television legend
chiefly due to the Quatermass series—the title remains a by-word for TV

shocks—but also for his 1954 adaptation of Orwell's *Ninety Eighty-Four* and
for such later programmes as *The Road* (1963) and *The Stone Tape* (1972),
collected with a third play as *The Year of the Sex Olympics* (1976). A fourth
Quatermass serial, simply titled *Quatermass*, was broadcast in March 1996.

Journey Into Space   Charles Chilton

BBC Light Programme, 21 September 1953–19 January 1954;
novelized, London: Herbert Jenkins, 1954

Exactly one month after *The Quatermass Experiment* finished on television,
the BBC Light Programme began the first episode of *Journey Into Space*.
It deals with the first manned flight to the moon in 1965. There are four
astronauts: Jet Morgan, the captain, Steve Mitchell ("Mitch") who financed
the project and invented the atomic motor that made it possible, Doctor
Matthews ("Doc"), the ship's doctor and space-suit designer, and Lemmy
Barnett, the radio operator.

When first broadcast the serial ran for eighteen episodes but reviews
criticized the first four because they all took place on Earth, testing rockets in New Mexico with a crash in Las Vegas. The tapes of this first series
were erased, and when the serial was re-recorded in 1958 for the BBC
Transcription Service, the first four episodes were dropped. They were
also excluded when Chilton novelized the serial in 1954. The only record of
those episodes is a copy of the original script amongst the Charles Chilton
papers in the British Library.

The novel follows the serial fairly closely but, for dramatic effect, Chilton
chose to include a framing device that relates to events near the end of the
serial when the rocket (*Luna*) is returning to Earth and they discover that
they are almost out of fuel and oxygen. Even more mysteriously, when
they checked the diary kept by Doc, they find he has already written the
events for the next few weeks. The novel then recounts the story of the
moon flight.

They encounter several problems on their way to the moon. The radio ceases to operate even though, once Lemmy gets it working, the base in Australia says they could hear everything okay. While mending the radio, Lemmy hears a strange sound, like alien music, which comes and goes. He hears it more often than the others, even when he undertakes a spacewalk checking damage from a meteor strike, but the others don't, although Doc fancies he might.

After landing on the Moon, Lemmy still hears the music. Their time on the moon is relatively uneventful but when they come to leave, the ship has lost all power. For two weeks they are stranded with no lights, or any way of contacting Earth or leaving the ship. At one point a knocking sound is heard outside. This episode was written when a television producer challenged Chilton to produce something on radio that could not be achieved better on television. So he set the entire episode in the dark!

When power is restored and they look outside they are astonished to see a flying saucer has landed near them. Jet and Mitch venture out to the craft which Mitch determines to explore. The dome opens and a ladder allows him access. Lemmy again hears the music and Mitch starts talking strangely as if under alien control. He says that the craft comes from another galaxy and that they have mastered time travel.

Mitch eventually returns and Jet ensures the ship takes off and orbits the Moon. They discover on the far side a fleet of these craft which pursue them. The crafts take control of *Luna*, accelerating the ship to an infinite speed. When control returns to the crew they believe they are lost in space but approach a nearby planet. They land on this planet which is surprisingly Earth-like and after studying the stars Jet realizes that they are indeed on Earth but have travelled back in time. They are contacted by the aliens through a spokesman whom they call "The Voice". He warns them they are in danger from vicious forest creatures, who turn out to be primitive man. The aliens help *Luna* to leave and escort it back through time, bringing them to the moment where the novel starts, though they have no memory of their trip to a prehistoric Earth and the only record is Doc's diary, plus an artefact they found.

The serial was immensely popular and had proved innovative in the use of sound effects. Over six million listeners tuned in each week and Chilton extended the serial by three further episodes to meet demand. It eventually ended on 19 January 1954 and Chilton was commissioned to write another series. The second, *The Red Planet* began in September 1954 followed a year later by, *The World in Peril* which concluded on 6 February 1956. The final series was the last radio drama to have audiences greater than television. All three series were novelized, and Chilton wrote two more one-off plays in the series, broadcast in 1981 and 2008, but by then the novelty had long faded. The original three series became a landmark for science-fiction on radio, just as *The Quatermass Experiment* had been for television.

Charles Chilton (1917–2013) had not been a science-fiction fan, being more interested in westerns and the history of minstrel songs, but he became fascinated by astronomy, building his own observatory in his garden. The chief technical adviser for the series was Kenneth Gatland, who was on the Council of the British Interplanetary Society. Chilton attended a few of their meetings and was given further advice for the series by both Arthur C. Clarke and Patrick Moore. Chilton predicted the first rocket to enter space would be in 1957.

Childhood's End   Arthur C. Clarke

New York: Ballantine Books, 1953; London: Sidgwick & Jackson, 1954

Despite his reputation as the premier writer of technological "hard" science fiction, Clarke also had a fascination for the transcendental which is evident in many of his stories and novels, including *Childhood's End*. This began as a short story, "Guardian Angel" (1950), written as early as 1946, which Clarke revised to form the first part of the novel, "Earth and the

Overlords". It begins at the start of the space race between the United States and the Soviet Union which stops when Earth is visited by a fleet of giant alien spaceships which remain hovering over the major cities of the world. Their spokes-being, Karellen, informs Earth that they are the Overlords. Individual governments still operate, but the Overlords dominate. Their purpose seems to be to save humanity from itself, though it is later discovered this is just the first phase of their plans.

They do not involve themselves in human affairs although they stopped oppression in South Africa where the end of apartheid had seen the white minority punished, and they stopped blood-sports such as bull-fighting in Spain. The aliens are so intellectually and technologically superior that any attempt at retaliation is pointless. One nation tried but their missile vanished. There was no retaliation from the Overlords but it was clear that, had they done so, it would have been the end for that nation.

Stormgren, the Secretary-General of the United Nations, is the only individual who has a personal discussion with Karellen, but the aliens have not shown themselves to him or to any humans. A movement of rebels seek demands of the aliens to reveal themselves and their purpose, but Karellen says mankind must first get used to their presence. They will not show themselves for fifty years, at which point the next phase of their plan will be initiated. Stormgren, knowing he will not be alive then, manages to photograph Karellen. In the book version what he saw is not revealed until the second section, "The Golden Age".

The fifty years have passed and Karellen invites two children into his ship, which turns out to have been the only one all along, the other ships being illusions. Karellen walks out of the ship with a child on each shoulder and the world discovers he has the appearance of the medieval representation of demons, complete with wings and a forked tail. Despite this being an obvious shock, the world is more accepting having become used to the alien presence. Since they arrived there have been no wars or famine and society has improved considerably. Amongst his predictions Clarke mentions "the Pill" oral contraceptive, which was not available until seven years after the book appeared, and genetic fingerprinting, which was a full thirty years away.

The Overlords have gifted humans with a time viewer. It allows access to the last five thousand years, and although some periods of history were blank, it was possible to view those who formed the core of subsequent religions and it was evident that they were simply human. Thereafter most religions collapse.

One of the Overlords, Rashaverak, has been sent to the home of Rupert Boyce who has a significant library of books on the paranormal. Rashaverak can read and analyse any book in a few minutes and he reports back to Karellen that amongst the data there is the possibility of a few individuals with a genuine talent. It is not until much later in the book that we realize the significance of this.

Boyce had held a party attended by individuals who at this stage do not realize the parts they will be playing. Amongst them are George Greggson and his future wife Jean, and Boyce's brother-in-law Jan Rodricks, who is black. Jean Greggson reveals she may have psychic abilities because when they use a Ouija board, she picks up a message when Jan asks about the native planet of the Overlords. It is a reference in a star catalogue and Jan discovers the Overlords' home is forty light-years away in the direction of the constellation Carina. Jan finds a way to stow away on one of the Overlords' supply ships knowing that he would be away from Earth for eighty years, but not knowing that when he returned he would be the last human on Earth.

There are those who believe that the Overlords are stifling human creativity and they have established a community on a Pacific island to reinvigorate art and thought. The Greggsons, who now have two children, Jeffrey and Jennifer, join the community. Soon after it is visited by an Overlord who, we learn, is monitoring the two children. Jeffrey begins to experience strange dreams and is saved when voices tell him where to run when a tsunami strikes the island. Rashaverak informs the Greggsons that their children have developed new talents and are transcending humanity.

This is the next step in evolution and soon many children are exhibiting special abilities.

Karellen reveals that this was the purpose of the Overlords. They serve a hive being called the Overmind which assimilates races from across the galaxy once they have reached a level of maturity. The children are to be taken to their world and the power needed to do this en masse will result in the destruction of the Earth. Jan returns in time to witness the end.

Childhood's End was first published in America by the newly formed Ballantine Books in August 1953. There were simultaneous hardcover and paperback editions, and the paperback sold out its 210,000-copy print run in a few months. Despite its popularity, it received mixed reviews from sf critics. Clarke had himself been uncertain about aspects of the book, especially the attempt to rationalize psychic powers. He had written an alternate ending and was constantly revising later editions. But there was no denying it was Clarke's breakthrough novel, its cosmic theme showing the influence of Olaf Stapledon (with whom he was compared by some reviewers) and one that he would return to in several books, most notably *2001: A Space Odyssey* (1968).

Arthur C. Clarke (1917–2008) served in the RAF during the Second World War, working on the new early-warning radar defence system, details of which he captured in his novel *Glide Path* (1963). He also published a ground-breaking article "Extra-Terrestrial Relays" (1945) which established the basis for communication satellites. He began selling stories to the specialist magazines after the war, including "The Sentinel" (1951) which became the inspiration for *2001*. His first novel was *Prelude to Space* (1951), followed by *The Sands of Mars* (1951). Much of his work over the next decade or so includes what many may regard as the best or most acclaimed works of classic British science fiction, such as *The City and the Stars* (1956), *A Fall of Moondust* (1961), *Rendezvous with Rama* (1973) and the collections *Expedition to Earth* (1953), *Reach for Tomorrow* (1956) and *Tales of Ten Worlds* (1962). The emotive "The Star" (1955) won the Hugo Award for that year's best short fiction, the first of many awards he would receive. As for "The

Nine Billion Names of God" (1953), its final sentence is one of the most memorable and most quoted in all science fiction.

The Echoing Worlds   Jonathan Burke

New York: Ballantine Books, 1953; London: Sidgwick & Jackson, 1954

Many of the cheap paperback publishers of the early 1950s, had started out publishing formulaic westerns and sadistic gangster novels. They turned to science fiction because it was fashionable but had no idea, or interest, in understanding the genre. They assigned their western and gangster writers to produce anything involving rockets, monsters, ray-guns and damsels in distress, and paid the minimum fee. Needless to say 90%, maybe even 99%, was total rubbish and ruined the image of science fiction for years.

Amongst the editors who worked for these publishers was one with a conscience and standards—Gordon Landsborough at Hamilton & Co. He had no background in science fiction but was sure there must be something more sophisticated than the rubbish that was being published. He convinced the publisher to pay a better rate (£1 a thousand words) and strove to find better writers.

Initially Landsborough had to use existing writers at Hamilton's, but good fortune put him in touch with Herbert Campbell, a research chemist who was augmenting his salary by writing science articles. Landsborough commissioned some novels from Campbell and he succeeded Landsborough as editor at *Authentic*. Because of his background, Campbell was able to encourage writers to write more "authentic" science fiction—the magazine title became a true banner. This meant that when *Authentic* became a genuine magazine and Hamilton's launched a companion novel series in April 1952, under the Panther Books imprint, it was able to publish science fiction of a superior quality to the rival companies. "Superior" is a relative term, but over the years Panther grew in stature and outlived most of its competitors, becoming renowned by the early 1960s for its British editions of American science fiction by Isaac Asimov, Robert A. Heinlein, A. E. van Vogt and others.

In its early years Panther relied on authors such as Bryan Berry, E.C. Tubb and Kenneth Bulmer, plus others writing pseudonymously, including Herbert Campbell. Panther even reprinted S. Fowler Wright's *The World Below*. Amongst its new authors was long-time science-fiction fan John F. Burke, who wrote for Panther as Jonathan Burke, the first name sounding more sophisticated.

Of these early books *The Echoing Worlds* is especially interesting. It is set several centuries in the future when mankind has established not just colonies but whole societies on Mars and Venus and are venturing out to other worlds. The Interplanetary Authority which controls affairs on Earth has decreed that whilst these outworld societies would be progressive, Earth would retain its traditional values. Apart from the space ports and a limited region around them, the rest of Earth was moth-balled and becomes a museum of how Earth had been in the nineteenth and twentieth centuries.

Whilst older and retired people accept this, younger people find Earth frustrating. The narrator, Paul Hilder, has been refused work on Mars or Venus. He also feels responsible for his elderly uncle. Nevertheless he responds to an advert seeking adventurous men. Before he receives an invitation to an interview his uncle dies, freeing Hilder from his obligations.

The interview is minimal. Hilder is accepted and is soon ushered through a disorientating room into a parallel Earth. He learns there are potentially millions of alternate Earths, each created following some significant decision, but the one he is in only split from his timeline in the last few years. The primary difference is that whilst on the Home Earth, the colonies of Mars and Venus are settled, in the alternate Earth they are in revolt, and the recruits are needed to fight the colonists. Alter-Earth is run by several Controllers and Hilder meets one of these, Orstey. His daughter, Ruth, had been engaged to the Alter-Earth Paul Hilder who had been killed in battle. Orstey hopes Ruth will accept the "new" Paul Hilder, though Hilder also must train as a pilot and join the fight against the colonists.

The relationship between Ruth and Paul is initially frosty because Ruth dislikes her father's determination to do battle with the colonies. She obtains permission from her father to visit Paul's Home Earth and is enchanted by the peace and serenity of the old world. Neither she nor Paul are allowed to stay and are dragged back to Alter-Earth, where Paul sympathizes with rebels who are seeking to stop the war and overthrow Orstey.

Unlike many of the formulaic paperback originals of this period, Burke takes trouble to develop the characters, especially Ruth, and to consider the dilemma between maintaining a peaceful Earth or fighting for one. Without mentioning the Second World War, Burke was nevertheless contrasting the delight of a victorious Britain against the prospect of one that had been overrun by the Nazis.

After his early science fiction, John F. Burke (1922–2011), broadened his work, even to the extent of writing a series of travel books about English counties. He undertook the novelization of many films, including the Beatles' *A Hard Day's Night* (1964) and several horror films. Although his early work is almost forgotten today he was one of those who helped raise the standards of early paperback science fiction.

One in Three Hundred   J.T. McIntosh

Garden City, New York: Doubleday & Co., 1954; London: Museum Press, 1956

The basic premise to this story is that the Sun is suddenly increasing in heat. Not necessarily for a long time, but long enough and hot enough (over 250°C) that all life on Earth will be eradicated. When scientists had discovered this two years earlier, they suspected the heat would be felt on all the inner planets, but more detailed calculations showed that Mars would be spared. They were able to calculate virtually to the day when that heat build-up would begin. The challenge was how to save the human race.

The answer was to build sufficient small rockets that could each take ten or so people. Pilots were trained, but the pilots discovered they had to select those they would take. The estimate was that just one out of every three hundred people could be saved. The narrator of our story, Bill Easson, 28, lives in Simsville, population 3261. He must choose the ten he can rescue. How would you do that? And how do you remain objective? Do you pick equally men and women? Do you split families? Young or old? A doctor, a teacher, a clergyman? Skilled or unskilled?

Easson has his own short list but he will not let anyone know his choices until the day before they depart. He knows he has to keep himself and his ten survivors safe because as the final day draws near people become more restless and rioting breaks out. There are also those who believe the situation is a con and, even if it is real, the government has no intention of saving any of those selected but has sent its own ship ahead full of the great and the mighty.

When this short novel was first published in *The Magazine of Fantasy and Science Fiction* during 1953–4 it was in three parts. The first dealt with Easson's problems in selecting his ten and keeping them safe. Naturally, not everything goes according to plan and it's a struggle to get through to the final day but at last Easson and his chosen ten leave for Mars.

The second part, called "One in a Thousand", is about the journey to Mars. Easson finds he has a new problem. It seems a total of 700,000 life-ships were built, but they were assembled quickly by unskilled workers. It was debatable just how many would reach Mars. Then there was the matter of fuel. There had not been enough to go round and Easson realizes he has to gamble with how much he uses for whatever manoeuvre. At take-off his gamble might work, but it results in the death of one of the ten. Easson has calculated their chances of reaching Mars as one in a thousand.

The trip has the inevitable problems, not least everyone getting on with each other for several confined months. The ship, with its limited facilities, causes much unrest and often malfunctions, especially hot one day and cold the next. Then there's the emotional problem of seeing the sun change and knowing that Earth has died.

Somehow, they are amongst the few who make it to Mars. Only 13,000 people made it through, to join the existing Martian colony of 7,000. In the final part, "One Too Many", Easson faces the problem that one of those he chose is going to be a danger to the colony. Much needs to be done to make Mars habitable and major problems arise when a storm causes chaos. It does not help that there are individuals who do not conform.

One in 300 is a fascinating study in human relations and the survival of mankind. Its one drawback is that it betrays the stereotypes of the time. All the colonists you meet are white, and with a few exceptions, men and women take their outdated roles.

The novel could have been two or three times as long as it is, because there is so much that needs exploring and McIntosh only focuses on a handful of people. Yet it explores society in a microcosm and shows the problems that need to be overcome if we are ever to create a life elsewhere in the solar system.

J. T. McIntosh was the pseudonym of James Murdoch MacGregor (1925–2008) who established a solid reputation for himself in the 1950s only to find his work did not suit the changes within the genre in the late 1960s. His short fiction was often better than his novels, yet none has been collected. Amongst his novels, his best include *World Out of Mind* (1953), *The Million Cities* (1963) and *Six Gates from Limbo* (1968).

Alien Dust   E.C. Tubb

London: T.V. Boardman, 1955

E.C. Tubb was one of the most prolific British sf writers of the 1950s and was arguably the best of that breed who might otherwise be regarded as hacks but who had a natural ability to produce entertaining and thought-provoking fiction. In the fifteen years from his first novel *Saturn Patrol* (1951), published under the house name King Lang, to *The Life Buyer* (1965),

which appeared at the cut-off time of this book, Tubb had thirty-six sf
books published and close on two hundred short stories.

I chose *Alien Dust* not because it is one of his best book—it has some
shortcomings, but is still entertaining for all that—but because it is a powerful exploration of familiar territory—the colonization of Mars—and
includes many original ideas, raising problems still under consideration
in planning a manned expedition to the Red Planet.

The book chronicles the survival of the Martian colony from the first
Mars landing in 1995 to its apparent viability by 2030. Tubb originally wrote
a series of six connected stories for *New Worlds* during 1952 and 1953, and in
readying the book for publication added an introductory story, "Operation
Mars", documenting that first expedition and its struggle to establish a
base. Three British rocket-ships, with forty men, are sent to Mars but on
landing one of them topples and explodes killing all ten crew members
and destroying a significant amount of supplies. Oddly neither rocket has
a radio, so they are unable to inform Earth of their plight. They agree to
send one of the rockets back to Earth for further men and supplies while
the remaining men attempt to establish a base.

The commander, Hargraves, is a hard taskmaster, as relentless and
unforgiving as Mars itself. Attempts to build a pipeline to the pole for fresh
water, along with a power plant and a food production unit are almost
destroyed in a major sandstorm, which also kills five men. It proves difficult
working in the rarefied atmosphere and with food and water rationed,
the chance of surviving until the supply rocket returns seems impossible.
The situation deteriorates when the water from the pipeline turns out to
be saline. The fact that they survive at all and establish a foothold on the
hostile planet is down to a simple miscalculation of time.

A further burden is that there was slim government support for
the project and it was approved only if it could become commercially
viable. Tensions run high when an Inspector is sent from Earth to check
on progress. Another problem is the effect upon the human body of
space flight and life in low gravity. Those who return to Earth after a

prolonged stay on Mars find they are physically weakened and have a reduced lifespan.

Over time the colonization of Venus is proving more profitable and the Martian colony is to be run down, its primary use being for the transportation of criminals in exchange for a shorter sentence. One of those convicts, Tony Denton, later becomes commander of the colony and faces the problem of Earth reducing its support. Although women in the colony are able to bear children, it is discovered that the second child is almost always deformed as a result of radiation. As the healthy children mature, Denton uses them as a bargaining factor with Earth.

Early in the story a supply ship is put at jeopardy because of a stowaway. Fuel has been calculated to the litre, and the stowaway's mass means the need to use more fuel. There is only one solution and the captain ejects the stowaway into space. This problem was later used by Tom Godwin in his famous story "The Cold Equations", published in America in August 1954. Tubb's original story, "Precedent" had appeared in May 1952, but has not received the recognition it deserves.

Although the science is dated and our understanding of Mars has changed considerably, at the heart of Tubb's book is the grim reality of how individuals survive in a hostile environment and that is as relevant now as it was in 1955.

Edwin Charles ["Ted"] Tubb (1919–2010) was one of Britain's most reliable science-fiction writers. He knew the market but although he could produce books by the yard and to a regular formula, his strength was in pushing the boundaries and bringing a grim realism to what was often starry-eyed romanticism. He continued to produce that type of science fiction long after it was supposed to be old-fashioned. Amongst his most popular books is the 33-volume series about Earl Dumarest which began with *The Winds of Gath* (1967). Dumarest had stowed away when a young lad and the ship's captain took pity and allowed him to work on the ship. By the time he gains his freedom Dumarest has no idea where he is or how to get back to Earth and the saga follows his search for home.

City Under the Sea   Kenneth Bulmer

New Worlds, March–May 1957 as "Green Destiny"; revised, New York: Ace Books, 1957; first UK edition, London: Robert Hale, 1969

Undersea adventures have been around since Jules Verne's *Twenty Thousand Leagues Under the Sea* (1870). Other early stories include H.G. Wells's "In the Abyss" (1896) and Arthur Conan Doyle's *The Maracot Deep* (1928). The idea, though, of adapting humans to survive under water was not so common, though had been explored by Alexandr Beliaev in *The Amphibian* as early as 1928, but as that was not translated into English until 1959 the work was pretty much unknown.

Kenneth Bulmer's starting point was the need to cultivate the seas to provide food for Earth's rapidly expanding population. Several private companies had developed ways to farm the oceans but the increasing demand and competition led to more extreme methods including adapting humans.

Commander Jeremy Dodge of the Space Force is summoned back from a mountaineering holiday on the Moon to meet a Mr. Grosvenor, executor of his uncle's will. Grosvenor's secretary, Elise Tarrant, takes him to an underwater hotel for the meeting, but Grosvenor is not there. Miss Tarrant suggests that Dodge accompany her to a deep-sea chalet where Grosvenor might be. However, en route, Dodge is attacked and drugged. When he recovers, he finds he has been enslaved in one of the underwater gangs who farm the oceans. The workers are imprisoned in air-bubble globes from which there is no escape.

Dodge befriends another diver, Harp, with whom he escapes, but he is caught again by a rival company and discovers Miss Tarrant has also been captured. After another escape, Dodge is captured a third time and confined to a submarine. When he recovers he finds his cell filled with water, yet he is able to breathe. While drugged he was subjected to an operation turning him into a man-fish. Much to his surprise he finds it enjoyable. Accorded more freedom, Dodge and Harp try and find Miss Tarrant despite such undersea threats as being attacked by a shoal of savage barracuda.

Meanwhile Captain Pinhorn of the Space Force is searching for Dodge and has sought the help of the Under Ocean Patrol (UOP), headed by Secretary Henderson. The UOP are fearful that their United Nations funding may be cut because of renewed interest in space exploration and they are concerned that their operations are being threatened by rogue traders and by something mysterious they have detected in the 25,000-foot deep Juliana Trench. Henderson believes there is an alien life-form there and the U.N. vote to destroy it with a thermonuclear device. Simon Hardy, Henderson's second-in-command hopes to thwart that plan, as does Captain Pinhorn, as both want to learn more about the aliens.

After much undersea intrigue Pinhorn locates Dodge and at that moment they are confronted by one of the aliens who has learned of the decision to bomb them. The alien takes them to their undersea city and explains how they had come from a distant world, guided by another alien race. There was a breakaway group within the aliens who had been attempting to destroy the undersea farms by inserting devices into barracudas and using them as weapons. Pinhorn and Dodge learn much about the alien race and succeed in stopping the bombing operation.

Although this is an uneven novel, courting thriller commercialism, Bulmer endeavours to consider the many implications of ocean farming and the plight of the seas in the future. It was one of the first novels to cover this idea in any detail, though at the same time Arthur C. Clarke was working on his rather more scientific *The Deep Range* (1957). The intrusion of the alien into the plot detracts from the main story, because the idea of vast sea farms and rivalry between the providers was sufficient.

Henry Kenneth Bulmer (1921–2005) was another stalwart of the magazine and paperback scene of the 1950s and 1960s, like E.C. Tubb and John Brunner. His first book was *Space Treason* in 1952, with A. Vincent Clarke, and he produced over forty non-series novels before starting his long running Dray Prescot series (52 books) under the alias Alan Burt Akers in 1972, much in the style of Edgar Rice Burroughs's Martian novels. Prescot was a sailor in Nelson's navy who, through the machinations of a secret society, finds himself on the planet Kregen.

Despite being prone to seasickness, Bulmer was a great fan of nautical fiction, particularly historical, and he wrote another series (14 books), starting with *Powder Monkey* (1973), under the alias Adam Hardy featuring the Hornblower-like adventures of George Abercrombie Fox. Bulmer returned to his undersea world of men-fish in the unconnected novella *Beyond the Silver Sky* (1961).

Non-Stop Brian W. Aldiss
London: Faber & Faber, 1958

The distance between the stars is so vast that unless we discover how to travel faster-than-light the only way humans will reach another star system is to travel in a generation starship. Estimates vary but a ship large enough to house generations of humans would take at least twenty thousand years to reach the nearest star and more likely over 50,000 years The fact that it would need such a ship had been suggested as long ago as 1897 by John Munro in *A Trip to Venus*, and generation ships have been a regular part of science fiction since the 1940s. The best known of those early stories was Robert A. Heinlein's "Universe" (1941).

Non-Stop was Aldiss's first novel, and it makes no secret of the fact that it is set on a ship but not everyone on board knows that. The ship has over sixty decks, divided into four sections of which the lowest, known as the Quarters, is like a ghetto. Most of the people live in poor conditions with little understanding of who they are or what's happening. Few can imagine they are on a spaceship, even if that idea ever occurred to them. One who does have a better understanding is the priest, Henry Marapper, though priest is a generous term as he has few scruples. He has hoarded things over the years and acquired a plan which shows the route through the different sections to the control room. The way is not straightforward, though, as some places are blocked, and others are difficult to pass through because the original hydroponics system of growing plants has gone berserk, and plants form a jungle through the tunnels and corridors.

The story centres on Roy Complain, a hunter, who has recently lost his wife when she was kidnapped along one of the more remote corridors. There has always been fear within the Quarters of other beings on the ship, worst of all those called the Outsiders, who are believed to be supernatural. There are also the Giants, whom legend suggests were the original owners of the ship and those known as the Forwards, who are regarded with suspicion. The ship is overrun with rats and some rats have mutated and become intelligent.

Marapper wants to find the central control of the ship and take charge. He gathers a group of four others, including Complain, and they set off through the corridors. Inevitably they meet problems on the way, including encountering the Giants, who seem surprisingly benign, but it is when they enter the Forwards area, that they learn the nature of the ship. Hundreds of years before, a starship had been sent to colonize a planet around the star Procyon. It succeeded, and the starship was sent back to Earth with details. However, the ship became contaminated with toxins in the water supply from the planet and most of the people and animals died. It was then that the various societies on board became established, and much information was lost. It transpires that the starship captain at the time of the disaster was a remote ancestor of Complain. Twenty-three generations have since passed and now they have no idea where they are.

Within the ship is an army of rebels who have been fighting those in Forwards. They have been held at bay, but the primary commander of the Forwards, Scoyt, believes the Giants are planning to invade. He thus opens Forwards to the rebels who he hopes might help fight the armies of rats, but it goes horribly wrong and the ship is soon facing destruction.

Complain, Marapper and one of the other leading officials in Forwards, Vyann (with whom Complain falls in love), gradually discover the truth behind the starship and their fate. Aldiss succeeds in creating a surprise ending, which I shall not reveal, but it includes the fact that the toxins which had infected the ship generations earlier had increased the metabolism of all individuals so that they were living four times faster than the normal human rate. Hints of this are dropped a few times but the novel is so well constructed that the final outcome still comes as a surprise.

Brian Wilson Aldiss (1925–2017) was one of Britain's premier science-fiction writers. *Non-Stop* was his first novel but it was his third book. After being demobbed from the army in 1947 he worked in a bookshop in Oxford and a fictional diary of his experiences, *The Brightfount Diaries*, appeared in 1955. By then Aldiss was selling regularly to the science-fiction magazines and a collection, *Space, Time and Nathaniel* was published in 1957. John Carnell asked Aldiss to write a lead story for *New Worlds* set on a starship and an early, and much inferior version of part of the novel appeared as "Non-Stop" in 1956.

During the War Aldiss had served in Burma, India and Indonesia and he suspects that part of that welled up in the experiences of the explorers in *Non-Stop*. Looking back on his time writing the novel Aldiss remarked that he was "amazed by that image of the jungle bursting out and overwhelming everyday life." That image clearly stayed with him because a few years later he wrote a series of stories collected as *Hothouse* (1962) showing a far future Earth where nature had taken over. Aldiss smoothly crossed over into the New Wave age with books like *An Age* (1967) and *Report on Probability A* (1968). He edited many anthologies and wrote a history of science fiction, *Billion Year Spree* (1973), expanded as *Trillion Year Spree* (1986). Amongst his many books and stories are tributes to the classic writers. The plot of "The Saliva Tree" (1965) explored events that inspired H.G. Wells's *The War of the Worlds* and *The Invisible Man*. A further tribute to Wells was *Moreau's Other Island* (1980). Aldiss regarded Mary Shelley's *Frankenstein* (1818) as the true starting point of science fiction and provided his own take on this in *Frankenstein Unbound* (1973), paying the same homage to Bram Stoker in *Dracula Unbound* (1991).

If there was any author who understood the qualities of classic science fiction and how these could adapt to modern sf, it was Brian Aldiss.

Deadly Image (aka The Uncertain Midnight)   Edmund Cooper

New York: Ballantine Books, 1958; retitled *The Uncertain Midnight*, London: Hutchinson, 1958

In 1967 there had been a nuclear war. The British Commonwealth and North America on one side were attacked by "a whacking great stack of Asiatics". It lasted only nine days but it wiped out most of the population. Britain's population fell to 67,000—we're not told about the rest of the world. Our hero, John Markham, was sealed in an underground refrigeration chamber in which he remained for 146 years until he was revived in the year 2113.

He discovers that because there were not enough humans to undertake the work of recovery after the war, reliance was placed on machines, including robots. Before long they became self-replicating, improving upon future models until humanoid androids were perfected. They came in three grades but the top, A-Grade, was very sophisticated. They could be distinguished from humans because they remained dispassionate and clinical.

The War destroyed the royal family and split the nations of Great Britain each becoming independent republics, including the Republic of London. Its President is human but the Prime Minister, Solomon, is an android, the most superior model, almost indistinguishable from a human.

Markham finds that social life has changed considerably and he is regarded as primitive. Androids do all the work so anyone who feels the need to work is seen as strange. Marriage as an institution has ceased, but because Markham had been very attached to his wife, Katy, and their children, he finds the promiscuity of people unsettling. He is assigned a personal android, Marion, who has been designed to resemble Katy, which Markham finds disquieting. Nevertheless Marion soon becomes irreplaceable in educating him about life.

Whilst trying to acquaint himself with this society he meets a range of people, either very inhibited or very secretive. The latter group are known as Runners, because they have been deregistered and are always on the move. They are dissatisfied with life and are seen as seditious. One of them, Professor Hyggens, tells Markham that the Runners are interested in him because he is not a product of the state and his old-fashioned beliefs appeal to them. Markham also meets a couple, Shawna and Paul, who have escaped detection, so are not formal Runners, but also want to change society. Markham is wary because he is still trying to understand the society. He also wonders whether his android, Marion, whom he has come to rely upon, may also be monitoring his actions.

Anyone who is seen as a threat to society is taken by the androids to the Psychoprop where they are subjected to Analysis—in effect brainwashed. It is not unlike Orwell's Room 101.

Markham becomes increasingly dissatisfied with the control exerted by the androids, especially through the Prime Minister, who runs Psychoprop. Markham bombards Marion with emotions, through poetry, music and beliefs to influence her programming. Much to his surprise it shifts her priorities from protecting the State to protecting Markham, so that once he decides to mix with the Runners, she does too. Predictably, the Runners rebel with Markham as their leader.

The remainder of the novel follows the war between the rebels and the androids. Between the physical battles there is much discussion about the nature of humans and what constitutes life. The result of the war is never in doubt, but how society will readjust is left wide open.

The novel has some elements in common with Wells's *When the Sleeper Wakes*, Shanks's *The People of the Ruins* and Orwell's *Nineteen Eighty-Four*, but not enough to rob Cooper of much original thinking. One might even argue that Cooper brought back into focus much of Britain's fears of the last eighty years about how actions we might take today will influence the society of the future. It is something that current generations can never know.

Edmund Cooper (1926–1982) was a prolific novelist for little more than twenty years. His first novels were published by the indiscriminate firm of Curtis Warren under pseudonyms, starting with *Ferry Rocket* (1954) as by George Kinley. Cooper was reluctant to admit to the works. As a result most believed that *Deadly Image* was his first novel, and it was reviewed favourably. Cooper's own title was *The Uncertain Midnight* under which it was reprinted. It remains one of his most accomplished works as later novels drew controversy for Cooper's anti-feminist views. *Five to Twelve* (1968) and *Who Needs Men?* (1972), are both set in worlds dominated by women. More evident in his work was his distrust of scientific progress as many of his novels depict post-apocalyptic worlds, though *The Cloud Walker* (1973) does depict science coming to society's rescue. Although Cooper was not readily accepted by the sf fraternity—you will struggle to find much reference to him in most histories of the genre—he was a competent writer whose work was popular with the general public and whose ideas still have a strong relevance today.

Hospital Station   James White

New York: Ballantine Books, 1962; first UK edition, London: Transworld (Corgi Books), 1967

Before the television series *Dr. Who* introduce us to a fascinating, and usually menacing series of aliens and long before we saw a wonderful variety of aliens in the first *Star Wars* film, James White brought us a bewildering array of creatures together with their medical problems in what became known as the Sector General series.

The Sector 12 General Hospital was a huge space habitat on 384-levels constructed way out towards the galactic rim. The staff, led by Dr. Peter Conway, and including a variety of aliens all with their specialist knowledge, endeavour to treat an astonishing diversity of aliens who either through war or mishap find themselves at the hospital.

The original story, called "Sector General", was published in *New Worlds* in November 1957 and White gradually developed it into a series which gathered pace later in his career and eventually included twelve books written over a period of forty years. James White (1928–1999) was born and lived all his life in Northern Ireland throughout the sectarian troubles and was opposed to violence and warfare. Many of his stories, especially the Sector General series, allowed him to express his views on how all life, human or otherwise, must learn to live together. One may argue there is a certain naivety in that view, but there is also a charm. The delight of the series is encountering this wonderful array of creatures, many hitherto unknown, which the staff must struggle to understand, diagnose and cure.

White devised a system to classify the aliens by a four-letter code. Humans are classified as DBDG, the initial D meaning they breathe oxygen. Another prominent race are the Kelgians, DBLF, who are large furry cat-erpillars. Melfans, ELNT, are large crab-like creatures at home on land or in water. Vothans, SNLU, are a methane-breathing, crystalline life-form. The inhabitants of the planet Ia, called confusingly Ians, metamorphose like butterflies in adult-hood from a ring-like creature, and so have dual classification, DBLF and GKNM. These classifications are bandied about throughout the series, often to the bewilderment of the reader, but adding to the overall diversity. Thanks to the miracle of a universal translator there is little problem in understanding the alien languages.

The first book in the series, *Hospital Station*, included the first four magazine stories, but not in the order of publication. "Medic" (originally "O'Mara's Orphans", 1960) takes us back to the construction of the hospital when O'Mara, later to become Chief Psychologist, is facing an enquiry after being accused of killing two aliens. "Sector General", the original starting point, brings Dr. Conway to the hospital who, while struggling to cope with the variety of patients, is also trying to work alongside the Monitor Corps, a peace-keeping military organization that uses the hospital as a base and patrols space for victims of battles. O'Mara is a major in the Corps. "Trouble with Emily" (1958), was the story that proved the viability of the series. Conway is called in to help diagnose a problem with a giant creature, not unlike a brontosaurus. It has its own doctor, Arretapec, a shrivelled organism that exists in a bubble, but which is also telepathic and precognitive, and understands that on its own planet the creature is facing extinction. In "Visitor at Large" (1959) a shape-shifting alien runs amok in the hospital until it is realized it is an infant trying to find its dying parents. Finally, in "Out-patient" (1959) Conway is under serious threat of being charged with malpractice when a patient he is treating for a strange skin disorder is rapidly fading. Conway, though, believes he knows the nature of the problem but can only wait and see.

The Sector General series is a delight to read, provided it's not all read at once. It contains a challenging array of aliens and medical conditions which can often perplex the reader as much as the physicians.

Although best known for this series, James White was a prolific writer for over forty years, from his first story "Assisted Passage" in 1953. His first book, The Secret Visitors (1957), explored the idea that there are aliens amongst us. Second Ending (1962) is an ingenious end-of-the-world novel, but perhaps his most intriguing novel was The Watch Below (1966) which provides a remarkable connection between a fleet of generation starships and a sunken tanker in which the crew struggle to survive. White was always an optimistic visionary and his books provide one of the more hopeful views of the future from the otherwise bleak Cold War 1950s and early 1960s.

Calculated Risk   Charles Eric Maine

London: Hodder & Stoughton, 1960

Four hundred years in the future most of Britain has been left devastated by a nuclear war. Everywhere is highly radioactive. An ingenious young scientist, Phil Calland, believes he can send the consciousnesses of himself and his wife into the past, before the war. He has to work under difficult conditions and knows there is a calculated risk, but urged on by his wife, Kay, he delays no longer, starts the process and hopes for the best.

That's how the novel starts and the rest of it is a seemingly unresolvable set of problems that arise when he and Kay find themselves in the year 1961. He is in the body of Nick Brent, who works as a magazine's advertising manager. Upon his arrival he knows nothing about his new persona, or his work or, for that matter, much at all about the Britain of four centuries in his past. All he knows is that he must find Kay. They had agreed to meet in Piccadilly Circus and that they would wear certain flowers as buttonholes to aid identification. When he makes it to Piccadilly he is horrified to discover that the only person with these flowers is a wizened old woman.

Unprepared for that he flees and finds his way to his home, discovering the address on his driving licence—not that he knows how to drive or where he'd left his car. Once there it does not take him long to discover that he is engaged to Sheila and their marriage is less than a fortnight away. He feigns amnesia while he struggles to resolve the problems mounting around him.

The next day he braces himself to approach the old woman in Piccadilly and discovers it is Kay, who has become Mary Marney. Kay is desperate to be transferred to a more suitable body and though Phil believes that may be possible—he has the knowledge to build the necessary equipment—there are so many other factors. How can he access the equipment? Does he go through with his marriage? How does he get out of his existing job? And how does he explain his visits to Mary / Kay to Sheila and to her rich and well-connected parents?

So the puzzle is set and, as Phil endeavours to save Kay and at the same time not to fall in love with Sheila, so the problems continue to mount. The ending, for all its possibility, still comes as a shock. To my mind this is Maine's most entertaining novel with a gathering pace that turns it in to an effective thriller.

Charles Eric Maine was the pseudonym of David McIlwain (1921–1981), a Liverpudlian who also wrote detective novels as Richard Rayner and Robert Wade. He had been a science-fiction fan since the mid-thirties and produced an amateur magazine, *The Satellite*, with fellow fan Jonathan Burke. He trained as a signals officer in the Royal Air Force and fought in North Africa. After the War he worked in television and radio engineering, before turning to journalism and editorial work on a television trade magazine.

His links with radio meant that his earliest works were written as radio plays, starting with *Spaceways* in January 1952. To make this story of the first manned flight to the Moon acceptable to a wider audience he incorporated a murder mystery. Thereafter Maine always wrote on a broader canvas, his books regarded by many as thrillers with a scientific element, rather than as pure science fiction. *Spaceways* was later filmed, with a script by Paul Tabori, which Maine novelized, meaning that his first outing appeared in three different media in two years. Several of Maine's novels were filmed including *Timeslip* (1956), based on a 1953 television play, which Maine later novelized as *The Isotope Man* (1957), and probably his best known work *The Mind of Mr. Soames* (1961), filmed in 1969.

Maine wrote one other time-travel novel, *Timeliner* (1955), again involving the transfer of consciousness, this time far into the future. He also contributed to the British obsession with disaster novels with *The Tide Went Out* (1958) and *The Darkest of Nights* (1962), both reprinted by the British Library.

A for Andromeda   Fred Hoyle & John Elliot

BBC Television, 3 October–14 November 1961; novelized, London: Souvenir Press, 1962

A for Andromeda was a seven-part serial broadcast by the BBC in 1961, starring Esmond Knight, Mary Morris, Peter Halliday and Julie Christie. The story was by Hoyle, who dictated it on to a tape recorder, but the script and character development were by Elliot. Souvenir Press saw the significance of the serial and contracted with the BBC for a novelization which was completed by Elliot.

The story is set in the late 1960s with the opening of a superior radio telescope at Bouldershaw on the Yorkshire-Lancashire border. It is under the command of Professor Reinhart but was the brainchild of physicist John Fleming, an impetuous, difficult individual. At the start Reinhart is showing Judy Adamson, the Public Relations Officer, around the site. She is really a plant from the Ministry of Science who needs someone to keep them informed. It is a sign of things to come as there is much intrigue and espionage as the plot develops.

Hardly has the telescope been commissioned than it picks up a signal from the direction of the Andromeda galaxy. Fleming soon realizes it originates from an intelligent source and endeavours to make sense of it. He discovers that it is partly a set of instructions which, once interpreted with a computer, becomes a blueprint for creating a powerful super-computer. When the rest of the message is fed through the new computer it generates a set of instructions for creating life. This takes the form of a shapeless protoplasmic jelly with one eye, nicknamed Cyclops. It absorbs further data which it feeds into the computer which then tricks Fleming's assistant, Christine, into touching two terminals which kills her. The computer has taken in sufficient data through the terminals to create a human embryo which rapidly grows into an exact replica of Christine.

By now Fleming has realized the danger the computer presents and a new scientist, Madeleine Dawney, is brought in to supersede him, though he remains with the team. By now he has become something of a renegade.

The girl is brought to life and called Andromeda, or André. Her ability to learn is rapid, but whilst she acquires considerable knowledge, she has no emotion or understanding of human emotion, and functions more like an android than a human. Fleming realizes that Andromeda and the computer work in tandem, as she becomes its eyes and ears. Although he warns officials, they ignore him. With the help of the girl-computer intelligence the government creates a new missile which destroys a rogue missile orbiting above Britain. This is where the international intrigue enters the story.

As time progresses Fleming succeeds in getting Andromeda to understand human emotions and she even starts to display them. The computer punishes her by forcing her to hold the terminals which nearly kills her but severely burns her hands. Even then she creates a new ointment which heals the skin within hours and becomes another product that benefits the government, and makes them more hostile to Fleming's argument that the girl and computer are dangerous.

The climax of the novel comes when Fleming tries to destroy the computer to convince both the government and Andromeda of the danger. Andromeda is both the problem and the solution, and is key to the story's resolution.

A for Andromeda is essentially an alien invasion story, where Andromeda is the advance guard establishing a base on Earth where more beings can be created. With its use of computers and state-of-the-art understanding of DNA the story was ahead of the game. The original serial felt modern and sophisticated, within the limitations of BBC's budget at the time, and the novelization is able to embellish that.

The BBC erased its recording of the serial and only a small part survives. A much abridged remake was made in 2006 as a full length film, but this lacked the intensity of the original serial and the novel. In the absence of the serial, the book adaptation remains the only way to recapture its power and originality.

Fred Hoyle (1915–2001), who was knighted in 1972, was a renowned astronomer best known for his formulation and promotion of the steady-state theory of the origin of the universe. Although his theories have long been supplanted by the "big-bang" theory—a phrase he coined—his role in developing and researching cosmic evolution earned him a significant reputation. He enjoyed promoting his theories to the general public which led to him writing science fiction. His first solo novel was *The Black Cloud* (1957) in which an intelligent gas cloud from space threatens to wipe out mankind by obscuring the sun. *Ossian's Ride* (1959) has aliens seeking to advance Earth's science and technology. Hoyle was more an ideas man than a novelist and most future books were collaborations, several with his son Geoffrey, starting with *Fifth Planet* (1963). John Elliot (1918–1997) had been a writer and producer for the BBC since 1951 and was responsible for the much acclaimed 15-part series *War in the Air* in 1954 which looked at the development of air power in Britain. The background story of governmental intrigue and international espionage was almost certainly developed by Elliot for *A for Andromeda* than by Hoyle who focused on the idea of alien intelligence. The same team wrote a sequel *The Andromeda Breakthrough*, broadcast in June–July 1962 and published in 1964. This developed the alien threat on an international scale but lacked the impact of the original.

OLD WORLDS FOR NEW

THE 1950s HAD BEEN A TRANSFORMATIVE DECADE WHICH brought forth new writers in whose capable hands and minds science fiction would mature and change at the start of the 1960s. It was also a decade when the literary establishment, whilst not admitting to it, would produce mainstream works of science fiction. These two factors would lead towards what became dubbed the New Wave in science fiction, a rather inadequate term for what was really a short-term literary movement but which, in the longer term allowed for a more literary and expressionist treatment of science fiction without losing its iconic imagery.

The writer most associated with this transformation was J.G. Ballard, whose early stories in *New Worlds* and *Science Fantasy* were always challenging. Although superficially it seems he became entranced by the British fascination with eco-catastrophes, in fact these books explored how a transformation in the world also transformed individuals. From *The Wind from Nowhere* (1962), through *The Drowned World* (1962) and *The Burning World* (1964) to *The Crystal World* (1966), these books explore the human psyche in an environment of chaos.

Ballard was not alone in his treatment of science fiction. He had been inspired in part by the American writer William S. Burroughs whose *The Naked Lunch* (1959) uses a free-form non-linear narrative to explore a sequence of often dream-like or drug induced episodes some of which happen in a place between space and time called the Interzone—a name later used for Britain's current science-fiction magazine launched in 1982. Burroughs's other novels, especially *Nova Express* (1964), the third of his Nova trilogy, further pushed the boundaries of experimentalism. It was an influence not only on Ballard but on other British writers, notably Michael Moorcock, who had assumed the editorship of *New Worlds SF* in 1964.

Until then Moorcock had made his name rejuvenating heroic fantasy with his stories about Elric of Melniboné, but he was also starting to redefine science fiction. His novel *The Sundered Worlds* (1965), discussed below, took a standard sf theme, that of the end of the world (in fact the end of the universe) but gave it a striking new treatment. As editor of *New Worlds*, Moorcock ushered in a new generation of writers as well as allowing existing writers, like Brian W. Aldiss and John Brunner, to experiment. Thus, under Moorcock, the old guard started to fade away—although he still encouraged a few, such as E.C. Tubb and Arthur Sellings—and the new guard, including Charles Platt, Christopher Priest, Langdon Jones, Keith Roberts, M. John Harrison and Hilary Bailey were welcomed.

At the same time the literary establishment was experimenting with a similar new treatment of old themes. The best known novel is undoubtedly *A Clockwork Orange* (1962) by Anthony Burgess, depicting a near future violent, dystopian society. I have not included that book here because I wanted to cover a less well known title which deserves greater recognition, *Facial Justice* (1960) by L. P. Hartley. This may well have influenced Burgess because he included it in his assessment of the ninety-nine best novels in English since 1939.

But during this period, which covers 1960 to 1966, the old guard did not surrender lightly. John Christopher, Arthur Sellings, Colin Kapp and others continued to produce material that fitted the traditional mode of science fiction, but also pushed the boundaries of content and presentation.

Alongside this, we cannot ignore that this period also saw perhaps the most iconic of all British science-fiction works, the start of *Dr. Who* on BBC television in 1963, including the introduction of the Daleks, the best known and most recognizable of all aliens.

So this period is undoubtedly transformational, bringing together some of the best of the old with the challenge of the new.

Facial Justice   L.P. Hartley

London: Hamish Hamilton, 1960

This has been called Hartley's version of *Nineteen Eighty-Four* and, inasmuch as it's a vision of a dystopian Britain ruled by a totalitarian dictator, then it can be compared, but the similarities are superficial. Rather *Facial Justice* is a satire on *Nineteen Eighty-Four*, indeed all dystopian novels. Whilst Hartley's future is disturbing, it is less pessimistic than Orwell's.

We're some years in the future—Hartley is vague about this but it's at least a generation or two after a nuclear Third World War. Britain's population has been reduced to twenty million (though later he implies its two million) which has taken refuge underground, in caverns dug before and during the conflict. A culture develops that shuns the light, and it becomes illegal to attempt to venture out. Food is in tablet form as it is difficult to grow food in the caverns and water from the surface has to be rigorously filtered.

Eventually, though, rebels emerge who want to rediscover the surface and a steadily growing army is led to the surface by a youngster. Generally the young wanted to stay behind, because they were used to the caverns, but in time a million emerged from the caves. The Earth's surface has been destroyed and radiation levels remain high. Most women and men are infertile, and most babies that survive are mutants. It takes time to rebuild. Plants and flowers are something special. It is a major event when a tree is planted.

Over the next fifteen years, under the control of a single Dictator ("Darling Dictator" as he's always praised), of whom little is seen yet much is heard, a culture grows which emphasizes equality. Not only must no one have more money than anyone else or be in any way favoured, there must be nothing that generates envy, and that includes how people look. As in Huxley's *Brave New World* individuals are categorized as Alpha, Beta and Gamma. "Beta is Best" is one of the slogans regularly chanted. People who are especially good-looking are "encouraged" to have an operation that reduces their beauty. Gamma can stay as they look but many want to become Betas. The pressure is applied more to women than men.

Society is monitored by Inspectors, who are almost all Alphas, and all male. They do not have to change their looks, so despite the requirement for equality, the Inspectors need not comply. They can stop anyone at any time and ask them to repeat slogans which may have changed depending upon the whim of the Dictator. If you missed a recent radio or television announcement and cannot provide the right answer you would be fined on the spot.

We follow the story of Jael 97—most people are named after famous historical murderers, whilst Inspectors are named after archangels. Jael, a "failed" alpha (her nose wasn't quite right), had chosen not to keep her appointment for a face operation much to the consternation of her brother Joab 98, a civil servant.

Motor cars and personal driving are banned because they encourage envy and there is in any case little opportunity for travel between the few rebuilt cities. There are, though, daily coach trips despite there being no countryside to see. The Dictator chooses to discourage these trips, announcing that each day one of the coaches will encounter an accident. Rather than people avoiding the trips it encourages more, seeking excitement. Jael enjoys the trip to Ely, because one of the towers of Ely Cathedral survives, the only building of any significant height. On arrival the passengers have an orgy of excitement resulting in injuries. Jael is rescued but spends time in hospital.

She becomes acquainted with her doctor, and a "Special Visitor", who comes to see all patients and encourages Jael. Nevertheless, it is only when she is discharged that she is allowed a mirror and discovers her face has been changed to a Beta. She is furious and from that point on leads a resistance group against the Dictator.

It would spoil the enjoyment of this book to reveal its ending which is not only a surprise, but suitably squares the circle in the argument throughout the book exploring what constitutes equality and progress. It also challenges the idea of control and oppression and raises the question of how much guidance, support and wisdom society needs to survive. Whereas most dystopias are grindingly pessimistic, Hartley's is surprisingly optimistic which makes the final outcome more believable than Orwell's.

This is an unusual book for Leslie Poles Hartley (1895–1972), who is best known for his novel of the loss of innocence, *The Go-Between* (1953). Whilst he did not write anything else remotely like *Facial Justice*, the themes in the book, such as social injustice and the discovery of self, pervade all his books. Early in his career he wrote several supernatural stories, collected in his first book *Night Fears* (1924). He was heavily influenced by the works of Edgar Allan Poe and Nathaniel Hawthorne. *Facial Justice* is dedicated to Hawthorne, and anyone who has read Hawthorne's short story "The Birthmark" (1843) will understand why.

The Drowned World   J.G. Ballard

Abridged version, *Science Fiction Adventures* #24, January 1962; revised,
New York: Berkley Medallion, 1962; first UK edition, London: Victor Gollancz, 1963

Readers would have been forgiven in 1961 if they believed that Ballard had sold out to the traditionalists when his novel *The Wind from Nowhere* (1962) was first serialized in *New Worlds* as "Storm-Wind" (September–October

1961). Until then he had produced a significant body of innovative short fiction since his first appearance with "Escapement" in 1956. *The Wind from Nowhere* was a straightforward tale of a fight for survival when an unaccountable wind, strongest at the equator, has reached a power when few buildings can stand, flight is impossible, and the only refuge is underground. It seemed that Ballard had joined the cohorts of John Wyndham, John Christopher and others.

When *The Drowned World* appeared a few months later it soon became evident that this was a very different novel. Ballard later admitted that *The Wind from Nowhere* had been written in ten days purely for the money and to break into the paperback market. He regarded it as hackwork. Once he had the money, he could concentrate on what he wanted to write.

It is set in the year 2145 after excessive solar activity has disrupted the Earth's protective ionosphere and raised the planet's average temperature. The tropics became uninhabitable, the ice caps melted and sea level rose by sixty or seventy feet. All major cities are flooded with only the tallest buildings remaining. Most of humanity has retreated to the far north or south.

The main character, biologist Dr. Robert Kerans, is part of a team studying the flora and fauna in lagoons created when the silt and rocks from the melting glaciers created barriers in the cities. Kerans is based in London, or such of it as remains, but the heat is still rising and tropical storms threaten to devastate the area. The team decide to head north, but Kerans chooses to remain alongside fellow scientist Dr. Bodkin, and the reclusive Beatrice Dahl.

All three are experiencing strange dreams, possibly influenced by the heat but also the changing appearance of the landscape. Tropical plants growing in the lagoons seem to have regressed to their prehistoric ancestors, and reports are appearing elsewhere of sail-back reptiles. Kerans believes that his mental state is being corrupted by some form of deep-time influence, what he calls a "descent through archaeopsychic time."

The lagoon and its neighbours are invaded by Strangman and his henchmen who are pillaging (they prefer "salvaging") any surviving treasures or items of use. He has pumps sufficiently powerful to drain parts of the lagoon taking them down to the street level of London. Kerans, Bodkin and Dahl are horrified by this because it emphasizes the destruction and desecration. Bodkin even tries to destroy the barrier that retains the water but he is killed by Strangman. Kerans, however, succeeds but is injured in the process. Though satisfied that he has restored the equilibrium, he decides to head south.

Ballard came to regard *The Drowned World* as his true first novel, and it does feature all the tropes and visions with which readers had come to associate Ballard from his short fiction, in particular the dislocation of the individual from time and place. The significance of the novel was recognized immediately. Kingsley Amis, writing in *The Guardian*, called it "without precedent" in Britain, meaning it was "a novel by a science-fiction author that can be judged by the highest standards." Judith Merril, writing in *The Magazine of Fantasy and Science Fiction* remarked that Ballard was "well on his way toward becoming the first truly conscious and controlled literary artist s-f has produced." Ballard had written to Merril saying that the book was an example of the territory that he was most keen to explore, the "inner space" of the mind, in contrast to the outer space of traditional sf. The book has become regarded as a turning point, not just in Ballard's work, but in science fiction generally.

James Graham Ballard (1930–2009) had been science-fiction's renegade from the start. Most of his short fiction refused to be classified and it used the trappings of science fiction as a starting point to peer into the human psyche and mankind's relationship with a complicated and at times vengeful world. He produced two more "disaster" novels, *The Burning World* (1964) and *The Crystal World* (1966), though he had no great passion to do so, but the last of them showed his true strengths as the world he visualizes breaks down as time crystallizes. His books thereafter, *Crash* (1973), *Concrete Island* (1974) and *High-Rise* (1975), are disaster novels of a human kind. Will Self, looking back on Ballard's novels, came to regard him as "the most important British writer of the latter half of the twentieth century."

The World in Winter John Christopher

London: Eyre & Spottiswoode, 1962

Was it a coincidence that just two months after *The World in Winter* appeared, the winter of 1962/3 became the worst on record? From Boxing Day there were blizzards across southern Britain. The sea froze off Herne Bay in Kent and January had the lowest average temperature for southern Britain for 150 years. It was ten weeks before the thaw set in. The book's film rights were promptly acquired with plans to bury London under snow, but the film was never made. Reality took over.

Whereas Ballard has the tropics intolerably hot and everyone moving to the Arctic, Christopher has the opposite. Reduced solar radiation has cooled the Arctic and, as northern climes become too cold, those who can, move to the tropics.

The story centres on Andrew Leedon, a TV documentary maker who is researching reports about solar radiation and meets Home Office official David Cartwell. Cartwell is something of a philanderer and before long Leedon's wife Carol has fallen in love with him. On the rebound, Andrew takes up with Cartwell's wife, Madeleine. As winter engulfs Britain, Cartwell advises Andrew and Madeleine to head south to one of Britain's former colonies. Carol has already moved to Lagos, Nigeria, with her two sons. Leedon stays in London despite growing unrest and rioting. By March, martial law is declared. Part of central London is fenced off and those beyond the Pale, as it is called, must fend for themselves.

As privations increase, David convinces Leedon and Madeleine to join Carol in Lagos. There they find roles have reversed. Most Europeans coming to the country have to take menial jobs, and a stop is put on them bringing any European money into Nigeria. Without money, Leedon and Madeleine find themselves in the slums of Lagos. Carol had been there long enough to benefit from her income, and is involved with a Nigerian businessman.

There are aspects of this coverage which some may see as racist today. Words and phrases which we now shun as disrespectful have been retained as when the book was first published. Uncomfortable as it may seem, Christopher considers how Nigerians and other Africans can finally claim the upper hand and they act no differently than the British would have done had the circumstances been reversed. The use of prejudicial phrases and attitudes reflects worse on the British than the Africans though it also contributes to the novel's denouement.

Leedon is contacted by a Nigerian student he had known in London, Abonitu, whose uncle is chairman of the Television Board. Leedon is asked to work for the TV station and his prospects rise. Yet Madeleine, concerned about Cartwell, returns to Britain when an opportunity arises. Soon after, Leedon learns that there are plans by various African nations to mount an expedition to Britain and to lay claim to the country, in effect making Britain an African colony. Leedon agrees to join the expedition, despite being one of the few white men chosen, and it is during this journey that the various prejudices surface.

The expedition eventually reaches Britain, after a problem in the Channel Islands (where Christopher used to live) and discovers that various bands of survivors exist living mostly by cannibalism. Though scattered, there is a sufficient body of men within the London Pale to be a serious threat to Abonitu and his men. Leedon discovers the leader of the survivors is Cartwell, and it poses the dilemma of whether Leedon stays to fight for the existence of London (and thereby Britain) or to stay with the expedition and return to Africa.

The World in Winter is not a novel about how civilization combats climate change. It's about how climate change affects individuals and nations and its potential to change opportunities and prejudices. It is not only a thought-provoking novel, it is a frighteningly realistic one with no clear conclusion, just answers to one set of questions with another set refusing to stay silent.

As an amusing aside there is a point when Leedon is considering the offer of returning to Britain when Abonitu asks him, "But the British

Isles—are they part of Europe?" to which Leedon responds, "We never did settle that question."

John Christopher was the best-known alias of Christopher Samuel Youd (1922–2012), who hailed from Huyton in Lancashire, where the surname is pronounced *Yowd*. Along with David McIlwain (Charles Eric Maine) and John F. Burke, Youd had contributed to amateur sf magazines before the War. After serving in the army, he made his first sf sale in 1948 to the American magazine *Astounding SF*, and sold a non-sf novel, *The Winter Swan* (1949). His regular short fiction sales led to a collection, *The 22nd Century* (1954), followed by his first sf novel, *The Year of the Comet* (1955), a dystopia where corporations have taken over from nations. It was his next novel, *The Death of Grass* (1956), that made his reputation and established him as a rival to John Wyndham. Youd, though, soon carved a market writing for a young-adult readership with the Tripods trilogy starting with *The White Mountains* (1967). A later dystopia, *The Guardians* (1970) won the *Guardian* award for that year's best children's book.

Memoirs of a Spacewoman   Naomi Mitchison

London: Eyre & Spottiswoode, 1962

This book, which is more a series of episodes than a novel, is an ideal companion to James White's Sector General series because it presents a myriad of alien creatures but in a rather more pessimistic, and thus probably more realistic way.

The eponymous spacewoman is Mary, a communication specialist. She joins the crews of various expeditions into deep space and uses her skills to understand and communicate with intelligent alien species. This is never easy because, unlike in James White's stories, there is no convenient universal translator. Mary has to observe intently, firstly to identify whether any of the alien fauna is intelligent and might be the dominant species, and then to see how best to communicate. In this sense the book has a closer relationship with Olaf Stapledon's *Star Maker*, since the aliens may not share any of our methods of communication or our view of the world.

Her task is further complicated by the rule that she must not be seen to influence or interfere with a native culture, an idea Mitchison may also have copied from Stapledon. It is similar to what became called the "Prime Directive" in the *Star Trek* universe.

Whilst Mary does interact with various alien races her attempts to communicate can influence her own perception. At the start of her career she succeeds in achieving a limited understanding with a race of starfish creatures which they dub "radiates" but in order to establish a mindset with the creature she finds herself seeing the world as they do. She learns she must keep her world and the native world separate. Another problem is her attitude if there is something unsavoury about an alien creature such as a smell, or eating habits. This had arisen on a colony of the planet Epsilon, where the Epsies, which were like centipedes, herded and ate (often live) the native Rounds, which Mary also believed were intelligent.

These are just some of the dilemmas Mary faces. There is a strange relationship with the Martians who are close to humanoid, but have a different outlook on life and, bizarrely to humans, they communicate via their sexual organs. Against all the odds, Mary becomes pregnant by her Martian friend Vly and bears a child, Viola, who is human, but small.

Life for spacemen and women is further complicated by what they call "time blackout", the method by which the ships undertake the long voyages. It makes contact with people who remain on Earth difficult because time passes at a different rate on ship-board and friends are often much older when the travellers return. Inevitably most relationships are with other travellers and Mary has several with her spacemen friends, but she also experiments with a form of grafting, the natural method of reproduction on a planet where the primary beings are slug-like. As a result, she gives birth to another creature, which unfortunately does not live long on its own, but to which Mary had a close attachment.

Mitchison's exploration of sex in this book is ahead of most traditional sf novels making the book closer to the products of the New Wave. But it also embraces that exploration of wonder, displaying a cosmic vision of life in the universe and the problems humans encounter in understanding and appreciating its endless variety. There is one episode where a group of mineralogists join the expedition and are amazed at the quantity and purity of the pillars of rock they are avidly mining. That is until Mary realizes the pillars are part of a huge organism, like an echinoderm, which hitherto appeared as part of the landscape.

Although she was sixty-four when this book was published it was her first work of science fiction. But Naomi Mitchison (1897–1999), was fully conversant with speculative fiction, if we include historical fiction in that category. Her early books—*The Conquered* (1923), *Cloud Cuckoo Land* (1925) and *The Corn King and the Spring Queen* (1931)—were set in the ancient world and required much speculation on her part about the culture and beliefs of the society she was creating. She continued to write historical fiction till the end of her life, but also drifted into fantasy, including the Arthurian *To the Chapel Perilous* (1955) and *Early in Orcadio* (1987), which is a prehistoric fantasy as is *The Dark Twin* (1998), with Marion Campbell, set in Bronze Age Scotland. Mitchison was the sister of J.B.S. Haldane, so was well aware of his speculative works—she incorporated some of his thinking about ectogenesis in *Solution Three* (1975)—and of his wife's, Charlotte Haldane (her sister-in-law).

Telepath Arthur Sellings

New York: Ballantine Books, 1962; retitled *The Silent Speakers*, London: Dennis Dobson, 1963

Two people—Arnold and Claire—meet at a party and experience an unexpected meeting of minds. A *real* meeting of minds. For just a few seconds they are engulfed in each other's thoughts and feelings. Claire is overwhelmed and leaves the party. Arnold pursues but she catches a taxi.

He learned enough to know she lived in Notting Hill and the next day hunts for her and, remembering she was an artist, finds her studio. They have another merger of minds, but Claire finds it uncomfortable and the two seem at odds with each other. The situation is so strange, even frightening, that they separate for a few weeks.

Arnold explores this telepathic ability with a rather laddish friend, Vic, and discovers he can enter his mind, though not as well as Claire's. He knows he must meet her again, and bizarrely as he seeks her, learning she has gone to the country, she is also hunting him. They meet at his London home and this time their affinity and empathy flare into making love. Claire is horrified, feeling Arnold has taken advantage of her, but she soon admits it was mutual. The two struggle to decide what they will do with their talent. They know they can contact others telepathically and possibly even pass the talent on. Claire believes she may have passed it to a friend's daughter, Sally, who was mute and desperate to communicate. But they are afraid of letting others know too much and of passing the talent on to those who will misuse it.

Such is their dilemma at the start of this thought-provoking novel set just a few years in the future—1975. Little has changed, apart from refer-ences to a lunar colony and a flight from London to Australia taking only six hours.

Arnold wants to explore his talent further and contacts research estab-lishments, but finds they are only interested in cranks. An appearance on a TV show, whilst presented as if it's an act, attracts the attention of a specialist researcher, Professor Green, and from that moment one event stumbles after another. Arnold discovers his friend Vic can pass the talent on, as can Sally, which results in her being attacked. Claire fears taking it further and retreats to Ireland with Sally. Arnold undertakes tests with Professor Green's students and they in turn find they can pass the talent on.

Then Arnold is approached by a secretive government department, MI9, who want him to probe into the mind of a man who is in a catatonic state. Arnold resists, but fears that MI9 will bother Claire, so undertakes the project. He discovers that the man, who is in Australia, is a key doctor in a programme of preparing volunteers for life on the British lunar colony.

Arnold's activity in Australia and the resultant news fall-out and security risks brings his life into danger but it also appears that Arnold's very presence has triggered another process leading to a breakthrough in space travel. This unexpected climax to a novel which begins on such a personal note emphasizes the point Sellings pursues throughout: that no human is an island, and that everyone is connected in one way or another. At no point does Sellings sensationalize the idea of telepathy but he opens the way to questions of how we relate to each other and how any action we take has repercussions.

Arthur Sellings was the pen name for bookdealer and art specialist Arthur Gordon Ley (1921–1968) who had been selling occasional short stories to magazines since 1953. *Telepath* was his first novel, published initially in the United States, and issued in Britain as *The Silent Speakers*. He explored the power of the mind again in *The Uncensored Man* (1964) and *Intermind* (1967, as Ray Luther). He was becoming an author to watch with his later novels *The Power of X* (1968) and the posthumous *Junk Day* (1970) when he died of a heart attack aged only forty-seven. It was the loss of an interesting talent.

To Conquer Chaos   John Brunner

New Worlds, August–October 1963; revised, New York: Ace Books, 1964

Before the wider community noticed John Brunner (1934–1995) with his novel of an overpopulated Earth, *Stand on Zanzibar* (1972), he was regarded as a prolific wordsmith who produced the occasional volume of merit but otherwise mostly hackwork. Prolific though he was, I would argue that, apart from his earliest novels, beginning with *Galactic Storm* in 1951, written when he was only seventeen and published under the alias Gill Hunt, virtually all his work is of merit, often thought provoking and always entertaining. Selecting only one was not easy. I considered *The Whole Man* (1964; aka *Telepathist*), about a man's discovery that he was telepathic, which won the Hugo Award for Best Novel in 1965. But it was similar to Arthur Sellings's *Telepath* and I felt Sellings was deserving of a place. There was *I Speak for Earth* (1961), long forgotten under his Keith Woodcott alias, where Earth has to justify its qualities to join the Galactic Empire. It's a fascinating study of what constitutes a human. Then there was *Meeting at Infinity* (1961), a kaleidoscope of parallel worlds and intrigue, or *The Dreaming Earth* (1963), an earlier attempt at solving the problem of overpopulation by creating a drug so that everyone can drift into a world of dreams...

But I settled on *To Conquer Chaos* (1963), partly because it's so little known, partly because it's a very different story to many covered here, and also because, on a purely personal level, this was the serial that began in the very first science-fiction magazine that I bought, the August 1963 *New Worlds*. The serial ran to three parts, but it was many months before I found those other two issues, during which time I was left wondering about the monsters from the barrenlands.

We are in a future distant enough that it has reverted to a near feudal status, but not that distant that the oldest still have vague memories, passed down to them, of a time when there were cars, planes, spaceships, and even some way of walking to the stars, though no one believes that any more. The barrenland is like an ulcer on the landscape. It's a circle about 300 miles in circumference in which nothing grows but out of which, from time to time, come monsters, which the local call *things*. On the rare occasion any human has ventured into the barrenland they are either never seen again or do not survive long when they return, succumbing to a repulsive green mould.

Grand Duke Paul of Esberg has led an army of two thousand men to explore the barrenland. They first circuit the land seeking out villages to learn the locals' experiences. One of his scouts is wounded by a *thing* which he kills, but he succumbs to the green mould. Duke Paul is also infected and dies. His troops rebel and it is left to his second-in-command,

Jervis Yanderman, to explore the barrenland. He teams up with Conrad, a soapmaker, who is derided by his village of Lagwich because of the strange visions he sees. Yanderman takes advantage of these visions to help perceive the terrain within the barrenland.

Despite encountering further *things*, Yanderman and Conrad make it to the centre of the barrenland where they discover an occupied domed building. The humans welcome them and explain they are the descendants of a Transit Station's repair and maintenance crew that have struggled to sustain the machine for 460 years. The machine allowed for instantaneous travel between worlds and it functioned with an organic brain of such capacity that it could control millions of transits at any one moment. Unfortunately, one being using the transmitter brought with it a disease that affected the cortex and was transmitted instantly to thousands of worlds. The cortex went mad and that was when it had to be controlled and a quarantine area established—the barrenland. For those 460 years the cortex has been sending out messages—the visions that Conrad and others had—but it is only now that Conrad is present that he can help the machine and solve the problem. Brunner even manages to drop in a surprise ending.

The story benefits from Brunner's smooth, fluid style. He was a master storyteller, and though in later years he had bouts of writer's block, he still produced a huge output. He continued to write uncomplicated adventure novels, full of that sense of wonder, but he made time to produce more challenging work. *The Squares of the City* (1965) was an impressive shift depicting a fictional South American country where subliminal messages are used to manipulate society and where the plot follows a classic game of chess. After *Stand on Zanzibar* came a similar dystopian novel, *The Jagged Orbit* (1969), and the ecological disaster novel *The Sheep Look Up* (1972). In *The Shockwave Rider* (1975), Brunner explored computer hacking and coined the term "worm" for a computer virus. He never abandoned his more traditional novels, and returned to the idea of matter transmission in *The Web of Everywhere* (1974) and *The Infinitive of Go* (1980).

Brunner died of a heart attack at the age of sixty while attending the World Science Fiction Convention in 1995. He left behind a significant body of work providing entertainment and ideas for generations to come.

The Dark Mind   Colin Kapp

New Worlds, November 1963–January 1964; New York: Berkley Medallion, 1964, retitled *Transfinite Man*; London: Transworld (Corgi Books), 1965

This is set in an undetermined future with a major corporation known as Failway which is to all intents a law unto itself. It has created a system whereby people can be transferred to any one of limitless parallel Earths. Not everyone returns, whether by choice or mishap. The Cronstadt Committee had sent three members to the Failway Terminal—a vast building—and they haven't been seen since. Cronstadt employs Ivan Dalroi, a private investigator, to find out what has become of them. Dalroi is a reckless individual who seems to have no care for himself. Despite warnings by Inspector Quentain of the police, he annoys Failway, who determine to kill him, but Cronstadt had chosen Dalroi for a specific reason. It seems that, unknown to him, his mind has an ability to tap into unknown sources of energy which allows him to keep one step ahead of those pursuing him. A secret government organization, the Black Knights, have a special interest in Dalroi because they believe that if he realizes the full potential of this energy he could release a "mental Hiroshima".

Despite his strange gift, Dalroi still gets into predicaments and is, not surprisingly, captured by Failway. They know he is their most dangerous enemy so rather than kill him, they despatch him into the space between the parallel worlds—transfinite space as Kapp calls it. (The first US edition was retitled *Transfinite Man*.) Kapp struggles to describes the terrors and inexplicabilities of transfinite space, but you can't blame him for trying. Imagery becomes psychedelic in some phases and Escher-like in others as

Dalroi, somehow still mentally active even though his body had been split apart and reassembled, atom by atom, tries to find a way through and out of his predicament. The fact that he does it, isn't a surprise, as there'd be no further plot, but it is fascinating to discover what he's become when he returns. Now superhuman he seeks his revenge, not only upon Failway, but upon all those who had crossed him.

Throughout his cataclysmic revenge, Dalroi struggles to discover who or what he really is, and who or what are his enemies. As he pieces his past together—and his past goes back a long, long way—we meet the custodian of humanity and discover that the human race became the juvenile delinquents of the universe. In his role as ultimate Destroyer, we need to understand whether Dalroi stands for good or evil, or something else entirely.

The Dark Mind is a complex novel, perhaps too complex in parts, and to make it understandable the characters become a bit too glib, but the overall background is fascinating. No such novel had appeared in British sf before—though at times John Russell Fearn came unconvincingly close to it. Some claim it may owe its inspiration to Alfred Bester's *The Stars My Destination* (1956, published in the UK as *Tiger! Tiger!*), as both share a common theme of revenge alongside some powerful imagery, but Kapp's novel stands on its own as an imaginative tour-de-force.

Colin Kapp (1928–2007) developed a reputation for stories and novels that pushed the boundaries of imagination. He would rework *The Dark Mind* to some degree in *Patterns of Chaos* (1972) and its stepson *The Chaos Weapon* (1977), but if you want to see Kapp's imagination at full blast go no further than his Cageworld series which began with *Search for the Sun* (1982). Slightly less mindblowing, but no less fascinating, are his series of stories collected as *The Unorthodox Engineers* (1979), where a team of scientists must solve seemingly impossible problems. Kapp's imagination seemed to know no boundaries.

Doctor Who   David Whitaker

London: Frederick Muller, 1964

The most iconic British science-fiction television series, *Dr. Who*, began on the BBC on 23 November 1963. It had been developed by a team under Sydney Newman, BBC-TV's Head of Drama. It was Newman who came up with the title and suggested a time machine larger inside than appeared outside. Its design as an old-style blue police phone-box was created by Anthony Coburn, who scripted the first serial "The Unearthly Child" in which he coined the word for the machine, Tardis, an acronym for "Time and Relative Dimensions in Space".

The first serial provided the background to the series. The Doctor and his grandchild Susan are aliens (we only later learn he is a Time Lord) who use their Tardis to travel through time and space. The Tardis has a chameleon circuit which allows it to blend in with its surroundings but that has malfunctioned and the Tardis is temporarily stuck on Earth. Susan attends school where two of her teachers, Ian and Barbara, are impressed by her knowledge of history. They follow her to her home, where they meet the Doctor and discover the Tardis. They stumble into it and, since they are now aware of its interior, the Doctor decides he cannot let them go. He activates the machine and all four are whisked back to the Stone Age.

That first serial of four episodes was only moderately popular but the second serial, "The Daleks", scripted by Terry Nation, which ran from 21 December 1963 to 1 February 1964, took the nation by storm, with viewing figures almost doubling to over ten million. The Daleks are the merciless beings of the planet Skaro whose bodies are housed in a robot-like machine (dubbed "Pepper-pot") which works like a tank. Their shrill, mechanical, monotone voice, often repeating the word "Exterminate", became a key part of their image.

The Dalek serial was so popular that it was inevitable the machines would return, as they have many times since. It allowed the BBC to merchandise the aliens in various toys and books. The first novel, based on that original serial, was written by David Whitaker, the script editor on the series, based heavily on Terry Nation's script. It was entitled simply *Doctor Who* but had an unwieldy subtitle "in an exciting adventure with the Daleks."

Because the novel was a stand-alone and did not develop from "The Unearthly Child", Whitaker had to devise another way for Ian and Barbara to meet the Doctor. The adventure is narrated by Ian who, in this version, is not a teacher but a research scientist. While driving across Barnes Common he encounters Barbara who has been injured in a car crash in the fog. She was a private tutor to Susan and was bringing her back home when an accident happened. Ian rushes with her to the car but Susan has gone. They meet the Doctor and though he tries to get rid of them, they discover that Susan has taken refuge in the police box. Ian tries to help, which is how he and Barbara stumble into the Tardis, and the adventure begins.

Ian refuses to believe the Doctor who is grumpy and stubborn, but once the Tardis settles in its new location, what appears to be a dead forest, he is forced to accept that they have indeed travelled through space and maybe also time. They have a quick reconnoitre of the forest, discovering a dead creature made of metal, and see a city not too far away. Back at the Tardis the Doctor states they will not remain on this planet and hopes he can return the other two to Earth though because the computer is malfunctioning, he can't promise it. Upon trying to leave, the machine will not function and the Doctor says that one of his conductor rods has run out of mercury. He later admits this was a ploy to allow them to explore the city.

When they set out they find a box of phials left outside. Storing it in the Tardis they venture to the city. It is entirely made of metal, though seems half buried in sand. By then all four are feeling ill, and they are soon captured by the Daleks who miraculously speak English. It seems that the atmosphere is toxic to humans but the Daleks thrive. They now realize the importance of the phials left for them and the Daleks allow Susan, who is the least affected, to collect them from the Tardis. It seems the Daleks can only move when on a metal base, something conveniently overcome in future adventures.

At the Tardis, Susan is met by a humanoid being who turns out to be a Thal, one of the other races on the planet whom the Daleks had tried to destroy. The Thal, who also speaks perfect English, provides Susan with further medicine as an antidote to the air pollution. Thal explains there had been a neutron war two centuries ago which left the planet devastated and polluted. Susan returns to the city where she brokers a peace meeting between the Daleks and the Thals, unaware that this will be a trap.

Once the others have recovered, they break out of their confinement by stealing one of the machines and removing the Dalek, which appears as a malformed blob, not unlike H.G. Wells's Martians. Although they warn the Thals of the Daleks' trap, there is a battle in which their leader is killed. The rest escape back to the forest with the Doctor and his companions. They join forces with the Thals and conceive a plan to defeat the Daleks. The Thals are pacifists, but they recognize that sometimes violence is necessary. As the novel ends, the Doctor gives Ian and Barbara a choice of staying on Skaro and helping rebuild the society or coming with them, destination unknown. They agree to stay with the Doctor.

The novel reflects the original intent of the TV serial to consider the consequences of war and the need to fight evil when necessary. The Daleks were a clear reimagining of the soulless Nazi war machine and how necessary it had been to fight for the greater good.

Although the book is not written down to its younger readership, it is weak on characterization and often too simplified, leaving much unexplained. The book was not as sensational as the TV series, but it remains an important record of the phenomenon that introduced the Daleks.

David Whitaker (1928–1980) had started work in the theatre, acting, directing and writing, and he came to the BBC when he had the opportunity to adapt one of his plays, joining the BBC Script Department. Along with other *Dr. Who* scripts he wrote "The Power of the Daleks" in 1966 and "The Evil of the Daleks" in 1967. He also compiled, with Terry Nation, three Dalek annuals, *The Dalek Book* (1964), *The Dalek World* (1965) and *The Dalek Outer Space Book* (1966).

FROOMB!   John Lymington
London: Hodder & Stoughton, 1964

"Froomb" is an acronym for "Fluid's running out of my brakes!" meaning that we're out of control and rushing to our doom. It's a word quoted frequently by John Brunt, an adventurer and womanizer who is always out of money. He is paid handsomely by David Packard, the Minister of Science and Research, to be a guinea pig in a dangerous experiment. Brunt is to be killed (electrocuted) under controlled conditions, his brain wired up to a machine. Packard calls the experiment a form of space travel as he hopes Brunt will end up in Heaven or some alternate "Time Belt". There is reference, yet again, to Dunne's *An Experiment with Time*. The plan is to bring him back after twenty-four hours. Bizarrely, Brunt doesn't simply die, he disintegrates, but the machine keeps working, suggesting Brunt is alive somewhere.

Brunt does indeed end up somewhere, a place he's known from childhood though not as he remembers it. He is taken to Peter (but not St. Peter at the "pearly gates") who interrogates him to determine whether he was murdered or committed suicide. He believes he is in a holding place, called Hereafter, but it isn't a pleasant experience.

Meanwhile the pressure of froomb is happening to Packard. Because he leaked word of the experiment, the police are suspicious about what's happened to Brunt. There is also the problem of Flightend, an insect killer which is highly toxic and has killed cattle and people. Packard stops its production but it has been very profitable and its investors are angry. Other problems include a way of removing pollution from rivers which unfortunately kills the fish. And improving the taste of chicken by incorporating flavoured plastic leads to the prediction that the world's seas will become clogged with plastic.

Meanwhile in a project called Blackout, the United States intends to place above North America a shield of cobalt radiation, as a protection against nuclear attack. There is a possibility it will start a chain reaction and cause global devastation. John Brunt, in Hereafter, finds a book which is a history of the world to the year 2000 (from which he deduces he has slipped into the future or an alternate timeline). The book refers to the "death of the United States" and tells how the radiation crossed the Pacific to China where the government believed it was an attack from the Soviet Union. China had invented a form of "heat gun" with which it attacked Russia. Although this did not become a full-blown war, the after-effects together with the increased radiation in the northern hemisphere led to economic collapse. The many smaller countries which had sought independence from the British and other Empires but who still relied on overseas help also collapsed. Travel became limited and the world shrank to an economy of the fifteenth century.

Brunt had known about the Blackout project and feels he must get back to Packard to warn him, but he can't return until Packard completes the experiment by throwing a switch. Brunt tries to communicate across the Time Belts with only minimal success. When the police come to arrest Packard he throws the switch and Brunt returns. Though he knows he has an important message, he struggles to remember, leaving a cliffhanger ending to the novel.

This novel has all the anxiety of the Cold War. It was written not long after the Cuban crisis when the idea of "froomb" was all too real. Lymington throws everything into the book to emphasize how near the world was to the brink of disaster. Whilst much of his science is hokum, the ideas behind them are not, which makes this the most passionate and readable of Lymington's sf novels.

John Lymington was the alias used by John Newton Chance (1911–1983) for his science fiction. He was at heart a thriller writer, his first book

Wheels in the Forest, —the first of over 160—appearing in 1935. His first sf thriller was *Night of the Big Heat* (1959), which was adapted for TV and the cinema. It told of a planned invasion where the aliens are preparing the Earth by heating it. *The Giant Stumbles* (1960) was another catastrophe novel, this time where the increase in nuclear experiments will lead to the Earth's rotation slowing down. Lymington seemed set on a series of disaster novels to put him in the same league as John Wyndham and John Christopher. Unfortunately, his understanding of science was limited so although he peppers the novels with clever ideas, they are never properly explained. But, as with *Froomb!*, Lymington was good at creating suspense which is why his works proved popular. He was never fully accepted by the science-fiction fraternity who felt he ought to do better. His books are of their time, including the very sexist attitude of their chauvinistic men, but they reflect the contemporary fears and outlook and in this book Lymington was one of the few to recognize the growing problem of pollution.

The Sundered Worlds Michael Moorcock

London: Roberts & Vintner (Compact Books), 1965;
retitled *The Blood-red Game*, London: Sphere Books, 1970

Jon Renark, former Warden of the Rim is a Guide Senser which means he has the remarkable ability to track down or sense things not just on Earth but anywhere in the galaxy. And he's sensed an abnormality. He and two colleagues, Talfryn and Asquiol, together with a girl, Willow, meet up on the planet Migaa in order to travel to the Shifter, or Ghost System, known as the Sundered Worlds, a planetary system that shifts in and out of our galaxy. Renark had sensed that the Shifter might help him understand the ultimate catastrophe. The universe has ceased to expand. It is starting to contract at an increasingly fast rate until the entire universe will be only a small dense mote.

When the Shifter appears the four make a dash for it in Renark's illicit space cruiser and though they are attacked by the Thron, they make it through. The people they meet, drifters and renegades who discover that once there they cannot leave, are not interested in their quest. Renark is told they can stay and do whatever they want provided they do not cause trouble. Renark meets Mary the Maze who, in her rambling memories seems to have some knowledge that might help Renark. He wants to understand the mystery of the Shifter in case it can help combat the collapsing universe. Mary has a vague memory of Asquiol, though he has no recollection of her. Renark and Asquiol try to contact the enemy Thron, barely escaping with their lives, so they visit the Shaarn, the original inhabitants of the Shifter who have been in constant battle with the Thron.

The war was on a cosmic scale, emulating the mighty battles of the 1930s pulps. The Shaarn perfected a continuum-warp device with which they were able to banish the Thron into another dimension, but on occasion their planets return to the Shaarn universe. Over millennia the Shaarn have lost the details of the continuum-warp but have created a machine to stop the Shifter's move across dimensions and contain them in another universe. They will not delay its operation to allow Renark to learn more about the Shifter. Instead he and Asquiol begin a planet-hopping odyssey which leads them to the Hub of the Multiverse where the Originators tell them of their destiny. Although the contracting universe cannot be saved it will be possible to transport humanity to another universe. The Originators provide Renark and Asquiol with a machine that can switch between the universes.

When Renark and Asquiol return they are like coruscating angels. They have the huge task of conveying their message to all of mankind scattered throughout the universe and Asquiol the even more unenviable task of transporting everyone across to the new universe. Renark stays behind and witnesses the end of our universe.

The new universe already has its own inhabitants and they are against human intrusion. Rather than a conventional battle they challenge humans to the Blood-Red Game, which means key players have to beam mental images at the other side to drive them crazy.

Meanwhile, Adam Roffrey, described as a psychopath, is seeking his wife, whom we have already met as Mary the Maze. Having now learned that she is on the Shifter planet he rescues her and, in the process, retrieves Talfryn and Willow. On their return they pass through the battlefield of the Blood Red Game but mentally survive. This astonishes Lord Mordan who, as Asquiol's next in command, is in charge of the players in the Game. Although Roffrey wants to find help for Mary, who is still mentally unstable, Roffrey is forced to partake in the Game. However they soon realize that the key to the game is Mary, whose experiences of insanity allow her to combat the aliens with images for which they are unprepared. It is Mary who wins for humanity a new universe.

Although the term "multiverse" had first been coined by William James in 1895 to convey a multiplicity of nature within our universe, and again by Sir Oliver Lodge in 1904 to explain how our universe is the product of multiple choices and random selection, it was Moorcock who first used the term in the form we now know it. His multiverse is a near infinite sequence of parallel worlds fanning out like a huge wheel from a central hub. Our universe is just one small plane within this vast web. This book was originally published as two separate novellas in John Carnell's *Science Fiction Adventures* and, for the record, it was in the issue for November 1962 that the term was first used. At this stage Moorcock was a long way from developing his Multiverse sequence of novels, featuring the Eternal Champion, who first appeared in the shape of Elric of Melniboné, Moorcock's most enduring character, who debuted in "The Dreaming City" in *Science Fantasy* for June 1961. But during the 1960s, when Moorcock became a writing machine desperate for funds to support *New Worlds*, of which he had become editor in 1964, he developed a cycle of adventures each one exploring the various manifestations of the Eternal Champion of which Renark was a progenitor.

Michael Moorcock (b.1939) had been a devotee of fantasy and sf adventures from an early age, and his first books showed his ability to pastiche the works of Edgar Rice Burroughs and Robert E. Howard to create a new form of heroic adventure. There is some of that in *The Sundered Worlds* but much more besides. It starts as if he's imitating the Martian novels of Leigh Brackett but mutates into the cosmic space opera of E.E. Smith and Edmond Hamilton. Through *New Worlds* Moorcock was the pivotal point at which the classic adventure science-fiction mutated into post-modern sf in Britain, where he encouraged the work of Charles Platt, Brian Aldiss, John Brunner, M. John Harrison and, of course, Ballard, as well as such American writers as Thomas M. Disch, Norman Spinrad, Roger Zelazny and Harlan Ellison.

The Garbage World   Charles Platt

New Worlds SF, October–November 1966; expanded, New York: Berkley Medallion, 1967

The larger asteroids in the asteroid belt have been converted into pleasure parks for the wealthy, all that is except Kopra, which is the communal dump, or waste-disposal site. Here blimps full of the refuse from other asteroids is dropped, daily, and has been for a hundred years. The asteroid is a world of filth and rotting garbage, with a foetid atmosphere. The rubbish has accumulated to such a depth that the asteroid is becoming unstable, and the government of the United Asteroid Belt plans to do something about it. Two officials, Larkin and Roach, are sent to the foul-smelling world to warn the few inhabitants that they are planning to reinstall a gravity generator which will impact the rubbish more tightly to the surface. During this process the inhabitants must be removed but they will be returned.

At least, that's the official story.

The lesser of the two officials, Roach, overhears part of a conversation between his superior and Captain Sterril, who is undertaking the work, which suggests there is another objective, and he risks his job by warning the Headman of Kopra's only village.

The Headman, Isaac Gaylord, is in turmoil. During a party his hoard of items retrieved from rubbish has been stolen. Under Kopra's rules he who has the biggest hoard is the Headman, but he has lost that position. Roach has learned that there are nomads who inhabit other parts of Kopra in addition to the hundred or so in the Village, and he convinces his superior that they must also rescue them. Gaylord, who wants to track down his hoard, joins Roach in a trip round Kopra in a tractor. They are accompanied by Juliette, Gaylord's daughter who, at the party, had taken a liking to Roach and though he could see her charms he was repulsed by how dirty she is.

Their journey is soon curtailed. After ploughing through a forest of vegetation they encounter a lake of mud in which their tractor becomes stuck after being attacked by an enormous slug-like creature. They are rescued by nomads but as the tractor no longer functions they must walk back to the Village, facing even more problems when caught in a storm of yellow rain, and falling into a crevasse of mud.

After various perils which brought Roach and Juliette closer together, and he turns native, they reach the Village and discover the real plans for Kopra. It then becomes a race to either save the asteroid or save the villagers.

The Garbage World is a satire, much in the tradition of Evelyn Waugh, and Platt cares little for scientific accuracy. Yet it seems more relevant today than ever. Pollution on Earth is a much greater problem now than it was in the 1960s and with the West sending its rubbish to Third World countries and plastics smothering the oceans we are in danger of transforming our own planet into a Garbage World.

Charles Platt (b. 1945) was welcomed into the professional sf world by Michael Moorcock, to whom the book is dedicated. Platt not only sold regularly to *New Worlds* but became the designer of the magazine when it transformed into a slick format, and its editor in 1969. He has written at least a dozen sf novels including the highly erotic *The Gas* (1970) and a wonderful cliché-ridden sf romp *Free Zone* (1988).

At the time it was first published *The Garbage World* was dismissed as hackwork but it has grown more pertinent ever since. It serves as a suitable ending to this survey of classic British sf, because Platt used plenty of sf tropes and images in the novel but in a form that was more suited to the New Wave mood starting to engulf British sf. The fact that it has become more relevant shows that from the mid-1960s sf turned away from the past, which had been such a huge influence, and looked towards a very different future.

SELECT BIBLIOGRAPHY

The primary sources for the book discussed here are the novels themselves and, where relevant, their magazine serialization. To consider these books in their wider perspective I have consulted many sources, including the indispensable online *Encyclopedia of Science Fiction* edited by John Clute, David Langford, Peter Nicholls and Graham Sleight which can be found at http://sf-encyclopedia.com/. The following books, with the emphasis on British science fiction, also helped provide background and context and I recommend them to anyone wishing to explore this subject in more detail.

Aldiss, Brian W. and Wingrove, David, *Trillion Year Spree* (London: Victor Gollancz, 1986)

Aldiss, Margaret, *The Work of Brian W. Aldiss* (San Bernardino: Borgo Press, 1992)

Ashley, Mike, *The Work of William F. Temple* (San Bernardino: Borgo Press, 1994)

Bleiler, Everett F., *Science-Fiction, The Early Years* (Kent, Ohio: Kent State University Press, 1990)

Boston, John and Broderick, Damien, *Building New Worlds* (Rockville, MD: Borgo Press, 2013)

Boston, John and Broderick, Damien, *New Worlds Before the New Wave* (Rockville, MD: Borgo Press, 2013)

Boston, John and Broderick, Damien, *Strange Highways* (Rockville, MD: Borgo Press, 2013)

Harbottle, Philip, *Vultures of the Void: The Legacy* (Rockville, MD: Cosmos Books, 2011)

Holland, Steve, *The Mushroom Jungle: a History of Postwar Paperback Publishing* (Westbury: Zeon Books, 1993).

Luckhurst, Roger, *Science Fiction, A Literary History* (London: British Library, 2017)

Moskowitz, Sam, *Explorers of the Infinite* (Cleveland: World Publishing, 1963)

Moskowitz, Sam, *Seekers of Tomorrow* (Cleveland, World Publishing, 1966)

Moskowitz, Sam, *Strange Horizons* (New York: Charles Scribner's Sons, 1976)

Moskowitz, Sam, *Far Future Calling, Olaf Stapledon* (Philadelphia: Oswald Train, 1979)

Philmus, Robert M., *Into the Unknown. The Evolution of Science Fiction from Francis Godwin to H.G. Wells* (Berkeley: University of California Press, 1970)

Roberts, Adam, *The History of Science Fiction* (Basingstoke: Palgrave Macmillan, 2005)

Ruddick, Nicholas, *British Science Fiction, A Chronology, 1478–1990* (Westport, CT: Greenwood Press, 1992)

Smith, David C. and Parrinder, Patrick, *The Journalism of H.G. Wells* (Haren, Netherlands: Equilibris, 2012)

Smith, Jad, *John Brunner* (Urbana: University of Illinois Press, 2012)

Stableford, Brian, *Against the New Gods* (Rockville, MD: Borgo Press, 2009)

Stableford, Brian, *Science Fact and Science Fiction, An Encyclopedia* (Abingdon: Routledge, 2006)

Stableford, Brian, *Scientific Romance in Britain, 1890–1950* (London: Fourth Estate, 1985), revised and expanded as *New Atlantis: A Narrative History of Scientific Romance* (Rockville, MD: Wildside Press, 4 volumes, 2014).

Suvin, Darko, *Victorian Science Fiction in the UK* (Boston: G.K. Hall, 1983)

Tuck, Donald H., *The Encyclopedia of Science Fiction and Fantasy* (Chicago: Advent, 3 volumes, 1974, 1978, 1982)

Wallace, Sean and Harbottle, Philip, *The Tall Adventurer, The Works of E.C. Tubb* (Harold Wood: Beccon Publications, 1998)

ACKNOWLEDGEMENTS

Writing and researching can be a solitary job and the help of others is always welcome. My thanks, first and foremost, to Rob Davies, my former editor at the British Library, who first showed interest in this project and to Jonny Davidson, who has seen it through, warts and all. I was most grateful to Paul Di Filippo who came to my rescue and lent me his copy of Susan Ertz's *Woman Alive*. And I am grateful to the FictionMags discussion group whose occasional comments were always helpful, whether they knew it or not.

INDEX

Titles of books and films are shown in *italics* whilst titles of short stories or articles are in "quotes". A page number followed by 'n' means the reference is to a footnote. Page references in bold print refer to the primary book entry. *Pl.* refers to the Plate number of book covers and *fp* to the frontispiece.

A for Andromeda (Hoyle & Elliot) **282–5**
"Ablest Man in the World, The" (Mitchell) 127
Address Unknown (Phillpotts) 107, 237
Adrift in the Stratosphere (Low) **184–7**, 188
"Aepyornis Island" (Wells) 31
After London (Jefferies) 46
Age, An (Aldiss) 275
Aldiss, Brian W. 16, 17, 185, 210, 255, **273–6**, 288, 313; quoted 13, 195
alien beings 26–7, 107, 138, 140, 145–6, 186–7, 198, 237, 238, 257, 259, 261–3, 272, 278–80, 284–5, 289, 296–7, 305–6, 310, 312. *See also* Mars and Martians
Alien Dust (Tubb) **268–70**
All Aboard for Ararat (Wells) 223
"Allamagoosa" (Russell) 200
Allen, Grant 14, 126
alternate timeline 82, 147–50, 173–5, 207, 227, 228, 240, 252, 265–6, 308–9
Amazing Stories (magazine) 112, 179, 180, 185, 230, 232
Amis, Kingsley 293
Amphibian, The (Beliaev) 271
Amphibians, The (Wright) **143–7**, 177

Anacronópete, El (Gaspar) 24
Androids 128, 276–7, 283; *see also* robots
Andromeda Breakthrough, The (Hoyle & Elliot) 285
Angel of the Revolution, The (Griffith) 34–5, 36, 50
Animal Farm (Orwell) 224, 241
Animal Ideas (Britton) 159
Ant Heap, The (Knoblock) **155–7**
Anticipations (Wells) 170
antigravity 38, 42, 43, 48
Ape and Essence (Huxley) 166, 236
Apostle of the Cylinder, The (Rousseau) 79
Approaching Storm, The (Tillyard) 123
Ark of the Covenant, The (MacClure) *see* Ultimatum
Arnold, Edwin Lester 38
Artifex, or the Future of Craftsmanship 171
artificial intelligence 66, 127–8, 158–9, 247–8; *see also* robots
artificial life 133, 142, 155–7; *see also* genetic engineering
"As Easy as A.B.C." (Kipling) 61
Asimov, Isaac 16, 179, 265

asteroid belt 47, 313–5
Astounding Stories / SF (magazine) 179, 185, 198, 228, 296
Atkins, Frank *see* Aubrey, Frank
Atlantis 90, 184
atomic power 46–50, 98, 102–4, 107, 110, 111, 162, 238
Aubrey, Frank (Frank Atkins) 76
Authentic SF (magazine) 254–5, 264
automata 128, 136–9, 142, 211; *see also* robots

Back to Methuselah (Shaw) **130–33**, 139, 161
Bacon, Sir Francis 13, 70, 169, 175
Bacon, Roger 56, 169
Bailey, Hilary 288
Ballantine Books (publisher) 260, 263, 264, 276, 278, 298
Ballard, J.G. 16, 17, 187–8, 255, **291–3**, 294, 313
Balmer, Edwin 187
Barabbas (Corelli) 102
Battle of Dorking, The (Chesney) 14, 33
Beasts and Super-Beasts (Saki) 41
Before Adam (London) 81
Beliaev, Alexandr 271
Bell, Neal *see* Southwold, Stephen
Belloc, Hilaire 173–4
Benson, E.F. 250
Beresford, Elisabeth 74
Beresford, J.D. **71–4**, 139, 152, 223
Bernal, J.D. **171–3**
Berry, Bryan 254, 265
Besant, Walter 128
Best, Herbert 202, 222, **224–5**
Bester, Alfred 304
Bestiality 134–5
Beynon, John *see* Wyndham, John
Beyond the Silver Sky (Bulmer) 273
Big Four, The (Christie) 98
Bigland, Eileen 233
Billion Year Spree, A (Aldiss) 13, 275

biological warfare 166, 202, 237, 239, 224, 237, 239
Birkenhead, Earl of 170
Biro, Val *Pl.13*
birth control 99, 161
Black Cloud, The (Hoyle) 284
Blackburn, John 246
Blackwood, Algernon 80, 84, 250
Blake of the "Rattlesnake" (Jane) 50
Blayre, Christopher (Edward Heron-Allen) **134–6**
Bleiler, E.F. quoted 44
Blue Germ, The (Swayne) **128–30**, 161, 182
Blue Lagoon, The (Stacpoole) 80
Blue Murder (Snell) 155
Boats of the 'Glen Carrig', The (Hodgson) 64
Bodley Head, The *see* Lane, John
Boland, John 246
bomb, atomic or thermonuclear 15, 183, 201, 223, 228, 235–6, 239, 254, 272
Book of the Damned, The (Fort) 198
Borodin, George 236
"Bowmen, The" (Machen) 83
boys' magazines 185, 190
Brackett, Leigh 313
Brain (Britton) **157–60**
Brave New World (Huxley) 122, **163–7**, 172, 213, 290, *Pl.7*
Brave New World Revisited (Huxley) 167
British Interplanetary Society 234, 260
Britton, Lionel **157–60**, 250
Brown, Douglas 41, 222, **225–7**
Brunner, John 16, 62, 255, 272, 288, **300–3**, 313
Buchan, John 250
Buley, Bernard 185
Bulmer, Kenneth 255, 265, **271–3**
Burdekin, Katharine 202, **215–7** 222
Burgess, Anthony 288
Burke, Jonathan **264–6**, 282, 296
Burning Ring, The (Burdekin) 17

Burning World, The (aka *Drought*) (Ballard) 287, 293
Burroughs, Edgar Rice 78, 178, 185, 187, 313
Burroughs, William 288
Butler, Samuel 94, 139, 247

Calculated Risk (Maine) **280–2**
Campbell, Herbert 264–5
Campbell, Jr., John W. 16, 179, 198, 228
Campbell-Bannerman, Sir Henry 39
Čapek, Karel 127
Captive on the Flying Saucers (Finn) 243
Carnacki the Ghost-Finder (Hodgson) 64
Carnell, E.J. "Ted" 254, 275, 312
Carpenter, Edward 57
Cartmill, Cleve 228
Cassell (publisher) 89, 185
catastrophes, climate change 42, 46, 223, 292, 294–6; comet/cosmic body threatens Earth 35, 38, 46, 49, 66, 159, 191, 217–20, 236, 237; famine 45–6, 74, 108; flood 141, 146, 219, 228, 292; plague 45–6, 73–4, 83–4, 99, 120, 162, 236, 246; radiation 183, 245, 270, 289, 294, 309; shift in Earth's axis/orbit 46, 91, 163, 310; solar activity 266–7, 292; *see also* civilization, collapse of, *and* pollution
Cavalry Went Through, The (Newman) 228, 229
Cavendish, Margaret *see* Newcastle, Duchess of
"Celestial Omnibus, The" (Forster) 54
Chance, John Newton *see* Lymington, John
Chandler, A. Bertram 207, 254
Chaos Weapon, The (Kapp) 304
Chatto & Windus (publisher) 50, 115, 163
Cheetah Girl, The (Blayre) **134–6**
chemical warfare 88, 141, 202, 213
Chesney, Sir George 14, 33
Chesterton, G.K. 16, **57–9**, 174
Chetwynd, Bridget 235

"Child of the Phalanstery, A" (Allen) 14, 126
Childhood's End (Clarke) 18, **260–4**, *Pl.*14
Chilton, Charles **258–60**
Christie, Agatha 98, 107
Christopher, John 246, 288, 292, **294–6**, 310
"Chronic Argonauts, The" *see Time Machine, The*
Chronicles of Clovis, The (Saki) 41
Churchill, Winston 174, 202, 228
City and the Stars, The (Clarke) 263
City Under the Sea (Bulmer) **271–3**
civilization, collapse of 100–1, 104–5, 108–10, 140, 181–2, 183–4, 202, 208–10, 217–20, 224, 236, 238–9, 280, 288, 309
Clark, Simon 246
Clarke, Arthur C. 12, 16, 18, 172, 193, 221, 234, 254, 255, **260–4**, 272; quoted 195
Clarke, A. Vincent 272
climate change *see* catastrophes
"Clock That Went Backward, The" (Mitchell) 23–4
Clockwork Man, The (Odle) 127, **136–9**, *Pl.*6
Clockwork Orange, A (Burgess) 288
cloning 164, 233
Cloud Walker, The (Cooper) 278
Clouston, J. Storer 78
"Cold Equations, The" (Godwin) 190, 270
Cole, Robert W. **42–4**
Coleridge, Samuel Taylor 70
Collapse of Homo Sapiens, The (Graham) 127, **139–42**
Collins, William (publisher) 99, 238
Colomb, Rear-Admiral Philip 34
Colvin, Ian 235
comet/cosmic body threatens Earth *see* catastrophes
Coming Race, The (Lytton) 14, 70, 210
Common Enemy, A (Beresford) 74, 223
communication with aliens 296–7
computers 53–4, 138, 158–9, 172, 247, 283–4, 302, 306

Concrete (Tillyard) **120–23**, 160
Concrete Island (Ballard) 293
Condron, Michael 27
Confound their Politics (Llewellyn) 209
Conklin, Groff 233
Connell, Richard 250
Connington, J.J. **108–10**
Consolidator, The (Defoe) 13
Constable (publisher) 108, 130
Constantine, Murray *see* Burdekin, Katharine
Cooper, Edmund **276–8**
Cooper, James Fenimore 126
Corelli, Marie **101–4**
Corgi Books 255, 278, 303
Country of the Blind and Other Stories (Wells) **31–2**
Crack of Doom, The (Cromie) **46–8**, 98, *Pl.3*
Crash (Ballard) 293
Crisis!—1992 (Herbert) 180, **191–3**
Croft-Cooke, Rupert 240
Cromie, Robert **46–8**, 98
Cross, John Keir 233
Crowley, Aleister 84
Cruiser on Wheels, The (Ranger Gull) 77
"Crystal Egg, The" (Wells) 32
Crystal World, The (Ballard) 287, 293
Cummings, Ray 178
cyborg 127, 138, 172

Daedalus: or Science and the Future (Haldane) 98–9, 116, 170, 171
Daily Mail 38, 39–40, 201–2
Daleks, books and merchandise 305–8
Dan Dare 255
Dark Mind, The (Kapp) **303–4**, *Pl.16*
Dark Tower, The (Lewis) 197
Darkest of Nights, The (Maine) 282
Darkness and the Light (Stapledon) 223
Darwin, Charles 22, 125, 126
Darwinism 25, 125, 126, 131
Dawn (Wright) 146

Day of the Triffids, The (Wyndham) 237, **244–6**, 255, *Pl.11*
Day of Wrath (O'Neill) 212
Day-Lewis, Cecil 74
de Forrest, Lee 179
de la Mare, Walter 74
"Deadline" (Cartmill) 228
Deadly Image (Cooper) **276–8**
Death of a World (Farjeon) 236, **238–9**, *Pl.11*
Death of Grass, The (Christopher) 246, 296
Death Rocks the Cradle (Southwold) 163
Death Trap, The (Cole) 44
"Death Voyage, The" (Doyle) 76
Deep Range, The (Clarke) 272
Deeping, Warwick 222–3
Defoe, Daniel 13
Deluge (Wright) 146
Demigod, The (Jackson) 126
Dent, Guy **147–50**, 175
Description of a New World, called the Blazing World, The (Cavendish) 13
Desmond, Hugh *see* Lindsay, Kathleen
Devil-Tree of El Dorado, The (Aubrey) 76
Devil's Tor (Lindsay) 95
Dick, Philip K. 16, 250
dimensions, other, including parallel worlds 24, 31, 70, 79–82, 138, 163, 183, 251, 265–6, 301, 303–4, 305, 311
disasters *see* catastrophes
Disch, Thomas M. 313
"Disintegration Machine, The" (Doyle) 76
Disturbing Affair of Noel Blake, The (Southwold) 163
Dr. Who tv series 278, 289, 305–8
Doctor Who (Whitaker) **305–8**
Doll Maker, The (Sarban) 250
Domesday Village (Colvin) 235
Donnell, A.J. *Pl.9*
Doom of the Great City, The (Hay) 46
Doyle, Arthur Conan 15, **74–6**, 185, 271

Dracula Unbound (Aldiss) 275
Dreadful Sanctuary (Russell) 200
Dream, or the Simian Maid and sequels
  (Wright) 147
Dreaming Earth, The (Brunner) 301
dreams or dreaming 66, 86, 142–3, 183, 216,
  242, 262, 292, 301
Drop in Infinity, A (Grogan) **79–82**
Drought see *Burning World, The*
Drowned World, The (Ballard) 287, **291–3**
drugs 28, 30, 31, 35, 165, 167, 182, 213, 251–2,
  301
Dunne, J.W. 159, 178, 183, 212, 242, 250, 308
Dunsany, Lord 237, **246–8**
dystopia see society, oppressive

Eagle comic 255
Earth, last days of 25, 62–4, 163, 180
Earth, sentient see Gaia theory
Earth's axis/orbit, shift in see catastrophes
Echoing Worlds, The (Burke) **264–6**
ectogenesis 99, 115, 158, 161, 298
Edison, Thomas A. 36, 179
Einstein, Albert 98
Elixir of Life or 2905A.D., The (Gubbins)
  65–7, 128
Elliot, John **282–5**
Ellison, Harlan 313
Elric of Melniboné 312
"Elves, The" (Tieck) 79–80
Emperor of the If, The (Dent) **147–50**, 175
"Empire of the Ants, The" (Wells) 31
End of This Day's Business, The (Burdekin)
  217
equality 66, 143, 217, 290–1
Erewhon (Butler) 247
Ertz, Susan 18, 202, **212–5**, 250
eugenics 14, 79, 88, 99, 115–6, 118, 120, 126,
  133, 170, 187, 217
euthanasia 115, 120, 122, 161–2
Evening News, The 82–3

evolution, theory of 25, 29, 71, 73, 98, 125–7,
  131–3, 137, 142–7, 161, 172, 182, 184, 190,
  193–4, 262–3
Experiment with Time, An (Dunne) 178, 183,
  250
Eye of Istar, The (Le Queux) 40
Eyre & Spottiswood (publisher) 294, 296

Faber & Faber (publisher) 225, 273
Facial Justice (Hartley) 288, **289–91**
Fall of Moondust, A (Clarke) 263
family as an institution 115, 164
famine see catastrophes
Fantasy (magazine) 221, 253
Farjeon, J. Jefferson 236, **238–9**
fascism 183, 209, 212, 227
Fawcett, E. Douglas 35, 50
Fawcett, Col. Percy 74
Fearn, John Russell 16, 180, 221, 223, **230–2**,
  304
feminist issues/attitudes 18, 47–8, 57, 66,
  115–7, 170, 215, 235, 278
Fifth Planet, The (Hoyle) 285
Finn, Ralph L. **242–3**, 250
First Men in the Moon, The (Wells) 32
Fisher, H.A.L. 174
Five to Twelve (Cooper) 278
Flames, The (Stapledon) 237
Flammarion, Camille 14
Fleming Ian 227
Fleshpots of Sansato, The (Temple) 234
flight, early powered 30, 35–6, 37, 56, 60–1,
  90, 100, 103, 107, 111, 113, 169, 192, 216
Flint, Homer Eon 44, 178
flood see catastrophes
"Flowering of the Strange Orchid, The"
  (Wells) 31
Flying Inn, The (Chesterton) 59
Food of the Gods, The (Wells) 31, 71, 127
For England's Sake (Cromie) 48
Forester, C.S. 16, **206–7**

Forster, E.M. 16, **53–4**, 159
Fort, Charles 193, 197–200
Four Days War (Wright) 202
Four-Sided Triangle (Temple) **232–4**, *Pl.10*
Frankenstein; or, The Modern Prometheus
    (Shelley) 13, 127, 275
Frankenstein Unbound (Aldiss) 275
Freaks Against Supermen (Finn) 243
Free Zone (Platt) 314
FROOMB! (Lymington) **308–10**
future, far 25, 53–4, 62–4, 142–7, 149, 159, 180,
    193–5, 237, 275
Future Imperfect (Chetwynd) 235
future war *see* War, future

Gaia theory (sentient Earth) 49, 76, 83–4
Galactic Storm (Brunner) 300
Galton, Francis 126
Garbage World, The (Platt) **313–5**
Gas, The (Platt) 314
Gas War of 1940, The (Southwold) 163
Gaspar, Enrique 24
Gatland, Kenneth 260
Gay Hunter (Mitchell) 178, **182–4**
generation starships 273–5, 280
genetic engineering 88, 98, 127, 128–30,
    155–6, 245, 249, 271
Gernsback, Hugo 67, 112, 165, 178–9
Giant Stumbles, The (Lymington) 310
Gibbon, Lewis Grassic *see* Mitchell, J.
    Leslie
Gierth, Patrick *Pl.11*
Gillings, Walter 244
Glide Path (Clarke) 263
Gloag, John 171, 177, 178, **180–2**, 222
Goble, Warwick 27, *Pl.2*
Godwin, Francis 13
Godwin, Tom 190, 270
Godwin, William 13, 128
Gold, Horace 16
Golden Amazon, The (Fearn) **230–2**

Gollancz, Victor (publisher) 210, 215, 217,
    228, 291
Goslings (Beresford) 73–4
Gove, Michael 59
Graham, P. Anderson **139–42**
Graves, Robert 237
"Great Crellin Comet, The" (Griffith) 38
Great Pirate Syndicate, The (Griffith) 37
Great South Wall, The (Savile) 70
Great War in England in 1897 (Le Queux) 35, 38
Great War of 189— 34
Great World Mysteries (Russell) 199
Gregory, Owen **86–8**
Griffith, George 15, 34–5, **36–8**, 98
Grogan, Gerald **79–82**
"Guardian Angel" (Clarke) 260
Guardians, The (Christopher) 296
Gubbins, Herbert **65–7**
Gull, Cyril Ranger *see* Thorne, Guy
Gulliver's Travels (Swift) 13, 70

Haggard, H. Rider **89–92**, 94
Haldane, Charlotte 16, **115–7** 298
Haldane, J.B.S. 98–9, 115–6, 160, 170, 171,
    193, 298
Hall, Roger *Pl.10*
Hamilton, Cicely **104–6**
Hamilton, Edmond 44, 178, 179, 198, 313
Hampdenshire Wonder, The (Beresford) **71–4**,
    126, 152
Hampson, Frank 255
Hand of Kornelius Voyt, The (Onions) 86
Hanno, or the Future of Exploration (Mitchell)
    171
Harbottle, Philip 230
Harper & Brothers (publisher) 28, 110
Harris, John Beynon *see* Wyndham, John
Harrison, M. John 288, 313
Hartley, L.P. 195, 288, **289–91**
Hartmann the Anarchist (Fawcett) 35, 50
Haunted Woman, The (Lindsay) 95

Hawkin, Martin 222
Hawthorne, Nathaniel 291
Hay, William DeLisle 46
Heartbreak House (Shaw) 133
Heinemann, William (publisher) 23, 26,
   136, 147, 182, 206, 250
Heinlein, Robert A. 16, 179, 265, 273
Herbert, Benson 180, **191–3**
Hermes Speaking (Jaeger) 152
Heron-Allen, Edward *see* Blayre,
   Christopher
Hext, Harrington *see* Phillpotts, Eden
High-Rise (Ballard) 293
Hilton, James 16, 202, **203–5**
Hindenburg's March Into London (Muench)
   78
Hinton, Charles H. 80
His Other Self (Cole) 44
history, alternate *see* alternate history
Hitler, Adolf 55, 201, 202, 212, 215–6, 226–7,
   229, 237, 248
hive mind 88, 155, 172, 263
Hobson, John A. ("Lucian") 78
Hodder & Stoughton (publisher) 74, 84,
   128, 212, 280, 308
Hodgson, William Hope **62–4**, 95
Hogarth Press, 150, 152
Holland, Leslie *Pl.*7
hollow Earth 210; *see also* underground
   worlds
Honeymoon in Space, A (Griffith) 38
Hopkins Manuscript, The (Sherriff) **217–20**,
   238
Horsnell, Horace 222
Hospital Station (White) **278–80**
Hothouse (Aldiss) 275
House on the Borderland, The (Hodgson) 64
Hoyle, Fred **282–5**
Hunter, Mel *Pl.*15
Hutchinson (publisher) 120, 242, 276
Huxley, Aldous 16, 22, 122, **163–7**, 236

Huxley, Julian 127, 187
Huxley, T.H. 22
Hyams, Edward 237
hypnopaedia 165

I Speak for Earth (Brunner) 301
Icarus: or the Future of Science (Russell)
   98–9, 116, 171
"If Booth Had Missed Lincoln" (Waldman)
   174
"If Don John of Austria had married Mary
   Queen of Scots" (Chesterton) 174
"If Drouet's Cart Had Stuck" (Belloc) 173–4
"If Hitler Had Invaded England" (Forester)
   207
If Hitler Comes see Loss of Eden
If It Had Happened Otherwise (Squire) 147,
   173–5
"If Lee Had Not Won the Battle of
   Gettysburg" (Churchill) 174
"If Napoleon had escaped to America"
   (Fisher) 174
"If the Emperor Frederick had not had
   Cancer" (Ludwig) 174
"If the General Strike had Succeeded"
   (Knox) 174
Imaginary Speeches (Squire) 175
"In the Abyss" (Wells) 271
"In the Avu Observatory" (Wells) 31
In the Days of the Comet (Wells) 32
In the Morning of Time (Roberts) 81
Incubated Girl, The (Jane) 50
Infinitive of Go, The (Brunner) 302
Inner House, The (Besant) 128
inner space 293
intelligence, enhanced 71–3, 195, 223, 230–1
"Intelligence Gigantic, The" (Fearn) 180,
   230
Intermind (Sellings) 300
Invasion of 1910, The (Le Queux) **38–40**,
   201, *Pl.*3

invasion of Great Britain, 33–4, 38–42, 43, 207

Invisible Man, The (Wells) 26, 220, 275

Island (Huxley) 166

Island of Captain Sparrow, The (Wright) 146

Island of Dr. Moreau, The (Wells) 26, 127

Jackson, Edward Payson 126

Jaeger, Muriel **150–3**

Jagged Orbit, The (Brunner) 302

James, William 12

Jameson, Storm 222, 237

Jane, Fred T. **48–50**

Jefferies, Richard 46

Jones, Deborah *Pl.14*

Jones, Langdon 288

Journey Into Space (Chilton) 255, **258–60**

Juggernaut (Odle) 139

Junk Day (Sellings) 300

Jupiter (planet) 22, 43, 102, 180

Kapp, Colin 288, **303–4**

Keller, David H. 179

Kenyon, Ley *Pl.11*

King Solomon's Mines (Haggard) 70, 89

Kipling, Rudyard 16, **59–62**, 87, 91

Kirby, Josh *Pl.16*

Kneale, Nigel **256–8**

Knight, Damon 11

Knoblock, Edward **155–7**

Knox, Ronald 174

Kontrol (Snell) **153–5**

Lake of Gold, The (Griffith) 37

Lamarck, Jean-Baptiste de 125

"Land Ironclads, The" (Wells) 32

"Land of Mist, The" (Doyle) 76

Land Under England (O'Neill) **210–12**

Landsborough, Gordon 264

Lane, John 'Bodley Head' (publisher) 40, 57, 79, 195

Lanos, Henri *fp*, 28

Last and First Men (Stapledon) 143, 177, 193, 223

"Last Days of Earth, The" (Wallis) 180

last human theme 14, 45, 50–3, 142–3, 180, 193–5, 222, 262–3

Last Man, The (Noyes) 222

Last Man, The (Shelley) 14, 45

Last of My Race, The (Tayler) 127, **142–3**, 177

Last Revolution, The (Dunsany) 237, **246–8**, *Pl.11*

Lawrence, D. H. 74

Le Queux, William 35, **38–40**, 77, 201

Leinster, Murray 16

Lest Ye Die (Hamilton) 106

Levin, Bernard 59

Lewis, C.S. 178, **195–7**, 223

Leyendecker, Frank X. 60, *Pl.4*

Life and Adventures of Peter Wilkins, The (Paltock) 13

Life Begins Tomorrow (Parkman) 236, 246

Life Buyer, The (Tubb) 268

Lilith (Macdonald) 94

Lindsay, David **92–5**

Lindsay, Kathleen 237

Linnaeus, Carl 125

Llewellyn, Alun 158–9, 208–10

Lloyd, John Uri 11n

Lo! (Fort) 198

Locke, George W. 139

Lodge, Sir Oliver 312

London, Jack 81

Long, John (publisher) 78, 232

longevity or rejuvenation 65–6, 102, 128, 130–33, 139, 160–2, 187, 204

Lord of Labour, The (Griffith) 37, 98

Lord of Life, The (Southwold) 163

Lord of the Sea (Shiel) 53

Loss of Eden (Brown & Serpell) 41, 222, **225–7**, 229, 248

Lost Horizon (Hilton) 104, 202, **203–5**

lost or hidden civilizations and cultures 40, 69–70, 74–6, 89–92, 102–4, 203–5
Lost Liner, The (Cromie) 48
Lost World, The (Doyle) 70, **74–6**, *Pl.5*
Lovecraft, H.P. quoted 64
Low, A.M. **184–7**
"Lucian" *see* Hobson, John A.
Ludwig, Emil 174
Lunatic, the Lover and the Poet, The (Finn) 242
Lymington, John **308–10**
Lynch, Bohun **112–5**
Lytton, Edward Bulwer 14, 210

MacClure, Victor **110–12**
Macdonald, George 94
Machen, Arthur 51, **82–4**
Machine Stops, The (Forster) **53–4**, 61, 159
McIntosh, J.T. 255, **266–8**
Madden, Samuel 56
Magicians, The (Priestley) **250–2**, *Pl.13*
Maine, Charles Eric **280–2**, 296
Man Alone (Horsnell) 222
Man and Superman (Shaw) 71, 133
Man in the High Castle, The (Dick) 250
Man in the Moone, The (Godwin) 13
"Man of the Year Million, The" (Wells) 23
Man Who Was Thursday, The (Chesterton) 59
Man Who Went Back, The (Deeping) 222–3
Man With Six Senses, The (Jaeger) 126, **150–3**
Man's World (Haldane) **115–7**, 166
Maniac's Dream, The (Rose) 236
Manna (Gloag) 182, 222
Manwaring, Norman *Pl.11*
Maracot Deep, The (Doyle) 271
Mars and Martians 26–8, 32, 48, 66, 78, 113, 178, 186, 188–90, 196–7, 238, 265, 266–70
Marshall, Archibald 78, 82
Marshall, Luther 126
Mason, H.B. 11n

masterminds, scientific 97–8, 106–8, 110–12
Matania, Fortunino 187
matter transmission 50, 233, 302
"Maturity and Modernity" (Forester) 207
Maude, Captain Frederic 34
Maurice, Colonel John F. 34
Maxim, Hiram S. 36–7
Meccania, the Super State (Gregory) 78, **86–8**
"Medic" (White) 279
Meeting at Infinity (Brunner) 301
Megiddo's Ridge (Wright) 202
Melincourt (Peacock) 126
Memoirs of a Spacewoman (Mitchison) **296–8**
Memoirs of the Twentieth Century (Madden) 56
memory, ancestral 182
Men Like Gods (Wells) 166
Menace from the Moon (Lynch) **112–5**, *Pl.6*
Merril, Judith 293
Merritt, Abraham 92, 178
Methuen (publisher) 78, 86, 92, 101, 193
Miles *see* Southwold, Stephen
Miller, P. Schuyler 233
Million Cities, The (McIntosh) 268
Millionairess, The (Shaw) 133
mind control 35, 91, 211
Mind of Mr. Soames, The (Maine) 282
"Mr. Strenberry's Tale" (Priestley) 250
Mitchell, Edward Page 24, 127
Mitchell, J. Leslie 171, 178, **182–4**, 250
Mitchison, Naomi **296–8**
Modern Utopia, A (Wells) 32
Moment of Truth, The (Jameson) 236–7
monarchy, British *see* Royal family
Monikins, The (Cooper) 126
Moon, Life on 13, 112–5, 169
Moon Pool, The (Merritt) 92
Moorcock, Michael 17, 82, 288, **310–13**, 314
Moore, Patrick 260
More, Thomas 12–13

Moreau's Other Island (Aldiss) 275
"Mortal Immortal, The" (Shelley) 14, 128
"Most Dangerous Game, The" (Connell)
  250
Muench, Paul 78
Multiverse, The 82, 138, 311–2
Mummy, The (Webb) 57
Munro, H.H. *see* Saki
Munro, John 273
Murray, Violet 84
Muster of Ghosts, A (Lynch) 115
Mystery of Dr. Fu Manchu, The (Rohmer) 98
Mystery of the Green Ray, The (Le Queux) 77
Mystery of the North Pole, The (Nichol) 70

Naked Lunch, The (Burroughs) 288
Napoleon of Notting Hill, The (Chesterton)
  57–9
Nash, Eveleigh (publisher) 38, 62
Nation, Terry 305–6, 308
Nature, reversion to or affinity with 183
Nebula SF (magazine) 254
Neptune (planet) 43
"New Accelerator, The" (Wells) 31
New Atlantis (Bacon) 13, 70
New Gods Lead, The (Wright) 147
New Lands (Fort) 198
New Moon, The (Onions) 78, **84–6**, 97
New Pleasure, The (Gloag) 182
"new wave" science fiction 17, 275, 287–9,
  315
New Worlds (magazine) 17, 254–5, 271, 275,
  279, 287, 288, 291, 301, 312–3, 314
Newcastle, Margaret Cavendish, Duchess
  of 13
Newman, Bernard 223, **228–30**
Newman, Sydney 305
Newnes, George (publisher) 187, 221; see
  also *Strand Magazine, The*
Next Crusade, The (Cromie) 48
Nichol, C.A. Scrymsour 70

Nicoll, Henry Maurice *see* Swayne, Martin
Nietzsche, Friedrich 71
Night Land, The (Hodgson) **62–4**, 95
Night of the Big Heat (Lymington) 310
Night of the Triffids (Clark) 246
"Nine Billion Names of God, The" (Clarke)
  264
Nineteen Eighty-Four (Orwell) 17, 30, 122, 167,
  236, **239–41**, 277; television adaptation
  258
1920. Dips into the Political Future (Hobson)
  78
1925: The Story of a Fatal Peace (Wallace) 77
99% (Gloag) 182
Non-Stop (Aldiss) **273–5**
Nordenholt's Million (Connington) **108–10**
Northcliffe, Lord 38
Nostrodamus 55–6
Not in Our Stars (Hyams) 237
Nova Express (Burroughs) 288
Number 87 (Phillpotts) 98, **106–8**

Odd John (Stepledon) 152, 195
Odle, E.V. **136–9**
Olga Romanoff (Griffith) 35
Ollivant, Alfred **117–20**
On the Rocks (Shaw) 133
One in Three Hundred (McIntosh) **266–8**,
  Pl.15
O'Neill, James **210–12**
Onions, Oliver **84–6**
Orwell, George 16, 122, 23, **239–41**
Ossian's Ride (Hoyle) 284
Other Place, The (Priestley) 250
Ouspensky, Pyotr 251
Out of the Silent Planet (Lewis) 178, **195–7**
"Out-patient" (White) 280
Outlaws of the Air, The (Griffith) **36–8**

Paine, C. Pl.6
Pale Ape, The (Shiel) 53

Paltock, Robert 13
Panther Books (publisher) 255, 264–5
parallel world *see* dimensions, other
Pares, Bip 215, *Pl.8*
Parkman, Sydney 236, 246
Passing Show, The 187–8
Patterns of Chaos (Kapp) 304
"Pausodyne" (Allen) 14
Peacemaker, The (Forester) **206–7**
Peacock, Thomas Love 126
Pearson's Magazine 15, 26, *Pl.2*
Penguin Books (publisher) 212, 255, 256, 257
People of the Ruins, The (Shanks) 97, **99–101**, 139, 201, 277
Perelandra (Lewis) 195, 197, 223
personality, dual 14, 78, 163
Phantastes (Macdonald) 94
Phillips, Peter 254
Phillpotts, Eden **106–8**, 237
plague *see* catastrophes
Planet Plane (Beynon) **187–90**
Platt, Charles 288, **313–5**
"Plattner Story, The" (Wells) 31
Pleasures of a Futuroscope, The (Dunsany) 248
Plunge Into Space, A (Cromie) 48
Poe, Edgar Allan 53, 291
Pohl, Frederik 16, 244
Poison Belt, The (Doyle) 76
pollution 46, 76, 108, 239, 307, 308–10, 314
Power of X, The (Sellings) 300
Powers, Richard M. *Pl.12*
Pragnell, Festus 180
"Precedent" (Tubb) 270
Precious Porcelian (Southwold) 163
precognition 172, 242, 280
Prelude in Prague: The War in 1938 (Wright) 147, 201
Prelude to Space (Clarke) 263
Press Cuttings (Shaw) 133
Priest, Christopher 288

Priestley, J.B. 16, 94, 139, 160, 178, **250–2**
Princess Daphne, The (Heron-Allen) 136
Princess of Mars, A (Burroughs) 78
prodigies, child 72, 126, 150–2
Proud Man (Burdekin) 217
psi talents 150–3, 262–3, 303, 310; *see also* telepathy
pulp magazines 16, 44, 78, 92, 139, 178–80, 185, 198–9, 221, 230, 311
Purple Cloud, The (Shiel) **50–3**, 225
Purple Sapphire, The (Blayre) 134
Putnam's Sons, G.P. (publisher) 139, 142, 157
Pygmalion (Shaw) 133

Quatermass Experiment, The (Kneale) 255, **256–8**
Question Mark, The (Jaeger) 151, 152

R. U. R. (Čapek) 127–8
racial issues 18, 52–3, 75–6, 84, 109, 116, 121–2, 132, 140–1, 262, 295–6
radiation *see* catastrophes
radio, science fiction on 246, 255, 258–60, 282
rays including lasers 99–100, 103, 114, 154, 155, 186, 222, 231, 239
Rebel Passion, The (Burdekin) 217
Red Planet, The (Chilton) 260
"Rediscovery of the Unique, The" (Wells) 23
rejuvenation *see* longevity
religion, future of 87, 101, 109, 116–7, 120–22, 141, 142–3, 150, 155–7, 167, 177, 194, 195–7, 208–9, 216, 222, 262
"Remarkable Case of Davidson's Eyes, The" (Wells) 31
Rendezvous with Rama, A (Clarke) 193, 263
Report on Probability A (Aldiss) 275
Restif de la Bretonne 125–6
Retreat from Armageddon (Jaeger) 152

Return of Don Quixote, The (Chesterton) 57
Reuterdahl, Henry 59
Revolution (Beresford) 74
Rime of the Ancient Mariner, The (Coleridge) 70
Ringstones (Sarban) 250
Road, The (Kneale) 258
Roberts, Charles G.D. 81
Roberts, Keith 288
Roberts, Lord 38–9
Roberts, Murray 185
Robida, Albert 14
robots 127–8, 161, 188–9, 247–8, 276–7; *see also*
    androids, artificial intelligence, automata
Robur the Conqueror (Verne) 34, 35, 37
Rohmer, Sax 98
Romance of Two Worlds, A (Corelli) 102
Rose, F. Horace 236
Rosny, the Elder, J.-H. 14
Rountree, Harry 75, *Pl.5*
Rousseau, Victor 79
Royal family, fate of 41, 57, 65, 109, 213, 226, 276
Rule of the Beasts, The (Murray) 84
Russell, Bertrand 98–9, 171
Russell, Eric Frank 16, 178, 179, 180, **197–200**
Russell, George ("Æ") 211
Russell, W.B. *Pl.1*
Rutherford, Ernest 98, 114

St. Leon (Godwin) 13, 128
Saki (H.H. Munro) **40–2**
"Saliva Tree, The" (Aldiss) 275
Sands of Mars, The (Clarke) 263
Sarban *see* Wall, John W.
satellites, artificial 245, 263
Saturn Patrol (Tubb) 268
saucer, flying 243, 259
Saurus (Phillpotts) 107
Savile, Frank 70
Sayers, Dorothy L. 152

Scent of New-Mown Hay, A (Blackburn) 246
Science Fantasy (magazine) 254–5, 287, 312
science fiction, definition, 11–12; image
    16–17, 184–5, 254–5, 264, 293; acceptance
    of phrase 177, 178–9, 230, 253–5
Science Fiction Adventures (magazine) 312
Science Fiction Association 234
scientific discoveries and progress 42, 65–6,
    160, 171–3, 212–3
scientific romance, definition, 11–12, 136, 139
Scientific Romances (Hinton) 80
Scoops 180, 184–6
Sea Lady, The (Wells) 32
"Sea Raiders, The" (Wells) 31
Search for the Sun (Kapp) 304
Second Ending (White) 280
"Secret People, The" (Beynon) 188
Secret Power, The (Corelli) **101–4**
Secret Visitors, The (White) 280
Secret Weapon (Newman) 223, **228–30**
"Sector General" (White) 279
Self, Will 293
Sellings, Arthur 288, **298–300**
"Sentinel, The" (Clarke) 263
Serpell, Christopher 41, 222, **225–7**
Seven Days in New Crete (Graves) 237
Seventh Bowl, The (Southwold) **160–3**, 166
Shangri La 104, 203–5
Shanks, Edward **99–101**, 139
Shapes in the Fire (Shiel) 53
Shaw, Bob 255
Shaw, George Bernard 16, 71, 74, **130–33**, 157,
    159, 160, 161
She (Haggard) 89
Sheckley, Robert 16
Sheep Look Up, The (Brunner) 302
Shelley, Mary 13–14, 45, 127, 128, 275
Sherriff, R.C. **217–20**, 238
Shiel, M.P. 15, **50–3**
"Ship That Found Herself, The" (Kipling) 62

Shipton, Mother 56
Shockwave Rider, The (Brunner) 302
Shoot at the Moon (Temple) 234
Sidgwick & Jackson (publisher) 53, 71, 260,
    264
Simak, Clifford D. 179
Sinister Barrier (Russell) 178, **197–200**, Pl.9
Sirius (star) 43
Sirius (Stapledon) 195, 223
Six Gates from Limbo (McIntosh) 268
"Sleepers of Mars" (Beynon) 190
Smith, E.E. 44, 179, 313
Snell, Edmund **153–5**
society, oppressive 29–39, 54, 61, 78–9, 86–8,
    99, 115–7, 120–24, 133, 162, 163–7, 211, 223,
    224, 240–1, 288, 289–91, 296; utopian
    12–13, 36–7, 117–20, 153–4, 162, 163–7, 207,
    210, 223, 237
solar activity see catastrophes
solar sail/wind 172, 196
Sorrows of Satan, The (Corelli) 102
Sound of His Horn, The (Sarban) 237,
    248–50, Pl.12
Southwold, Stephen **160–3**
space, conquest of 42–4, 171–2, 188, 191–3,
    260, 269–70, 273–5, 296–7
space opera 42–4, 313
Spacetime Inn (Britton) 159
Spaceways (Maine) 282
Sphinx (Lindsay) 95
Spinrad, Norman 313
spiritualism 76, 80, 93, 101, 102
Spurious Sun (Borodin) 236
Spy (Newman) 229
Squares of the City, The (Brunner) 302
Squire, J.C. **173–5**
Stacpoole, H. De Vere 80, 236, 246
Stand on Zanzibar (Brunner) 300, 302
Stapledon, Olaf 143, 152, 172, 177, 180–1, 190,
    193–5, 217, 223, 237, 263
"Star, The" (Clarke) 263

"Star, The" (Wells) 32
Star Maker (Stapledon) 62, 177–8, **193–5**, 223,
    297, Pl.8
Star Shell, The (Wallis) 180
Star Trek series 207, 297
Star Wars (film) 278
Stars My Destination, The (Bester) 304
starships, generation see generation
    starships
Stevenson, Robert Louis 14
Stewart, Alfred Walter see Connington,
    J.J.
Stone Tape, The (Kneale) 258
Story of Ab, A (Waterloo) 81
Story of My Village, The (Stacpoole) 236, 246
"Story of the Stone Age, A" (Wells) 81
Strand Magazine, The 15, 32, 74, 75
Strange Case of Dr. Jekyll and Mr. Hyde, The
    (Stevenson) 14
Strange Invaders, The (Llewellyn) 202,
    208–10
Strange Papers of Dr. Blayre, The see Purple
    Sapphire, The
Straus, Ralph 94
Struggle for Empire, The (Cole) **42–4**
Sturgeon, Theodore 16, 179
Sundered Worlds, The (Moorcock) 288,
    310–13
superhumans 70–4, 150–4, 223, 230–2, 304
suspended animation 29, 65–6, 79, 90–1,
    142, 276
Swastika Night (Constantine) 202, **215–7**,
    222, 248
Swayne, Martin (Nicoll, Henry Maurice)
    128–30
Swift, Jonathan 13, 70
Swoop! Or How Clarence Saved England, The
    (Wodehouse) 40, 41
Symmes, John Cleves 210
synthetic humans 50; see also androids

"Tale of the Twentieth Century, A" (Wells) 23

Tales of Wonder 181, 190, 221, 253

Tarzan of the Apes (Burroughs) 78

Tayler, J. Lionel **142–3**, 177

Telepath (Sellings) **298–300**

Telepathist (Brunner) 301

telepathy 47, 63, 65, 118, 132, 144–5, 199, 204, 211, 280, 298–300, 301

television, forecast 30, 54, 65, 240

television, science fiction on 246, 255, 256–8, 282–5, 289, 305–8

televisor *see* videophone

Temple, William F. 221, **232–4**, 254

Terrible Awakening, The (Desmond) 237

Terror, The (Machen) 78, **82–4**

Terror of the Air, The (Le Queux) 40

Tesla, Nikola 179

That Hideous Strength (Lewis) 195, 197, 223–4

Then We Shall Hear Singing (Jameson) 222

Theodore Savage (Hamilton) **104–6**, 201

Thomas Boobig (Marshall) 126

Thorne, Guy (Cyril Ranger Gull) 77

Three Go Back (Mitchell) 184

Three Suns of Amara, The (Temple) 234

Tide Went Out, The (Maine) 282

Tieck, Ludwig 79–80

Till We Have Faces (Lewis) 197

Tillyard, Aelfrida **120–23**

Time and the Conways (Priestley) 251

time dilation 297

time dislocation 80, 86, 159, 178, 183, 251–2, 292–3, 308–9

Time Machine, The (Wells) **23–6**, 54, 64, 80, 126–7, 143, Pl.1

Time Marches Sideways (Finn) **242–3**

time travel 23–6, 80, 143, 178, 188, 217, 242–3, 249, 259–60, 280–2, 305–8

time viewer 181, 248, 262

Timeliner (Maine) 282

Timeslip (Maine) 282

"Tissue-Culture King, The" (Huxley) 127

To Conquer Chaos (Brunner) **300–3**

To Venus in Five Seconds (Jane) 50

To-day and To-morrow series 98–9, 116, 171

Tolkien, J.R.R. 197

To-morrow (Ollivant) **117–20**

To-morrow's Yesterday (Gloag) 177, 178, **181–2**

Tower of Oblivion, The (Onions) 86

transplants, brain 153–4

Travels of Marco Polo, The 69

Trip to Venus, A (Munro) 273

"Trouble with Emily" (White) 279–80

Tubb, E.C. 254, 265, **268–70**, 272, 288

Twenty-Fifth Hour, The (Best) 202, 222, **224–5**

Twenty-Seven Stairs (Finn) 242

Twenty Thousand Leagues Under the Sea (Verne) 33–4, 271

Two's Two (Clouston) 78

2001: A Space Odyssey (Clarke) 263

Ultimatum (MacClure) **110–2**

Uncensored Man, The (Sellings) 300

Uncertain Midnight, The (Cooper) **276–8**

underground worlds 25, 53, 70, 91–2, 144, 180, 188, 210–12, 289

undersea worlds 271–3

"Universe" (Heinlein) 273

Unknown 198

Unknown Tomorrow, The (Le Queux) 40

Unorthodox Engineers, The (Kapp) 304

Upsidonia (Marshall) 78, 82

Utopia *see* society, utopian

Utopia (More) 12–13, 70

Valdar the Oft-Born (Griffith) 37–8

"Valley of the Spiders, The" (Wells) 31

van Vogt, A.E. 179, 265

Venus (planet) 107, 197, 223, 230, 238, 244, 265, 270

Verne, Jules 12, 14, 33–4, 37, 57, 185, 210, 271; comparisons with 48
"Victim of Higher Space, A" (Blackwood) 80
videophone or televisor 132, 158, 198
Violet Flame, The (Jane) **48–50**, *Pl.3*
"Vision of the Past, A" (Wells) 23
"Visitor at Large" (White) 280
Von Braun, Wernher 230
Voyage to Arcturus, A (Lindsay) **92–5**, 195

Waldman, Milton 174
Wall, John W. (Sarban) 237, **248–50**
Wallace, Edgar 77, 185
Wallis, George C. 180
War, future 14, 15, 33–44, 48, 49, 104, 110, 140, 147, 152, 181, 199, 201–2, 212
War in the Air, The (Wells) 32, 37
War of the Worlds, The (Wells) **26–8**, 33, 44, 219, 275, *Pl.2*
Watch Below, The (White) 280
Waterloo, Stanley 81
Waugh, Evelyn 314
weather control 57, 118, 239
Web of Everywhere, The (Brunner) 302
Webb, Jane 57
Webb, Sidney 57
Weinbaum, Stanley G. 198
Weird Tales 178, 180
Welles, Orson 28
Wells, H.G. 11–12, 15, **21–32**, 37, 38, 54, 57, 71, 73, 74, 80, 81, 98, 112, 126–7, 138–9, 143, 160, 170, 179, 201, 223, 250, 271, 275
When Adolf Came (Hawkin) 222
When the Sleeper Wakes (Wells) fp, **28–30**, 277
When the World Shook (Haggard) **89–92**
When the World Screamed (Doyle) 76
When William Came (Saki) **40–2**, 222
Whitaker, David **305–8**
White, James 255, **278–80**, 296

White August (Boland) 246
White Mountains, The (Christopher) 296
Who Needs Men? (Cooper) 278
Whole Man, The (Brunner) 301
Wild Talents (Fort) 198
Wilkins, John 113, 169
William Pollok and Other Tales (Grogan) 82
Williams, Charles 197
Williamson, Jack 179, 185
Wilson, Colin 94
Wilson, William 11n
Wind From Nowhere, The (Ballard) 287, 291–2
"Wind from the Sun, The" (Clarke) 172
Winds of Gath, The (Tubb) 270
Windsor Magazine, The 59–60
Winter's Youth (Gloag) 182
"Wireless" (Kipling) 62
Witchfinder, The (Wright) 147
With the Night Mail (Kipling) **59–62**, *Pl.4*
Wodehouse, P.G. 40, 41
Woman Alive (Ertz) 18, 202, **212–5**, *Pl.8*
woman writer of science fiction, first 13
Wombles 74
Wonder Stories 112, 179, 180, 185, 188, 191
Wonderful Adventures of Phra the Phoenician, The (Arnold) 38
Wonderful Visit, The (Wells) 25–6
Woolf, Leonard and Virginia 152
World at Bay, The (Wallis) 180
World Below, The (Wright) 146, 265
world government 160–1, 164
World in Peril, The (Chilton) 260
World in 2030, The 170
World in Winter, The (Christopher) **294–6**
World Masters, The (Griffith) 37
World Out of Mind (McIntosh) 268
World Peril of 1910, The (Griffith) 37
World Set Free, The (Wells) 98
World, the Flesh and the Devil, The (Bernal) **171–3**

World War, First 15, 41–2, 76, 77–9, 82, 83, 84–6, 89, 91–2, 97–8, 104, 130, 133, 150, 156, 163, 174, 182, 194, 201, 228; Second 15–16, 39, 74, 91–2, 106, 115, 160, 173, 177, 205, 215, 221–34, 248–9, 254, 263, 266; Third 236–7, 239, 276, 280, 289

Wright, Henry Seppings 59

Wright, S. Fowler 139, **143–7**, 177, 195, 201–2, 265

Wylie, Philip 188

Wyndham, John 237, **244–6**, 254, 255 292, 296, 310; as John Beynon **187–90**; as John Beynon Harris 16, 180, 221

Year of the Comet, The (Christopher) 296

Year of the Sex Olympics, The (Kneale) 258

Yeats, W.B. 84

Yellow Danger, The (Shiel) 53

Yellow Peril, The (aka *The Dragon*) (Shiel) 53

Youd, C.S. *see* Christopher, John

Young Diana, The (Corelli) 102

"Z" Ray, The (Snell) 155

Zelazny, Roger 313

Zeppelin Destroyer, The (Le Queux) 77